GW01080122

Chromosomes Today

Volume 7

OXFORD CHROMOSOME CONFERENCE

ORGANISED BY
Dr M. D. Bennett; Dr M. Bobrow
Dr P. Brandham; Prof. H. J. Evans
Prof. M. Fergusson-Smith
Dr C. E. Ford F.R.S.
Dr G. Hewitt; Dr Keith Jones
Prof. H. Rees F.R.S.; Dr R. Riley F.R.S.

This was the seventh of the International Chromosome Conferences inaugurated by C. D. Darlington and K. R. Lewis, held in Oxford in 1964, 1967 and 1970, in Jerusalem in 1972, in Leiden in 1974 and in Helsinki in 1977. The proceedings of the conferences have appeared under the title Chromosomes today, *volumes 1-6.*

CHROMOSOMES TODAY

VOLUME 7

Proceedings of the Seventh International Chromosome Conference held in Oxford, England, 26–31 August 1980

Editors

M. D. BENNETT *Plant Breeding Institute, Cambridge*

M. BOBROW *University of Oxford*

G. HEWITT *University of East Anglia*

London

GEORGE ALLEN & UNWIN

Boston Sydney

First published 1981

GEORGE ALLEN & UNWIN LTD
40 Museum street, LondonWC1A 1LU

ISBN 0 04 575 021 1

ISSN 0069–3944

British Library Cataloguing in Publication Data

Chromosomes today.
Vol. 7
1. Chromosomes – Congresses
I. Bennett, M. D. II. Bobrow, M.
III. Hewitt, G. IV. International Chromosomes Conference (*7th: 1980: Oxford*)
574.87′322 QH600

ISBN 0–04–575021–1

Printed in Great Britain by Mackays of Chatham.

Foreword

The first Oxford Chromosome Conference, as many will know, was organised by C.D. Darlington and K.R. Lewis and held in the Botany School in July, 1964. Its purpose was to bring together a representative international group of those concerned with the study of chromosomes, whatever their organism, methods and objective, in the confident expectation that all would profit by learning about the interests, ideas and discoveries of others whose work might otherwise not come to their attention. No similar gathering had been attempted before; because of the wide range of biological contexts in which chromosome study is relevent, spoken accounts of new research were scattered over many different meetings (and written reports over even more different periodicals).

At the time of the first Conference the mechanics of transmission and recombination were, of course, already well understood in their essential features, although a cloud of mystery still hung over the basis of spindle function and the nature of the centromere. At that time also chromosome study had long been established as a valuable aid to the taxonomist and student of evolution on the one hand and the plant breeder on the other. But the new sophistication in the use of biochemical and biophysical methods had only just started to make its impact on our knowledge of chromosome organisation and behaviour. The attempts to unravel the manner in which information borne by the chromosomes is read, conveyed to the cytoplasm and applied to the direction of development and the regulation of function were in their infancy, and the new attack by the electron microscopists on the problem of pairing in meiotic prophase had not even begun. The application of chromosome observations in medicine, both practice and research, and including that most intractable complex of problems, cancer, had scarcely commenced to gather momentum and was still nearly a decade removed from the enormous impetus to be given by the discovery of the simple banding methods that permit confident recognition of all individual human chromosomes. Experimentally, the use of distinctive "marker" chromosomes to trace cell lineages and relationships in grafted animals and chimaeras of all kinds was already established but still to come were the simple techniques for fusing mammalian cells from different species and cloning the resultant hybrids that eventually led, via enzyme-deficiency markers and the discovery of the amazingly convenient chromosome-loss phenomenon, to the recent enormous growth in the map of the human genome. Finally, the employment of chromosome methods in two further fields of applied biology, insect pest control and veterinary science, was still several years away.

The first Conference unquestionably achieved its purpose and there was a general desire for a new gathering of the same kind. Accordingly, the second Oxford Conference was held in 1967 and the third in 1970, both again organised by Professor Darlington and Dr. Lewis and held in the Botany School. The founders could not be expected to continue indefinitely with their labour of love and at the close of the 1970 Conference an offer from J. Wahrman to arrange the next one in Jerusalem was warmly accepted. A Conference was duly held in Jerusalem in 1972 and was followed by others in Leiden (1974) organised by P.L. Pearson and in Helsinki (1977) organised by A. de la Chapelle. At Helsinki it was decided that the Conference should come back to Oxford in 1980, but as the Seventh International Chromosome Conference.

The Conferences have had no formal standing and no continuing International Committee; at each one the arrangements adopted were those deemed best by the organisers. This gave those concerned with arrangements for the Seventh Conference the opportunity to experiment. By the time planning began the volume of new chromosome research had grown so great and its ramifications so wide that to maintain the primary aims of the original Conference some change in the pattern would have been necessary anyway. The Organizing Committee therefore decided to take the extreme step of confining oral presentations to plenary sessions at which a panel of invited speakers would present summaries of the current state of their own particular fields suitable for a general audience but including perhaps a few words addressed to the specialist. It was recognised that this decision would disappoint many and maybe cause some to stay away, but the alternative of accepting contributed papers and holding parallel sessions, would have had a fragmenting effect, tending to change the Conference into an aggregate of small specialist symposia when it was the unity of the subject it was desired to emphasize.

The decision to allocate ample time and provide conveniently located accommodation for poster sessions was a necessary compensation for the exclusion of contributed papers. This system of presenting new research results is still evolving and many are becoming adept at presenting evidence of technical competence, essential factual material, and conclusions, in a display that is quickly assembled and occupies a minimum of space. Its obvious advantage is that each viewer can determine his own programme and order of priority. It would be instructive if it were possible to compare per unit of time expended by the viewer/listener, the rate of acquisition of new 'take home' facts and ideas at good poster sessions and at parallel sessions of short contributed papers. Natural selection may provide the answer.

It is important to think also of the presenter of the poster. He may find it necessary to attend at his poster for two hours or more, but he is almost sure to have the benefit of relaxed discussion with those who are particularly interested in his work. New ideas, questions and viewpoints that had escaped his attention are more likely to emerge in these conditions than in the minimal, if indeed any, discussion that follows the short spoken paper.

Perhaps the most serious aspect of the wholesale substitution of the poster for the short spoken communication (and one that was considered carefully by the Organising Committee before reaching its decision) is the attitude of some scientific administrators that may even be written into institutional rules, namely to require an applicant for a travel grant to show that he will, or would expect to, present a paper. Should these remarks come to the attention of scientific administrators who apply such a rule, they are respectfully urged to consider the view that, at contemporary international Conferences, as much or more may be gained from presenting a good poster as from giving a short contributed paper, and if necessary, to change the rule accordingly.

The published proceedings of international conferences tend to be of ephemeral interest only and are rarely quoted in the general literature (though there are some renowned exceptions). The wise investigator will usually not consign valuable new research results to them. On the other hand they could provide a particularly suitable vehicle for short but authoritative reviews addressed to the non-specialist reader and accompanied by an up-to-date set of key references. The 30 invited speakers at the Oxford Conference were all requested to submit articles of this kind. Nearly all have done so and they appear in this volume. The organisers are grateful to them for their co-operation. It is hoped that these articles will be particularly well suited for those, and they must now be many, who feel that their grasp of other aspects of chromosome study, even those immediately peripheral to their own, is beginning to slip and who wish to bring themselves up-to-date again without having to spend time searching the literature or reading, at least in the first instance, heavy specialist reviews.

The Organising Committee is deeply grateful to Professor Darlington, the Honorary President, for his generosity and for the unique blend of distinction, understanding and wit he brought to the Conference.

Turning finally to a personal note, I wish to place on record my gratitude to the members of the Organising and Local Committees and the many volunteer helpers for their splendid support, and most of all to Dr. Martin Bobrow who took on the central responsibility for the Conference during my one-year absence in Leiden.

Professor A. Gropp of Lübeck and Professor U. Wolf of Freiburg-im-Breisgan have generously agreed to arrange the next Conference in West Germany, in 1983, at a place and date to be arranged.

C.E. FORD

Secretary-General

Contents

Conference members

Adair J Department of Biological Sciences University of Warwick Coventry CV4 7AL

Ahloowalia B S Agricultural Institute Oak Park Research Centre Carlow Ireland

Albanese R ICI Pharmaceutical Division Mereside Alderley Park Macclesfield Cheshire SK10 4OG

Al-Othman Sulaiman Kuwait Cytogenetic Centre PO Box 12086 Shamia Kuwait Arabia

Anderson D Central Toxicology Laboratory ICI Ltd Alderley Park Nr Macclesfield Cheshire UK S10 4TJ

Archidiacono N Cattedra di Genetica Medica c/o Istituto per l'Infanzia Ospedale Burlo Garofolo Via dell'Istria 65 Trieste Italy

Arlett C F MRC Cell Mutation Unit University of Sussex Falmer Brighton Sussex BN1 9QG

Arnason U Institute of Genetics Solvegatan 29 S-223 62 Lund Sweden

Ashley T Oak Ridge National Laboratory Biology Division Oak Ridge TN 37830 USA

Auerbach A D Memorial Sloan-Kettering Cancer Center 1275 York Avenue New York New York 10021 USA

Autio K Folkhalsan Institute of Genetics PO Box 819 SF-00101 Helsinki 10 Finland

Avivi L University of Tel Aviv Department of Human Genetics Sackler Medical School Tel-Aviv Ramat-Aviv Israel

Becher R West German Tumor Center Westdeutsches Tumorzentrum Innere Universitatsklinik (Tumorforschung) Hufelandstr. 55 4300 West Germany

Beek B Address unknown

Bennett M D Plant Breeding Institute Maris Lane Trumpington Cambridge CB2 2LQ

Berger R Laboratoire de Cytogenetique Centre G Hayem Hopital Saint-Louis 75475 Paris Cedex 10 France

Beverstock G C Instituut voor Anthropogenetica Sylvius Laboratoria Universiteit Leiden Wassenaarseweg 72 Leiden Netherlands

Bianchi N O Instituto Multidisciplinario de Biologia Cellular (IMBICE) CC 403 1900 La Plata Argentina

Bobrow M Department of Medical Genetics Old Road Headington Oxford OX3 7LE

Boue A Groupe de Recherches de Biologie Prenatale INSERM Chateau de Longchamp Bois de Boulogne 75016 Paris France

Boue J Same address as above

Bougourd S M Department of Biology University of York Heslington York YO1 5DD

Bowser-Riley S M Cytogenetics Infant Development Unit Birmingham Maternity Hospital Birmingham

Boyes B G Department of Anatomy Health Sciences Centre University of Western Ontario London Ontario N6A 5C1 Canada

Brandham P Jodrell Laboratory Royal Botanic Gardens Kew Richmond Surrey TW9 3DS

Breckon G MRC Radiobiology Unit Harwell Didcot Oxon
Britten R J Division of Biology California Institute of Technology Pasadena California 91125 USA
Brod E Med Diagn Institut 6238 Hofheim Wilhelmstr 2
Brook D MRC Clinical and Population Cytogenetics Unit Western General Hospital Crewe Road Edinburgh EH4 2XU
Brooker P C Genetics Department Royal Free Hospital School of Medicine 8 Hunter Street London WC1N 1BP
Buckton K E MRC Clinical and Population Cytogenetics Unit Western General Hospital Crewe Road Edinburgh EH4 2XU
Buhler E M Department of Genetics Basler Kinderspital Romergasse 8 CH-4005 Basel Switzerland
Bylsma J B Clinical Genetics Centre State University Utrecht PO Box 18009 3501 CA Untrecht The Netherlands
Cacheiro N L A Biology Division Oak Ridge National Laboratory P O Box Y Oak Ridge Tenessee 37830 USA
Callan H G Department of Zoology Bute Buildings The University St Andrews Fife KY16 9TS
Capanna E Institute of Comparative Anatomy Via Borelli 50 I-00161 Rome
Carson H L Department of Genetics University of Hawaii Honolulu Hawaii
Casey G Department of Cytogenetics and Immunogenetics Institute of Cancer Research and Royal Marsden Hospital Fulham Road London SW36JJ
Cattanach B M MRC Radiobiology Unit Harwell Oxon OXII ORD
Cavalier-Smith T Department of Biophysics University of London King's College 26-29 Drury Lane London WC2B 5RL
Cawood A H MRC Radiobiology Unit Harwell Oxon OXII ORD
Chaganti R S K Memorial Sloan-Kettering Cancer Center 1275 York Avenue New York New York 10021 USA
Chandley A MRC Clinical and Population Cytogenetics Unit Western General Hospital Edinburgh Scotland
Chaudhuri Laboratorium fur Experimentelle Radiologie 8042 Neuherberg bei Munchen Ingolstadter Landstrasse 2 W Germany
Chan Han-yuan Institute of Cell Biology Academia Sinica Shanghai China
Clarke G Department of Medical Genetics Old Road Headington Oxford OX3 7LE
Cocking E C School of Biological Sciences Department of Botany University Park Nottingham NG7 2RD
Connel J Division of Chemical Carcinogenesis Royal Cancer Institute Pollards Wood Research Station Nightingales Lane Chalfont St Giles Bucks HP8 4SF
Couturier J Institut de Progenese 15 rue de l'Ecole de Medecine F75270 Paris Cedex 06
Cremer T Institut fur Anthropologie und Humangenetik Im Neuenheimer Feld 328 D-6900 Heidelberg 1 Federal Republic of Germany
Crowther W Department of Zoology Oxford University South Parks Rd Oxford
Curtis C F Ross Institute London School of Hygiene and Tropical Medicine Keppel Street London WC1E 7HT
Daker M G Paediatric Research Unit Guy's Hospital Medical School London

Danford N Department of Genetics University College of Swansea Singleton Park Swansea SA2 8PP
Darlington C D Botany School Oxford University South Parks Road Oxford
de Capoa A Istituto di Genetica Citta Universitaria Piazzale Aldo Moro Rome Italy
de Grouchy J Laboratoire de Cytogenetique Humaine et Comparee U 173 INSERM Hopital Necker-Enfants-Malades 149 rue de Sevres 75730 Paris Cedex 15 France
de la Chapelle A Department of Medical Genetics University of Helsinki Haartmaninkatu 3 00290 Helsinki 29 Finland
Delhanty J D A Galton Laboratory Department of Genetics and Biometry Wolfson House 4 Stephenson Way London NW1 2HE
de France H F Clinical Genetic Centre PO Box 18009 3501 CA Utrecht The Netherlands
de Schepper G Institute for Human Genetics Sarphatistraat 217 Amsterdam The Netherlands
Dietrich A J Same address as above
Donald J Department of Cellular Pathology ICRF PO Box 123 Lincoln's Inn Fields London WC2A 3PX
Dreiss M Department of International Agriculture Steinstr 19 3430 Witzenhausen West Germany
Dutrillaux B Institut de Progenese de Medicine 15 rue de l'Ecole 75006 Paris
Dyban A P Institute for Experimental Medicine Acad Med Sci USSR Kirovsky 69/71 Leningrad 197022 USSR
Dyer A F Botany Department University of Edinburgh Scotland
Engelhardt P Institute of Genetics Salomonkatu 17 SF-00100 Helsinki 10 Finland
Esponda P Instituto de Biologia Celular (CSIC) Madrid 6 Spain
Essen-Moller J Institute of Molecular Cytogenetics University of Lund Tornavagen 13 S-223 63 Lund Sweden
Evans E Sir William Dunn School of Pathology South Parks Road Oxford
Evans G M Department of Agricultural Botany School of Agricultural Sciences University College of Wales Penglais Aberystwyth Dyfed SY23 3DD
Evans H J MRC Clinical and Population Cytogenetics Unit Western General Hospital Crewe Road Edinburgh Scotland
Evans R R Pathology Department Royal Hospital for Sick Children Edinburgh
Feldman M Plant Genetics The Weizmann Institute of Science Rehovot Israel
Ferguson-Smith M Royal Hospital for Sick Children Yorkhill Glasgow Scotland
Ferraro M Istituto di Genetica Citta Universitaria Piazza Aldo Moro Rome
Finaz C INSERM U 162 Hopital Debrousse rue Soeur Bouvier 69322 Lyon France
Finch R A Plant Breeding Institute Maris Lane Trumpington Cambridge
Finnegan D J Department of Molecular Biology University of Edinburgh King's Buildings Mayfield Road Edinburgh EH9 3JR

Fischer P Institute of Cancer Research University of Vienna Borschkegasse 8a A-1090 Vienna Austria

Flavell R Plant Breeding Institute Maris Lane Trumpington Cambridge CB2 2LQ

Fletcher H L School of Biological Sciences University of East Anglia Norwich NR4 7TJ

Ford C E 156 Oxford Road Abingdon Oxford

Fredga K Institute of Genetics Solvegatan 29 S-223 62 Lund Sweden

Fuge H Abt Zellbiologie Fachbereich Biologie Universitat D-6750 Kaiserslautern Federal Republic of Germany

Gamperl R Institute of Medical Biology and Human Genetics University of Graz Harrachgasse 21/8 A-8010 Graz Austria

Gebhart E Institut fur Humangenetik und Anthropologie D-852 Erlangen Bismarckstr 10 W Germany

Geneix A Laboratoire d'Histologie Embryologie Cytogenetique Faculte de Medecine BP38 63001 Clermont Ferrand Cedex

Geraedts J P M Instituut voor Anthropogenetica Sylvius Laboratoria der Ryksuniversiteit Leiden Wassenaarseweg 72 Leiden Netherlands

Gibby M Department of Botany British Museum (Natural History) Cromwell Road London SW7 5BD

Godward M B E Department of Plant Biology and Microbiology Queen Mary College University of London Mile End Road London E1 4NS

Gosalvez J Departamento de Genetica Universidad Autonama de Madrid Spain

Gosden C M MRC Clinical and Population Cytogenetics Unit Western General Hospital Crewe Road Edinburgh Scotland

Goyanes V J Juan Canalego Hospital Rubine 17-20A La Coruna Spain

Gropp A Institut fur Pathologie der Medizinischen Hochschule Lubeck D-2400 Lubeck Ratzeburger Allee 160

Grzeschik K H Institut fur Humangenetik Vesaliusweg 12-14 D4400 Munster Germany

Haas O A Institute for Cancer Research University of Vienna Borschkegasse 8a A-1090 Vienna Austria

Hagemeijer A Department of Cell Biology and Genetics Erasmus University PO Box 1738 3000 DR Rotterdam The Netherlands

Haglund U Department of Medical Cell Genetics Karolinska Institute Box 60 400 S-104 01 Stockholm Sweden

Hansmann I Institute of Humangenetics Nikolausberger Weg 5a 3400 Gottingen Federal Republic of Germany

Harnden D G Department of Cancer Studies University of Birmingham Birmingham 15

Hartmann-Goldstein I Genetics Department Sheffield University Sheffield S10 2TN

Hassold T J Department of Anatomy and Reproductive Biology 1960 East-West Road Biomed A204 Honolulu Hawaii 96822

Hauschteck-Jungen E Zoologisches Institut Winterthurerstr 190 8057 Zurich Switzerland

Hauser-Urfer I Allgemeine Botanik ETH Zentrum Zytologie Universitatsstr. 2 CH-8092 Zurich Switzerland

Hellkuhl B Institut fur Humangenetik Vesaliusweg 12-14 D-44 Munster West Germany

Hens L Instituut voor Morfologie-Vrije Universiteit Brussel Laarbeeklaan 103 B-1090 Brussels Belgium

Heslop-Harrison J S Plant Breeding Institute Maris Lane Trumpington Cambridge CB2 2LQ

Hewitt G School of Biological Sciences University of East Anglia Norwich

Hilder V A Department of Biological Sciences University of Warwick Coventry

Hope R Imperial Cancer Research Fund PO Box 123 Lincoln's Inn Fields London WC2A 3PX

Hopkin J M University of Birmingham 117 Bournbrook Road Selly Park Birmingham B29 7BY

Hopkin J E Same address as above

Howell R T SW Regional Cytogenetics Centre Southmead Hospital Bristol

Jacky P B Department of Medical Genetics University of British Columbia Mather Building UBC Vancouver B C V6T IW5

Jacobs P A Dept of Anatomy and Reproductive Biology University of Hawaii School of Medicine Honolulu Hawaii 96822 USA

Jaworska H Institute of Molecular Cytogenetics University of Lund Tornavagen 13 S-223 63 Lund Sweden

Jenderny J Institute of Humangenetics Nikolausberger Weg 5a 3400 Gottingen FRG

John B Dept Population Biology Research School of Biological Sciences ANU Canberra Australia

Jonasson J A Institute of Medical Genetics V Agatan 24 S-75220 Uppsala Sweden

Jones G H Dept of Genetics University of Birmingham PO Box 363 Birmingham B15 2TT

Jones K Jodrell Laboratory Royal Botanic Gardens Kew Richmond Surrey

Jones R N Department of Agricultural Botany University College of Wales Penglais Aberystwyth

Kakati S Dept of Genetics and Endocrinology Roswell Park Memorial Institute 666 Elm Street Buffalo New York 14263 USA

Kaluzewski B Laboratory of Genetics Institute of Endocrinology Medical Academy of Lodz 3 Sterling st 91-425 Lodz Poland

Kennaugh A Paterson Laboratories Christie Hospital and Holt Radium Inst Withington Manchester M20 9BX

Kenton A Jodrell Laboratory Royal Botanic Gardens Kew Richmond Surrey

Kim M A Institut fur Humangenetik Vesaliusweg 12 4400 Munster W Germany

Kirsch-Volders Lab of Humangenetics Vrye Universiteit Brussel Pleinlaan 2 B1050 Brussels Belgium

Klasterska I Institute for Radiation Biology Wallenberg Laboratory S-10691 Stockholm Sweden

Klinger H P Dept of Genetics Albert Einstein College of Medicine 1300 Morris Park Avenue Bronx NY 10461 USA

Lacadena J-R Departamento de Genetica Universidad Complutense de Madrid Madrid 3 Spain

Laemmli U K Dept of Biochemical Sciences Princeton University Princeton NJ 08540 USA

Lafourcade P Hopital de la Salpetriere 47 bd de l'Hopital 75651 Paris France
Laird C Dept of Zoology University of Washington NJ15 Seattle Washington 98195 USA
Lange W Foundation for Agricultural Plant Breeding PO Box 117 6700 AC Wageningen The Netherlands
Law C N Plant Breeding Institute Maris Lane Trumpington Cambridge CB2 2LQ
Lawler S Dept of Cytogenetics and Immunogenetics Institute of Cancer Research Royal Marsden Hospital London SW3 6JJ
Lecher P E Lab de Cytogenetique UER Sciences Universite Clermont Fd BP 45 63170 Aubiere France
Lemeunier F CNRS Laboratoire de Biologie et Genetique Evolutives CNRS 91 190 61 F sur Yvette France
Levan G Department of Genetics Stigbergsliden 14 S-41463 Gothenburg Sweden
Lin Zhong-ping Institute of Botany Academia Sinica Shanghai China
Linde-Laursen I Risø National Laboratory Agricultural Research Dept DK-4000 Roskilde Denmark
Linnert G Institute of Applied Genetics of the Free University D-1000 Berlin 33 Albrecht-Thaer-Weg 6
Lyon M Genetics Section MRC Radiobiology Unit Harwell Oxford OX11 ORD
Madan K Institute of Human Genetics Cytogenetics Laboratory AZVU Free University De Boelelaan 1117 Amsterdam The Netherlands
Malet P Laboratoire d'Histologie Faculte de Medicine BP 38 63001 Clermond Ferrand Cedex France
Mandel J-L Unite 184/INSERM Faculte de Medecine 11 rue Humann Strasbourg France
Marchant The Botanical Garden University of British Columbia 6501 Northwest Marine Drive Vancouver BC V6T IW5
Marino J S Museo Nacional Ciencias Naturales Castellana 80 Madrid 6 Spain
Marks G E John Innes Institute Colney Lane Norwich NOR 70F
Mattei J F Centre de Genetique Medicale Service du Professeur Giraud Hopital d'Enfants de la Timone 13385 Marseille Cedex 4 France
Mattei M G Same address as above
Maudlin I Tsetse Research Laboratory Dept of Veterinary Medicine University of Bristol Langford House Langford Bristol BS18 7DU
Mehdipour P Cytogenetics Dept Nuffield Wing School of Medicine University of Liverpool L69 3BX
Mello-Sampayo T Gulbenkian Institute of Science Apt 14 2781 Oeiras Codex Portugal
Merani M S IMBICE Anatomie Comparata di Roma Las Heras 3892 Buenos Aires Argentina
Mikkelsen M John F Kennedy Institute Dept of Medical Genetics GL Landevej 7 DK 2600 Glostrup Denmark
Miller O J Columbia University 701 West 168th Street New York NY 10032 USA
Miller D A Same address as above
Mindek G J Strahlenbiologisches Institut der Universitat Zurich August Forel Str 7 CH 8029 Zurich Switzerland

Mitelman F Department of Clinical Genetics Lund University Hospital S-221 85 Lund Sweden
Mittwoch U Dept of Genetics and Biometry Galton Laboratory Wolfson House 4 Stephenson Way London NW1 2HE
Mizuno S Dept of Applied Biological Science Faculty of Science & Technology Noda (278) Japan
Moens P Dept of Biology York University Downsview Ontario Canada M3J IP3
Mohandas T Division of Medical Genetics (E-4) Harbor-UCLA Medical Center Torrance California USA
Moreau N 53 Avenue Rockefeller 69003 Lyon France
Morescalchi A Institute of Histology and Embryology of the University Via Mezzocannone 8 80134 Napoli Italy
Moses M J Box 3011 Dept of Anatomy Duke University Medical Center Durham North Carolina 27710 USA
Murken J Address unknown
Nakai S Division of Genetics National Institute of Radiological Sciences 9-1 4-CHOME Anagawa Chiba-Fhi Japan
Narayan R K J Dept of Agricultural Botany University College of Wales Aberystwyth Dyfed Wales SY23 3DD
Neitzel H Institut fur Humangenetik Nuebuerweg 6 D-1000 Berlin 19 Germany
Oakley H Dept of Genetics University of Birmingham Edgbaston Birmingham
Obe G Institut fur Genetik Arnimallee 5-7 D-1000 Berlin 33 W Germany
Ockey C H Paterson Laboratories Christie Hospital and Holt Radium Inst Withington Manchester M20 9BX
Olivieri G Istituto di Genetica Fac Scienze Citta Universitaria 00185 Roma Italy
Olmo E Institute of Histology and Embryology Via Mezzocannone 8 80134 Naples Italy
Oud J L Institute of Genetics Dept of Cytogenetics and Population Genetics Kruislaan 318 1098 SM Amsterdam The Netherlands
Owen M Dept of Botany Plant Science Laboratories The University of Reading Whiteknights Reading
Papes D Dept Botany Rosseveltov trg 6 YU 41001 Zagreb PO 933 Yugoslavia
Parker J S Queen Mary College Mile End Rd London E1 4NS
Parrington J M Galton Laboratory Wolfson House 4 Stephenson Way London NW1 2HE
Passarge E Institut fur Humangenetik Jufelandstrasse 55 4300 Essen 1 W Germany
Paulson J R MRC Laboratory of Molecular Biology Hills Road Cambridge CB2 2QH
Peacock J CSIRO Division of Plant Industry PO Box 1600 Canberra City ACT 2601 Australia
Pearson P L Instituut voor Anthropogenetica Sylvius Lab Wassenaarseweg 72 Leiden Netherlands
Perry P MRC Clinical and Population Cytogenetics Unit Western General Hospital Edinburgh EH4 2XU
Pimpinelli Istituto di Genetica Facolta di Scienze Universita da Roma 00100 Roma Italy
Pinfield C L Department of Genetics University of Birmingham PO Box 363 Birmingham B15 2TT

Plagens U Zool Inst 8700 Wuerzburg Rontgenring 10 Fed Rep Germany

Prantera G Istituto di Genetica Faconta Di Scienze Universita di Roma 00100 Roma Italy

Probeck H D Institute of Humangenetics Nikolausberger Weg 5a 3400 Gottingen Federal Republic of Germany

Quack B Centre Departemental de Transfusion Sanguine Faubourg Mache 73000 Chambery France

Raman R Cytogenetics Laboratory Dept of Zoology Banaras Hindu University Varanasi 221005 India

Ramsay G Botany Dept University of Edinburgh The King's Buildings Mayfield Road Edinburgh EH9 3JH

Rees H School of Agricultural Sciences University College of Wales Penglais Aberystwyth SY23 3DD

Reeves B R Department of Cytogenetics and Immunogenetics Institute of Cancer Research and the Royal Marsden Hospital Fulham Road London SW3 6JJ

Retief A E Dept of Cytogenetics Tygerberg Hospital PO Box 63 Tyerberg 7505 South Africa

Riley R Agricultural Research Council 160 Great Portland Street London

Rocchi A Istituto di Genetica Universita di Roma 00185 Italy

Rocchi M Cattedra di Genetica Medica Istituto per l'Infanzia Ospedale Burlo Garofolo Via dell'Istria 65 Trieste Italy

Rommel M Dept of International Agriculture University of Kassel Steinstr 19 3430 Witzenhausen West Germany

Russo F Fisiologia animale Facolta di Medicine Veterinaria Universita di Napoli Italy

Sachs E Faculteit der Geneeskunde Erasmus Universiteit Rotterdam Postbus 1738 3000 DR Rotterdam Holland

Sachsse W Institut fur Genetik Johannes Gutenberg-Universitat 6500 Mainz

Salerno A Cattedra di Zoognostica Facolta di Scienze agrarie Universita di Napoli 80055 Portici Italy

Salk D Dept of Pathology School of Medicine University of Washington Seattle Washington 98195 USA

Santesson B Institute for Medical Genetics Vastra Agatan 24 S-752 20 Uppsala Sweden

Savage J R K MRC Radiobiology Unit Harwell Oxford OX11 ORD

Schell J Department of Genetics University of Ghent Ledegankstraat 35 900 Ghent Belgium

Schimke R T Dept of Biological Sciences Stanford University Stanford California 94305 USA

Schroder J Folkhalsan Institute of Genetics PO Box 819 SF00101 Helsinki 10 Finland

Schvartzman J B Biology Dept Brookhaven National Laboratory Upton New York 11973 USA

Schwanitz G Institut fur Humangenetik der Universitat Bonn Wilhelmstr 31 5300 Bonn 1

Schwarzacher H G Histologisch-Embryologisches Institut der Universitat Wien Schwarzspanierstrasse 17 A-1090 Wien Austria

Schweizer D Institute of Botany The University of Vienna Dept of Cytology Rennweg 14 A-1030 Vienna Austria

Seabright M Wessex Regional Cytogenetics Unit General Hospital Salisbury
Searle A G MRC Radiobiology Unit Harwell Oxon OXII ORD
Searle J B Dept of Genetics 2 Tillydrone Avenue Aberdeen AB92TN
Secker Walker L M Dept of Cytogenetics The Royal Marsden Hospital Fulham Road London SW3 6JJ
Serra A Universita Cattolica Facolta di Medecina e Chirurgia Istituto di Genetica Umana Via della Pineta Sacchetti 644 00168 Roma
Serville F Residence Dauphine 120 Avenue Louis Barthou 33200 Bordeaux France
Sharat Chandra H Microbiology and Cell Biology Laboratory Indian Institute of Science Bangalore 560 012 India
Sharma A Centre of Advanced Studies in Chromosome Research Dept of Botany University of Calcutta 35 Ballygunj Circular Road Calcutta 700019 India
Sharma A K Same address as above
Sharman G B School of Biological Sciences Macquarie University North Ryde NSW Australia 2113
Siegemund F Martin-Luther-Universitat 401 Halle (Saale) Domplatz 1 Germany
Smyth D Department of Genetics Monash University Clayton Vic 3168 Australia
Sorsa M Institute of Occupational Health Haartmaninkatu 1 SF-00290 Helsinki 29 Finland
Sorsa V Same address as above
Southern E M MRC Mammalian Genome Unit Dept of Zoology West Mains Road Edinburgh Scotland
Southern D I Zoology Dept Manchester University Manchester MI3 9PL
Sparkes R S Dept of Medicine UCLA School of Medicine Los Angeles CA 90024 USA
Speit G Abt Klin Genetik der Universitat Ulm Oberer Eselsberg D-7900 Ulm West Germany
Sperling K Institut fur Humangenetik Heubuerweg 6 D-1000 Berlin 19
Staessen C Vrije Universiteit Brussel Lab voor Antropogenetica Pleinlaan 2 1050 Brussel Belgium
Stahl A Laboratoire d'Histologie et Embryologie II Faculte de Medecine 27 boulevard Jean-Moulin F-13385 Marseille Cedex 4 France
Stengel-Rutkowski Nymphenburger Str 181 8000 Munchen 19 BRD
Stern H Dept of Biology B-002 University of California San Diego La Jolla California 92093 USA
Stevens D J G Paterson Laboratories Christie Hospital and Holt Radium Inst Withington Manchester M20 9BX
Stingo V Inst of Histology and Embryology Via Mezzocannone 8 Naples Italy
Sumner A T MRC Cytogenetics Unit Crewe Road Edinburgh EH4 2XU Scotland
Swindell J Paterson Laboratories Christie Hospital and Holt Radium Institute Withington Manchester M20 9BX
Sybenga J Dept of Genetics Gen Foulkesweg 53 6703 Wageningen The Netherlands
Takahashi E Division of Genetics National Institute of Radiological Sciences 9-1 Anagawa-4-chome Chibashi 260 Japan

Tan C C Fudan University Shanghai People's Republic of China
Tease C MRC Radiobiology Unit Harwell Oxon OXII ORD
Thomson E J MRC Clinical and Population Cytogenetics Unit Western General Hospital Crewe Road Edinburgh EH4 2XU
Tommerup N Dept of Medical Genetics GL Landevej 7 DK 2600 Glostrup Denmark
Toudic L Service de Pediatrie Genetique Medicale Hopital Morvan Brest 29200 France
Traut W c/o Ruhr Universitat Bochum Abt Biologie PO Box 102148 D4630 Bochum Germany
Valentino F Istituto di Genetica Universita di Roma 00185 Italy
Valerio D Cattedra di Zoognostica Facolta di Scienze Agraria Portici Italy
van Brink F Dept of Animal Cytogenetics and Cytotaxonomy University of Utrecht Padualaan 8 PO Box 80.061 Utrecht The Netherlands
Van Buul P P W Lab Radiation Genetics and Chem Mutag University of Leiden Sylvius Laboratories Wassenaarseweg 72 Leiden The Netherlands
van der Ploeg M Dept of Histochemistry and Cytochemistry Wassenaarseweg 72 AL 2333 Leiden The Netherlands
van Hemel J O Clinical Genetics Centre State University 3501 Utrecht The Netherlands
van Prooyen Knegt A C Lab voor Histo en Cytochemie Wassenaarseweg 72 AL 2333 Leiden The Netherlands
van Raamsdonk Dept of Biosystematics Transitorium III Padualaan 8 Utrecht The Netherlands
Vardi A Agricultural Research Organisation The Volcani Center Bet Dagan PO Box 6 Israel
Vega C E Service de Pediatrie et Genetique Medicale Hopital d'Enfants Groupe Hospitalier de la Timone 13385 Marseille Cedex 4 France
von Koskull H Laboratory of Prenatal Genetics Dept of Obstetrics and Gynaecology University of Helsinki Haartmaninkatu 2 0290 Helsinki 29
Vosa C Botany School Oxford University South Parks Road, Oxford
Wahrman J Dept of Genetics The Hebrew University of Jerusalem Israel
Walker S Cytogenetics Unit Nuffield Wing School of Medicine PO Box 147 Liverpool L69 3BX
Wallace B M N Dept of Genetics University of Birmingham PO Box 363 Birmingham B15 2TT
Wallace C Anatomy Department Medical School Hospital Street Johannesburg South Africa
White M J D Research School of Biological Sciences Australian National University PO Box 475 Canberra City ACT 2601 Australia
Prof. U Wolf The Institute for Human Genetics Albertstrasse 11 D-7800 Freiberg I Br W Germany
Wolff S Laboratory of Radiobiology University of California San Francisco California 94143 USA
Wolstenholme J Cytogenetics Laboratory Dept of Pathology Ninewells Hospital Dundee DD1 9SY Scotland
Wooley J C Biochemical Sciences Dept Princeton University New Jersey 08544 USA

Yao Xin Institute of Cell Biology Academia Sinica Shanghai China
Yoon J S Dept of Biological Sciences Bowling Green State University Bowling Green Ohio 43403 USA
Zakharov A F Institute of Medical Genetics Kashirskoye shosse 6a Moscow 115478 USSR
Zang K D Dept of Human Genetics University of Saarland 6650 Homburg/Saar Federal Republic of Germany
Zang Sichong Inst for Medical Cell Genetics Karolinska Institute 104 01 Stockholm Sweden
Zech L Institute for Medical Cell Genetics Karolinska Institute 10401 Stockholm 60 Sweden
Zergollern L Mose Pijade 131/11 41 000 Zagreb Yugoslavia
Zhang Yu-yan Institute of Cell Biology Academia Sinica Shanghai China
Zhimulev I Institute of Cytology and Genetics USSR Academy of Sciences Novosibirsk USSR

Cyril Dean Darlington FRS

1903–1981

We record with great sadness the death of Professor Darlington on 26 March 1981. He was the President of this Conference, and of its predecessors. It was he who founded the series of Chromosome Conferences and, with K R Lewis, organised the first three held in Oxford in 1963, 1966 and 1969.

Darlington published his first major work, *Recent Advances in Cytology* in 1932, at the age of 29. With remarkable clarity and style of drawing and interpretative diagrams, it integrated the previous welter of unrelated observations about chromosomes into a coherent whole. The second edition of this work contributed fundamental insights into chromosome mechanics and meiotic phenomena. His *The Evolution of Genetic Systems* has been described as '. . . among the really important biological books of the century'.

All who attended the Chromosome Conferences will remember his unique personality. His scholarship and wit created a legend in his own lifetime.

Chromosomes and organisms: the evolutionary paradoxes

C. D. Darlington

Botany School, Oxford

During the sixteen years since we began these meetings, great events have altered the shape of the world we live in. Molecular, microbial and ultra-microscopic discoveries have taken us from the edge of the great argument about life and put us right in the middle of it. This argument, as we know, is about structure, about development and, above all, about evolution.

We have long seen the chromosomes, not as the beginning of life, but as its central achievement. Now we can see that achievement as a profound and prolonged reorganisation of life, a nuclear revolution. We had been accustomed to argue from brief experiments to remote conclusions. Now we can go further and extend our view to the limits of time and space. But when we do so we find rules broken by exceptions and axioms dissolved, as I have ventured to put it, into component processes (7). To be more precise, earlier mechanisms of heredity and variation have been reconstructed, displaced or supplanted by this nuclear revolution. Vestiges of the pre-nuclear system are seen to survive in plasmids or transposable elements, in viruses, pro-viruses and plasmagenes. The organellar genomes, of the post-nuclear world are taking their place in symbiotic successions (9). Some of these survivals are massive and permanent. Others are so rare or so minute as to seem insignificant on an experimental time scale (4). But are they insignificant when we move onto the longer time scale of evolution?

It is on this longer scale that we have to look, for example, at our evidence of variation in the size of nuclear chromosomes and in their content of DNA. The two kinds of evidence are parallel and, within limits, concordant. According to both, apart from polyploidy and polyteny, the chromosomes vary over a range of perhaps $1:10^5$.

Long ago it was clear that there was some sense in this variation as between for example, yeast, the lily and the salamander (2). But it was also clear that there was some lack of sense. There were several stages in the argument.

In the first place, systematic comparisons suggested sharp changes in chromosome size of the order of ten or even a hundred (16, 20). In the second place, experimental comparisons showed smaller changes, doubling or halving of size (5). In the third place these observations were paralleled and supported by systematic (not experimental) observations of correspondingly large changes in DNA content (18, 22). None of these changes had been easily related to any genetic causes or effects. They also seemed to be unrelated to the well understood principle of random change in chromosome structure, whether spontaneous or induced by physical or chemical treatments.

This conflict, involving chromosomes, molecules, and organisms, has been so clear as to deserve the name of the c-value paradox (3). It contains however another paradox, namely that its investigators, molecular or microscopic, have apparently taken note of one or two of the three kinds of evidence. Taken all together we may see the problem as that of how chromosomes can multiply or divide their size without appearing to change their genetic character.

To attack this problem we need to look at the whole evidence of chromosome behaviour throughout nuclear organisms. When we do so we find that side by side with regular complements of chromosomes recombining by crossing over and segregation at meiosis there are a variety of chromosomes which evade or escape these restrictions. They are the supernumeraries enduring in populations as balanced polymorphisms but not necessary for any particular individual (6). Like gene mutations they arise everywhere but visibly survive, multiply and evolve only where by chance they prove useful (19).

Useful for what? B or m chromosomes are generally small and were thought at first to be inert, useless and even parasitic. The same conclusions have been reached about redundant, non-transcribing and heterochromatic sequences of DNA in the regular members of the complement (12, 17). When I attempted forty years ago to describe what they did as the "activity of inert chromosomes" I was told that this was a paradox and hardly suitable as a title of a paper submitted to the Royal Society (10,11). Now partly and gradually the paradox has been resolved: redundant chromosomes and sequences are indeed preserved by natural selection.

Take first the evidence of plants.

B chromosomes in Angiosperms affect most visibly the germination of seeds (21), the growth of pollen and its sterilisation by incompatibility (15). But more fundamentally they affect the pairing of chromosomes, first its initiation in zygotene; then the frequency and distribution of crossing over (23); hence the survival of hybrids, the evolution of polyploids and the isolation of species. They owe their value mainly to an increase of variance not connected with any decisive thresholds. Always their value is for the population, the continuing and future population.

Consider then the well established sex chromosomes of animals. They often share in varying degrees the character of the supernumerary. Their history was early seen to reflect their special disadvantages. As they develop they come to be composed of two parts; a pairing segment, with recombination in both sexes, and a differential segment with recombination in only one sex and hence in one chromosome, X not Y. In insects, as Wilson noticed, the Y chromosome, which is largely non-recombining, is often lost in evolution (24). Which, on Weismann's view of natural selection through recombination, was to be expected.

What are we to say, however, of examples where the Y chromosome turns the tables on its partner by increasing its size and maintaining its activity?

Here there are several paradoxes. The Y chromosome in *Drosophila* is without effective recombination even in its pairing segment. Yet it is often larger than X. And it carries a series of genes identifiable by their several effects on the activity of the sperm. The mechanism is seen in a lampbrush transcription of unique individuality. For, when all the other chromosomes are inactive in the prophase of meiosis in the male fly, DNA loops with RNA and protein attached arise at specific loci on the Y. This activity sustains the fertility of the fly and it does so in different ways in different species. In a word, it is at present actively evolving by means altogether of its own (14).

Here we have an evolutionary initiative on the part of the Cinderella of the genome. We do not understand it except as a property of highly replicated DNA. But it is no longer unique. Examples have recently accumulated of sex chromosomes annexing by interchange a large part of the autosome apparatus. In this way a recombining part of the nuclear genome is captured for non-recombination in the heterozygous sex; but it continues to recombine in the homozygous sex. Thus termites and centipedes, monotreme mammals and Angiosperm mistletoes, have established new systems of recombination (9). The effects of these systems, unperceived by their discoverers, are bound to be very like those I have ascribed to achiasmate meiosis in the Diptera and elsewhere or to male haploidy in the Hymenoptera: they represent two-tracks in heredity contrasted in their recombination (8).

Another example will show the immense versatility that is given to chromosome systems by the exploitation of repetitive or redundant material which neither transcribes nor recombines. In the Heteroptera segregation of the sex chromosomes is organised without chiasmata by their co-orientation at the second metaphase of meiosis. This manoeuvre evidently depends on differential timing of the replication and transcription of their centromeres. And it allows the most divergent developments in the determination of sex. In some groups the X chromosome is multiplied like a supernumerary (to the number of 14 in *Cimex*) and Y becomes the effective sex-determinant. In other groups X alone is effective and Y is lost altogether (5).

These paradoxes are to be understood, in the first place, in the light of the unique character of the chromosomes in evolution. This paradoxical character may be obvious to us but we have not yet made it clear to others who have not seen chromosomes as we see them. It depends on the diverse responsibilities which their evolution has imposed on them: they are responsibilities which are differently understood by different people. We think of the chromosomes as responsible for their own activities at all times. The experimental breeder thinks of them as responsible for the character of the organism. And the evolutionist (if he thinks of them) may hold them responsible for the species, its past and its future, its continuation and its continuity.

This is where we break with the Darwinians. They are embarrassed when we tell them that all reproduction is oriented to the future. We know that the inventions of diploidy, meiosis, incompatibility, and the whole genetic system, have their effects only through future generations. For the Darwinian, whether organismal naturalist or mathematical evolutionist, this principle has no place in his nomenclature. Did not Bateson ridicule Weismann's chromosome theory in 1905 for "dealing in futures"? (1) And did not Haldane, using Bateson's archaic language sixty years later, still declare that "natural selection is blind in the sense that no character is favoured because it may be useful a thousand generations hence"?(13).

This is one lesson. Another is that responsibilities for present and future are not separate: they are bound up together in the chromosomes. Neither are they concordant responsibilities; on the contrary, they are inherently conflicting. Why? Because the chromosomes are ultimately responsible both for the continuity and for the discontinuity in life: the continuity which goes back to the molecular beginning; and the discontinuity which arises anew with each organism, each generation, and each species.

Thus, so long as evolution continues, there must always be conflict between the present and future needs of organisms and of species. They are conflicts for which the history of the chromosomes and the devices of the genetic system have only partly prepared them.

It does not therefore surprise us to find defects in the adaptation of the chromosomes. Again we disagree with the Darwinians. They expected to find perfection in nature. We may expect even in this Conference to find the evidence, not just of our own mistakes, but of nature's as well.

REFERENCES

1. Bateson, W. 1905. The Evolution Theory (Dr. August Weismann) in W. B. Naturalist, Cambridge U.P.: 1928.
2. Boivin, A. and Vendrely, R. & C. 1948. L'Acide desoxyribonucleique du noyau cellulaire, depositaire des caracteres hereditaires. C. R. Acad. Sci., Paris. 226:1061-1063.
3. Cavalier-Smith, T. 1978. Nuclear Volume Control etc. J.Cell.Sci. 34: 247-278.
4. Cullis, C. A. and Goldsbrough. 1980. DNA changes in flax genotrophs. John Innes Symp. 4: 91-98.
5. Darlington, C. D. 1965. Recent Advances in Cytology (3rd ed) Churchill, London. (Fig.12 and tables 10 and 79, Cimex)
6. Darlington, C. D. 1971a. The evolution of polymorphic systems. Ecological Genetics and Evolution. Ed. R. Creed, Blackwell, Oxford.
7. Darlington, C. D. 1971b. Axiom and Process in Genetics. Nature: 234, 521-525.
8. Darlington, C. D. 1972. The place of the chromosomes in the genetic system. (Two-track heredity.) Chromosomes Today. 4: 1-13.
9. Darlington, C. D. 1979. A diagram of evolution. (XY interchanges). Nature, 276: 447-452.
10. Darlington, C. D., and Thomas, P. T. 1941. Morbid mitosis and the activity of inert chromosomes (Sorghum). Proc. R.S. (B), 130: 127-150.
11. Darlington, C. D. and Upcott, M. B. 1941. The activity of inert chromosomes in Zea mays. J. Genet. 41: 275-296.
12. Doolittle, W. F. and Sapienza, C. 1980. Selfish genes, the phenotype paradigm and genome evolution. Nature, 284: 601-603.
13. Haldane, J. B. S. 1968. Science and Life. Pemberton, London.
14. Hess, Oswald. 1973. Genetic regulation revealed by Y chromosome lampbrush loops in Drosophila hydei. Chrs. Today, 4: 117-124.
15. Lewis, Dan. 1961. Chromosome fragments and mutation of the incompatibility gene. Nature 190: 990-991.
16. Marks, G. E. 1956. Chromosome numbers in the genus Oxalis. New Phyt. 55: 120-129.
17. Orgel, L. E. and Crick, F. H. C. 1980. Selfish DNA: the ultimate parasite. Nature, 284: 604-608.
18. Rees, H. 1972. DNA in higher plants: Brookhaven Symp.Biol. 26: 304-318.
19. Rees, H. 1974. B chromosomes. Sci.Prog.Oxf.: 61, 535-554.
20. Rothfels, K. et al. 1966. Chromosome size in Ranunculaceae. Chromosoma 20: 54-74.
21. Vosa, C. G. 1966. Seed germination and B-chromosomes in the leek (Allium porrum). Chrs. Today, 1: 24-27.
22. Wallace, D. C. et al. 1973. Genome size and evolution. Chromosoma. 40: 121-126.
23. Ward, E. J. 1973. Heterochromatic B chromosomes in maize affecting recombination. Chromosoma, 43: 177-186.
24. Wilson, E. B. 1925. The Cell in Heredith and Development (3rd ed.) Macmillan, N.Y.

CHROMOSOME ORGANISATION AT THE MOLECULAR LEVEL

DNA sequence organization and repeat sequences

R. Britten

California Institute of Technology, Carnegie Institution of Washington

An informal review of the status of DNA sequence organization as reflected by studies of repeated DNA sequences other than satellites. The subjects touched upon are: characteristics of repeats in eukaryotes; patterns of interspersion of repeats and single copy DNA; examination of specific families by recent techniques; presence of repeat transcripts in egg and nuclear RNA; mobility of some repeat families; conservation of some sequences over long periods of evolution; and evolutionary conservation of patterns of transcription. We know little about the significance of repeats. Nevertheless the complex patterns of transcription and the high degree of evolutionary conservation of some repeats suggest that the search for function is by no means hopeless. However, it is clear that there are many kinds of repeats, all of which are not likely to have equal significance and many possible roles must be considered.

CHARACTERISTICS OF REPEATS

In the earliest work it appeared likely that repetitive sequences were ubiquitous in eukaryotic genomes. By now it appears that the existence of repeats in the DNA can be taken as typical of eukaryotes and species such as yeast, which have few repeats, simply differ in their sequence organization from the majority. Yeasts do have moveable repetitive sequence elements that may turn out to be very common in eukaryotes as well as prokaryotes.

A small fraction of eukaryotic DNA consists of clusters of repetitive genes, such as those coding for histones or the ribosomal RNA cistrons. In addition, globin gene regions are organized in small clusters of genes and pseudogenes. However, at the criteria of precision of sequence relationship utilised in hybridisation studies most messenger RNA including the complex class is homologous to single copy DNA (Goldberg et al, 1973). Thus it appears that most genes effectively occur as few or single copies and most of the repetitive sequences observed with ordinary criteria are not genes.

The number of members in families of repeats ranges from several million down to very few. The very high frequency families of repeats are often organized in tandem and the resulting blocks of DNA may be purified and are normally called satellites. They are covered in other papers of this symposium.

In recent work with sea urchin repeats the frequency of repetition of about two dozen families was measured. The results show a broad distribution of frequencies up to about 10,000 copies and no discrete components are evident. After correction for the reduced sampling of lower frequency families during the cloning procedure it appears that there is an approximately uniform amount of DNA in the families in each decade of frequency. There are only a few large high frequency families while there are very many small low frequency families. In sea urchin DNA the median repeat family probably has less than 100 members. Many repeats are very divergent in sequence and reassociate to form duplexes of reduced thermal stability. Klein et al. (1978) showed that the individual families of repeats have characteristic degrees of divergence ranging from those in which all members are nearly exactly alike to those which show a 25 to 30C reduction in thermal stability compared to precise duplexes, which probably implies 25 or 30% sequence divergence.

The repetitive DNA of most higher organisms that have been studied consists of a majority of short repeats and a minority of longer repeats. The longer repeats have usually been recognized by the fact that after renaturation to repetitive cot large single strand specific nuclease resistant structures remain, which include, for example, about 7% of sea urchin DNA. The short repeats make up about 14% of the genome. This proportion is typical for many species that have been studied. Families in the long class are precisely repetitive while those in the short class show a lower thermal stability even after correction for the reassociated duplex length (Britten *et al.*, 1976). The sequences of the long and short repeats are principally distinct from each other though many families in each class may have a few members in the other class (Eden *et al.*, 1977; Moore *et al.*, 1981).

REPEAT AND SINGLE COPY DNA SEQUENCE ORGANIZATION

Studies of the organization of repeated sequences in eukaryotic DNA started with the observation of the interspersion of repeats among single copy sequences in calf DNA (Britten and Smith, 1970). Subsequent measurements indicated qualitatively that interspersion was important in mouse DNA and sea urchin DNA. Detailed measurements of DNA from the amphibian *Xenopus laevis* (Davidson *et al.*, 1973; Chamberlin *et al.*, 1975) and the sea urchin *S. purpuratus* (Graham *et al.*, 1974) showed that most of the single copy DNA occurred in segments averaging about 1 kb, interspersed with repeats a few hundred nucleotides in length. This has come to be called the short or *Xenopus* pattern of interspersion. Studies of the DNA of many more species indicated that similar patterns are widespread (Goldberg *et al.*, 1975).

There is some evidence (Eden *et al.*, 1980, and Eden, 1980) that birds have an intermediate pattern but studies have not been made for low frequency or very divergent repeats. There is evidence that short repeats occur in the region of structural genes in chicken (Cochet *et al.*, 1979).

Drosophila and some but not all Diptera appear to have a distinctly different pattern of interspersion (Manning *et al.*, 1975; Crain *et al.*, 1976) in which stretches of single copy DNA are much longer and the repeats average a few kilobases. The housefly (Crain *et al.*, 1976b) and the silk moth (Efstadiatis *et al.*, 1976) have a short pattern of DNA sequence interspersion. Short repeats may be present in Drosophila DNA but are few in number.

Wensink *et al.* (1979) have observed a class of repeats in

Drosophila which occur in a "scrambled" arrangement in which members of families of fairly short repeats apparently occur in a variety of sequence environments. Observations of moveable sequence elements in Drosophila are reviewed briefly in a later section.

INDIVIDUAL FAMILIES OF SEA URCHIN REPEATS

The techniques of recombinant DNA and sequencing have been applied to the study of the DNA of several species and have confirmed the patterns of sequence organization for a few individual families of repeats. Particularly detailed examination has been made of a variety of repetitive families in the sea urchin genome. Selected examples of the individual repeat families studied by Klein *et al.* (1978) have been used for a variety of measurements including expression in egg RNA and nuclear RNA and their evolutionary changes (briefly reviewed below). Cloned repeat probes were used to screen libraries of *S. purpuratus* inserts in lambda phage. Many individual DNA fragments of several kilobases in length were selected, mapped and the locations of the repeats determined, followed by examination of the characteristics of the adjacent sequences (Anderson *et al.*, 1981; Scheller *et al.*, 1981). Restriction mapping, gel blots, reassociation kinetics, and electron micrographic heteroduplex analysis have yielded significant information about the sequence organisation of the appropriate neighbourhoods of the sea urchin genome.

Two of the families consist of a large set of short repeats which typically are imbedded in single copy DNA sequences. Of 13 inserts studied only one showed 2 copies of the repeat. Of 27 inserts examined for the second family only 3 showed 2 copies. Electron micrographic studies showed homology between these inserts only in short 200-300 nucleotide regions. These are typical examples of short interspersed repeat families.

A third family appears to occur commonly in tandem and in an interesting new pattern where individual occurrences are separated by many kilobases but are much closer together than random expectation. A total of 17 inserts were studied and 2 of these contained 4 copies in apparent tandem array. One insert had three copies. Two of the inserts showed two widely spaced copies of the repeat.

The fourth family of sea urchin repeats has a novel organization in which small precisely related subfamilies can be recognised as members of a large "superfamily". The subfamilies have from 5 to 35 members each and form stable duplexes which are about 5 kb long and melt about 4 C below perfect duplexes. Duplexes between different subfamilies melt 20 to 25 C below perfect duplexes and intermediate degrees of relationship are not observed within this superfamily. The subfamilies appear to be related to each other by sharing fairly short DNA sequences (Scheller _et al._, 1981; Posakony _et al._, in preparation).

STATUS OF ANALYSIS OF THE HUMAN GENOME

The first measurements of human DNA repeats (Britten, 1969) included hydroxyapatite fractionation of 0.5 kb fragments which had been reassociated at various cots. Fifty percent of such fragments were identified as approximately single copy, i.e. did not contain repeats with a frequency greater than about 30 copies. 11% of these fragments contained repeats with several thousand copies and 27% contained repeats with more than a few thousand and less than 100,000 copies. Finally, 6% of the DNA was bound at very low cot, including foldback and families with frequencies greater than 100,000 copies. Schmid and Deininger (1975) made similar measurements and observed that 51% of 0.6 kb fragments appeared to reassociate as single copy. A range of rates of reassociation was observed which suggests that 35% of the fragments contained members of families with frequencies from a few copies to a few hundred thousand copies.

Schmid and Deininger (1975) showed that about 90% of very long DNA strands (13 kb) contained repeats. About half of these fragments were bound at very low cot while perhaps a third appeared to contain repeats with 10,000 or less copies. Their work clearly shows that high frequency repeats and reverse repeats are widely interspersed through human DNA. Low frequency repeats may also be interspersed and would probably not have been detected by their methods. Measurements of the fraction of fragments which contain repeats as a function of fragment length (Schmid and Deininger, 1975) indicate that many of the interspersed single copy fragments average about 2 kb in length.

After correction of these observations for single copy DNA linked to repeats it appears that between 20 and 30% of the DNA consists of actual repeated sequences. Another third of the genome consists of single copy sequences in the range of a few kb in length. The remaining 30 to 40% of the genome probably consists of longer single copy regions. Most of these longer regions appear to contain foldback or reverse repeats with spacings of more than 10 kb. Very divergent repeats or repeats with less than 100 copies could also interrupt these longer single copy DNA regions. Electron micrographic studies suggest that many of the interspersed repeated sequences are about 300 nucleotides in length (Deininger and Schmid, 1976).

Houck *et al.* (1979) observed that unlabelled 2,000 nucleotide DNA fragments reassociated to cot 68 and digested with S1 yielded a 300 nucleotide band visible with ethidium bromide. They estimate that 5% of the mass of the genome is in this band. About ½ of this DNA can be digested with the restriction enzyme Alu 1 to yield a 170 nucleotide and a 120 nucleotide fragment. They estimate that this "Alu family" of repeats contains 3% of the genome and thus occurs in about 300,000 copies. Its reassociation kinetics suggest 50-100,000 copies. The Alu family is fairly divergent, as indicated by thermal stability and by sequencing of several members (Rubin *et al.*, 1980). This family is widely interspersed in the genome and members often occur in neighboring locations with reverse orientation. Thus, the single DNA strands self renature to form loops with a range of lengths averaging perhaps 1.5 kb (Deininger and Schmid, 1976). If all the copies were uniformly spaced in the genome they would be separated by an average of 10 kb of DNA. This figure is uncertain since the frequency is not accurately known. Many copies could, of course, be more compactly arranged.

Another estimate has been made of the fraction of human DNA repeats which is short and interspersed. For this study DNA was prepared from cultured human fibroblast cells that had been labelled with ^{3}H thymidine *in vivo* (T.H. Hall, T. Giugni and

R. Britten, unpublished). The DNA was sheared to 2000 nucleotides, reassociated to cot 0.1, treated with S1 nuclease and subjected to gel electrophoresis. About 3% of the total tracer was in a peak at about 350 nucleotides. In addition, a wide range of other fragment lengths were observed. Such a measurement repeated at cot 40 showed a large increase in the S1 resistant fragments larger than 400 nucleotides. The fraction in the 300 nucleotide region increased little. This observation appears to confirm the conclusion drawn by Houck et al. (1979) that most of the 300 nucleotide interspersed repeats are of very high frequency and many are probably members of the Alu family. It does suggest that the quantity in the family may be somewhat less than they estimated, using unlabelled DNA. This measurement also indicates that in addition to the Alu family, a much greater number of other repeats of lower frequency are interspersed in human DNA. The other repeat lengths appear longer, ranging from 400 nucleotides to 1 kb and possibly larger.

In a measurement done for quite different purposes, Wolf et al. (1980) digested human DNA with Bam H1 and inserted the resulting fragments into the plasmid pBR 322. The inserts averaged 5.4 kb in length and about 70% hybridised to "multiple bands" of digests of human DNA in Southern blots (Southern, 1975). In a set of cross homology tests only one of 18 of these inserts hybridised to any other of the set. While there are uncertainties as a result of special circumstances in this work it clearly suggests that most of these plasmids contained repeats and that most of these were not Alu family members.

Fritsch et al. (1981) have examined a 64 kb region of the human genome (containing the beta-like globin gene cluster) for repetitive sequences and have determined which fragments contain members of the Alu family. Their results may be summarised as follows: 10 fragments totalling 24 kb do not have any repeats that they could detect (they estimate a 50 copy limit); 8 fragments totalling 18 kb contained an Alu family number; 9 fragments totalling 22 kb contained other repeats but not an Alu family member. In addition, they state that their procedure would not have detected other repeated sequences on fragments which contained an Alu repeat. The measurements of human DNA sequence organization are far from complete but the limited data suggest the following summary. Short period interspersion of repeat sequences from 0.3 to 1 kb and single copy sequences averaging 2 kb is present in 50 to 60% of the genome. Among the interspersed sequences the 300 nucleotide Alu family is very prominent. Its 100,000 to 300,000 members may be spaced as little as 10 kb apart on average. Reversed copies are often near each other and this pattern is transcribed yielding nuclear RNA exhibiting interspersed duplex regions. Many other repeated sequences are interspersed in human DNA and the evidence suggests that they could form the majority. Many of the other interspersed repeats are also transcribed into nuclear RNA (Fritsch *et al.*, 1981).

TRANSCRIPTION OF REPEATS

The characteristics of the RNA which is transcribed from repeats supply the strongest indication of the importance of repeats in the genome. Repeat transcripts are universally present in nuclear RNA and it has been known for many years that there are large qualitative and quantitative differences among the repeats represented in the RNA of different tissues and stages of development. Detailed measurements have been made of the expression of particular families of sea urchin repeats in mature egg RNA and nuclear RNA from gastrula stage embryos and from adult intestine tissue (Costantini *et al.*, 1978; Scheller *et al.*, 1978). Large differences in concentration were observed for different repeats and large changes were observed for certain families. These are the strongest contrasts yet observed for any class of macromolecules during differentiation and development. Transcripts of both strands of each family of repeats were present in both egg RNA and nuclear RNA.

Recent measurements (Posakony *et al.*, unpublished) show that there are high concentrations of only a few sizes of transcripts in egg poly A+ RNA. The set of transcript sizes is entirely different for the two strands indicating that the two strands are represented in egg RNA as a result of different specific events of asymetric transcription. Most maternal RNA coding sequences are linked to repeats in sea urchin poly A+ RNA (Costantini *et al.* 1980)

When sea urchin egg poly A+RNA (mostly maternal messenger RNA) is renatured, complex branched structures are observed. These structures result from the renaturation of complementary repeat sequences on different RNA molecules while interspersed single copy regions remain single stranded (Costantini *et al.*, 1980). Human tissue culture cell nuclear RNA also renatures to form complex structures (Federoff *et al.*, 1976), as does the poly A+ egg RNA of the amphibian *Xenopus laevis* (M. Chamberlin and E. Davidson, unpublished). In the human genome the "Alu repeat" is transcribed into nuclear RNA (Jelinek *et al.*, 1980). The transcription of reverse repeats also occurs and leads to the formation of RNAse resistant duplexes in the nuclear RNA. Fritsch *et al.* (1981) used double stranded RNAse resistant RNA as a probe and showed that several of the non-Alu repeats in the beta-like globin gene region are represented in the Hela cell nuclear RNA, in addition to many transcripts of the Alu repeat.

The significance of the observations of specific transcription is uncertain. It has been proposed that the complementary repeats in the RNA can form duplexes *in vivo* which affect processing of the RNA and thus gene expression (Davidson and Britten, 1979). It is unlikely that these sequences occur only accidentally in the transcribed regions. The striking modulation of representation of certain repeat families suggests specific control of the transcription of repeats since the total single copy complexity of nuclear RNA shows little modulation during development.

EVOLUTIONARY FREQUENCY CHANGE AND MOBILITY

Recent measurements show that many repeat families change rapidly in frequency during sea urchin evolution (Moore *et al.*, 1978) and that many repeats are mobile elements in Drosophila DNA. Transposable elements have been studied in bacteria for many years and are also important in yeast (e.g. Roeder *et al.*, 1980; Scherer and Davis, 1980).

Studies of cloned repeats in Drosophila have led to identification of moveable elements which are of well defined length, are precisely repeated (Potter *et al.*, 1979), have direct terminal repeats (Finnegan *et al.*, 1978) and show large variation in position and frequency among strains of *D. melanogaster* (Strobel *et al.*, 1979; Ilyin *et al.*, 1978). Another set of moveable elements in Drosophila have terminal reverse repeats and show considerable variation in length and position (Potter *et al.*, 1980). It is likely that mobile elements are of universal significance. Transformation often leads to the integration of genes that are unstable to deletion and it has been suggested that similar catastrophic events may occur for normal genes (Pellicer *et al.*, 1980). The role of moveable repeats in mammalian genetic instability remains uncertain. However, in yeast, maize and Drosophila insertion and deletion events are known to have important effects on genetic stability.

In sea urchins all repetitive sequence families appear to change in frequency on an evolutionary time scale (Moore *et al.*, 1978; Moore *et al.*, 1981), though some much more rapidly than others. Rapid evolutionary frequency change is not restricted to tandem arrays and satellites. One of the most rapidly changing families in the sea urchin genome consists primarily of short repeats which are interspersed throughout the genome. Therefore, some mechanisms of insertion and deletion must be responsible, moveable repeat elements may be involved.

A striking feature of repeat evolution is exhibited in the comparison of *S. purpuratus* and *Lytechinus pictus* which had a last common ancestor about 175 million years ago. It appears that there has been almost complete loss of the members of most families and these have been replaced by new families in both species. Nevertheless, the quantities and the frequency distribution of the repeats is about the same in both species. Such similarities or conservation of repetitive sequence patterns are common, and imply that there are selective forces which establish these patterns. Clearly, particular selective conditions are not universal since there is a great deal of variety in the quantities and frequency distributions that have been observed so far.

At this time direct measurements of evolutionary frequency changes of individual families of repeats have not been made among vertebrate species. However there is good evidence that rapid changes in frequency also occur in mammalian, including human, DNA. This statement is based on a large number of measurements of interspecies repetitive sequence relationships among vertebrates. In the earliest measurements (Bolton *et al.*, 1964) the fraction of repeats held in common between Rhesus monkey, a series of primates, mammals, birds and fish was determined. The result was a simple exponential decay of extent of relationship with time, accurately following the equation $H = \exp(-T/130)$ where H is the fraction of repeats held in common and T is the time in millions of years since the last common ancestor. Such an exponential decay or "single hit curve" apparently rules out base substitution as the primary mechanism for loss of repeat homology. Many base substitutions would be required to lose recognition of an individual repeat and a time lag would occur after separation of two species lines before the full rate of substitution would be reflected in loss of repeat homology ("multiple hit curve"). The observed exponential decay without lag is consistent with events of deletion or insertion of repeats as the primary events in the loss of homology. The effects of such processes have been directly observed in Drosophila and sea urchin DNA. Thus it is likely that they occur in vertebrate DNA including the human genome. We can estimate the rate (from the 130 million year decay period) to be equivalent to the loss and/or gain of one 300 base repeat per 50 years per human genome. Even if repeats have no specific function their insertion into or deletion from the genome would probably have deleterious genetic effects and these processes are likely to be an important source of genetic variation.

EVOLUTIONARY CONSERVATION OF REPEATS

It can be argued that potential functions of repeats would depend on their primary sequences. If this were so the repeats would be under significant selective pressure and evolutionary conservation of their sequences could be observed. In fact the evolutionary rate of change of the average sequence of families of repeats is much slower than that of single copy DNA (Harpold and Craig, 1978; Moore *et al.*, 1978). Certain families of repeats are very tightly conserved in sequences while others change more rapidly. Most striking among conserved families is the one represented in *S. purpuratus* by the clone CSp2108 (Scheller *et al.*, 1981). Very precisely related repeats are found in *Lytechinus pictus* which has a common ancestor shared with *S. purpuratus* no more recently than 175 million years. In this time most shared repetitive sequences have been lost and the single copy DNA has diverged so that only 20% homology may be measured. Nevertheless, there are repeats in *L. pictus* which are clearly members of one of the CSp2108 subfamilies in *S. purpuratus* and have not diverged by more than 10% in nucleotide sequence. This observation suggests that the sequence-dependent selection pressure for this family of repeats is very strong and thus several members of this subfamily may perform critical functions in both of these distant sea urchin species.

Cloned repeats from *S. purpuratus* were used to compare the concentration of transcripts in the eggs of *S. purpuratus* and *S. franciscanus* (Moore *et al.*, 1980). The eggs of these species contain different amounts of RNA and their genomes contain different numbers of copies of these cloned repeats. Some of these repeats are highly expressed in the eggs of both species and some are rare in both species. For each family of repeats tested the eggs of both species contain about the same number of transcripts per nanogram of total egg RNA. The two species had a last common ancestor about 20 million years ago and their single copy DNAs have a median divergence in sequence of about 20%. The observed evolutionary conservation of the patterns of expression in egg RNA appears significant when compared with the large genomic differences between these species.

SELFISH OR ALTRUISTIC ?

The answer to this question will probably be: "both or neither". For these paragraphs selfish refers to a set of repeats that offers no positive advantage by being present in the genome. It has its own life in the genome of one or more species and its properties, such as sequence and frequency, are determined only by its own survival. Altruistic is taken to mean that the selection pressure which governs the existence and sequence of a family of repeats is entirely due to the advantage it gives to the species. These definitions are clearly incomplete and possibly paradoxical but serve to point up the issue.

There are observations which suggest that some repeats are not under tight selection pressure from the point of view of the organism and its genome. An example would be the satellite which makes up 20 or 30% of the green monkey genome and is absent or quantitatively very different in closely related species. Such cases are numerous. However there are satellite families shared over great evolutionary distances. Mobility of sequence elements has raised the possibility of horizontal transfer and this sharing of sequences does not quite prove conservation. A direct test of horizontal transfer and its quantitative significance is needed.

In contrast many observations suggest strong selection pressure on individual repeats or on significant patterns of sequences or their expression: A) the similarity of repeat sequences in interspecies comparisons; B) the similarity of quantities and frequencies of repeats at great evolutionary distances for some but not all comparisons; C) the great differences in the concentration of transcripts of certain repeats in different sea urchin tissues; D) the conservation of the quantitative pattern of repetitive sequence expression in sea urchin egg RNA.

The following abstract argument has been an essential part of our strategy for more than a decade.

1). Repeats have enormous potentiality for control and for other relationships through their sequence homology.

2). The sequence elements that supply this potentiality are often not utilised. The very idea of potentiality requires a storehouse of unused elements, as well as mechanisms for producing, translocating and varying them. The idea of selfishness of the repeats may be helpful conceptually but will probably appear shallow in a broad view of the nature of evolution.

3). Where significant potentiality exists ("color coded hookup wire") it is likely to be utilised. In other words repeats may operate as regulatory elements when the opportunity arises and a selective advantage for the species results.

4). The ability to translocate and thus establish new regulatory relationships is a source of evolutionary variation.

Repeated sequences may have parasitized the genomes of all eukaryotes (Doolittle and Sapienza, 1980; Orgel and Crick, 1980) or are important functional elements of the genome (e.g. Britten and Davidson, 1969; Davidson and Britten, 1979). I feel it is much more likely that they have both roles (Britten and Kohne, 1966; Britten and Davidson, 1971).

REFERENCES

Bolton, E. T., R. J. Britten, T. J. Byers, D. B. Cowie, B. Hoyer, Y. Kato, B. J. McCarthy, M. Miranda and R. B. Roberts. 1964. C.I.W. Yearbook 63, 394.

Britten, R. J. 1969. C.I.W. Yearbook 67, 327.

Britten, R. J. and E. H. Davidson. 1969. Science 165, 349-358.

Britten, R. J. and E. H. Davidson. 1971. Quart. Rev. Biol. 46, 111-138.

Britten, R. J., D. E. Graham, F. C. Eden, D. M. Painchaud and E. H. Davidson. 1976. J. Mol. Evol. 9, 1-23.

Britten, R. J. and D. E. Kohne. 1966. C.I.W. Yearbook 65, 98.

Britten, R. J. and J. Smith. 1970. C.I.W. Yearbook 68, 378-386.

Chamberlin, M. E., R. J. Britten and E. H. Davidson 1975. J. Mol. Biol. 96, 317-333.

Cochet, M., F. Gannon, R. Heu, L. Maroteaux, F. Perrin and P. Chambon. 1979. Nature 282, 567.

Costantini, F. D., R. H. Scheller, R. J. Britten and E. H. Davidson. 1980. Nature 287, 111.

Costantini, F. D., R. H. Scheller, R. L. Britten and E. H. Davidson. 1978. Cell 15, 173.

Crain, W. R., E. H. Davidson and R. J. Britten. 1976b. Chromosoma 59, 1.

Crain, W. R., F. C. Eden, W. R. Pearson, E. H. Davidson and R. J. Britten. 1976. Chromosoma (Berl) 56, 309.

Davidson, E. H. and Britten, R. J. 1979. Science 204, 1052.

Davidson, E. H., B. R. Hough, C. S. Amenson and R. J. Britten. 1973. J. Mol. Biol. 77, 1.

Deininger, P. L. and C. W. Schmid. 1976. J. Mol. Biol. 106, 773.

Doolittle, W. F. and C. Sapienza. 1980. Nature 284, 601.

Eden, F. C. 1980. J. Biol. Chem. 255, 4854.

Eden, F. C., A. T. H. Burns and R. F. Goldberger. 1980. J. Biol. Chem. 255, 4843.

Eden, F. C., D. E. Graham, E. H. Davidson and R. J. Britten. 1977. Nucleic Acids Res. 4, 1553.

Efstratiadis, A., W. R. Crain, R. J. Britten, E. H. Davidson and F. C. Kafatos. 1976. Proc. Natl. Acad. Sci. U.S.A. 73, No. 7, 2289.

Federoff, N. and T. R. Wall. 1976. In Molecular Mechanisms in the Control of Gene Expression, 5. W. J. Rudder, D. P. Nierlich and C. F. Fox, eds. New York : Academic Press, 379.

Finnegan, D. J., G. M. Rubin, M. W. Young and D. S. Hogness. 1978. Cold Spring Harbor Symp. Quant. Biol. 42, 1053.

Fritsch, E. F., J. C-K. Shen, R. M. Lawn and T. Maniatis. 1981. Cold Spring Harbor Symp. Quant. Biol.- in press.

Goldberg, R. B., G. A. Galau, R. J. Britten and E. H. Davidson. 1973. Proc. Nat. Acad. Sci. U.S.A. 70, 3516.

Goldberg, R. B., W. R. Crain, J. V. Ruderman, G. P. Moore, T. R. Barnett, R. C. Higgins, R, A. Gelfand, G. A. Galau, R. J. Britten and E. H. Davidson. 1975. Chromosoma 51, 225.

Graham, D.E., B. R. Neufeld, E. H. Davidson and R. J. Britten. 1974. Cell 1, 127.

Harpold, M. M. and S. P. Craig. 1978. Differentiation 10, 7.

Houck, C. M., F. P. Rinehart and C. W. Schmid. 1979. J. Mol. Biol. 132, 289.

Ilyin, Y. V., N. A. Tchurukov, E. V. Ananiev, A. P. Ryskov, G. N. Yenikolpov, S. A. Limborska, N. E. Maleeva, V. A. Gvozdev and G. P. Georgiev. 1978. Cold Spring Harbor Symp. Quant. Biol. 42, 959.

Jelinek, W. R., T. P. Toomey, L. Leinwand, C. H. Duncan, P. A. Biro, P. V. Choudary, S. M. Weissman, C. M. Rubin, C. M. Houck, P. L. Deininger and C. W. Schmid. 1980. Proc. Natl. Acad. Sci., U.S.A. 77, 1398.

Klein, W. H., T. L. Thomas, C. Lai, R. H. Scheller, R. J. Britten and E. H. Davidson. 1978. Cell 14, 889.

Manning, J. E., C. W. Schmid and N. Davidson. 1975. Cell 4, 141.

Moore, G. P., F. D. Costantini, J. W. Posakony, E. H. Davidson and R. J. Britten. 1980. Science 208, 1046.

Moore, G. P., W. R. Pearson, E. H. Davidson and R. J. Britten. 1981 - submitted.

Moore, G. P., R. H. Scheller, E. H. Davidson and R. J. Britten. 1978. Cell 15, 649.

Orgel, L. E. and F. H. C. Crick. 1980. Nature 284, 604.

Pellicer, A., D. Robins, B. Wold, R. Sweet, J. Jackson, I. Lowy, and J. M. Roberts. 1980. Science 209, 1414.

Potter, S. S., W. J. Brorein, P. Dunsmuir and G. M. Rubin. 1979. Cell 17, 415.

Potter, S., M. Truett, M. Phillips and A. Maher. 980. Cell 20, 639.

Roeder, G. S. and G. R. Fink. 1980. Cell 21, 239.

Rubin, C. M., C. M. Houck, P. L. Deininger, T. Friedman and C. W. Schmid. 1980. Nature 284, 372.

Scheller, R. H., D. M. Anderson, J. W. Posakony, L. B. McAllister, R. J. Britten and E. H. Davidson. 1981. J. Mol. Biol. - submitted.

Scheller, R. H., F. D. Costantini, M. R. Kozlowski, R. J. Britten and E. H. Davidson. 1978. Cell 15, 189.

Scherer, S. and R. W. Davis. 1980. Science 209, 1380.

Schmid, C. W. and P. L. Deininger. 1975. Cell 6, 345.

Southern, E. M. 1975. J. Mol. Biol. 98, 503.

Strobel, E., P. Dunsmuir and G. M. Rubin. 1979. Cell 17, 429.

Wensink, P. C., T. Shiro and C. Pachl. 1979. Cell 18, 1231.

Wolf, S. F., C. E. Mareni and B. R. Migeon. 1980. Cell 21, 95.

Gene amplification and methotrexate resistance in cultured cells

Robert T. Schimke

Department of Biological Sciences, Stanford University, Stanford, CA

In this report we summarize the current status of studies on the mechanism(s) whereby cultured animal cells become resistant to the 4-amino analog of folic acid, methotrexate, as a result of stepwise selection, a resistance due to elevated levels of dihydrofolate reductase and associated amplification of DNA sequences coding for dihydrofolate reductase.

Selection of cells with elevated dihydrofolate reductase levels

Methotrexate (MTX) selectively inhibits dihydrofolate reductase (DHFR), an enzyme necessary for the generation of key precursors of nucleic acids. Cells can become resistant to MTX by three mechanisms: (1) an alteration in the enzyme such that MTX does not inhibit; (2) an alteration in inward MTX transport; (3) an increased capacity for cells to synthesize DHFR. The latter type of resistance is obtained characteristically upon stepwise selection of cells in progressively increasing concentrations of MTX in the medium. The resistant cells contain increased levels of DHFR proportional to the level of resistance (Alt et al, 1976). The elevated DHFR levels result from a corresponding increase in the DHFR gene copy number, i.e. gene amplification (Alt et al, 1978). This is observed in a number of cell lines of both hamster and mouse origin, and in highly aneuploid cells as well as those having a relatively stable karyotype (Schimke et al, 1979). We have proposed that DHFR gene amplification is an infrequent event and that various DNA sequences can undergo amplification randomly, and that amplification of specific sequences is detected only when cells are placed under appropriate selection conditions, i.e. MTX. The requirement for stepwise selection results from the fact that the amplifications occur in small steps, and hence cells with progressively more DHFR genes (and MTX resistance) are obtained only by the stepwise selection process (Schimke et al, 1978).

The amplified DHFR genes, increased DHFR levels, and MTX resistance can occur in either a stable or an unstable state. When cells with amplified genes are grown in the absence of MTX, some cell lines lose resistance rapidly, such that within 20 cell doublings the cell population has lost 50% of its resistance (and gene copy number). In other cell lines the genes persist when cells are grown in the absence of MTX (Alt et al, 1978). When cells are first selected for MTX resistance, characteristically the amplified genes are unstable, whereas when cells are grown for long periods under selection pressure, the population of cells that emerges has more cells with stably amplified DHFR genes.

Localization of amplified DHFR genes in stably and unstably amplified cells.

In stably amplified cell lines the DHFR genes are localized to a single region of a chromosome. In a Chinese hamster ovary cell line (Nunberg et al, 1978) and a mouse L5178Y cell line (Dolnick et al, 1979) the amplified genes are present on an expanded region called a homogeneously staining region (HSR) to which the amplified genes can be localized by *in situ* hybridization with DNA complementary to DHFR mRNA. Where it has been possible to determine, only one of the two homologous chromosomes contains the HSR (Beidler and Spengler, 1976, Dolnick et al, 1979). Preliminary results done in collaboration with Dr. Frank Ruddle of Yale Univ. indicate that the resident (non-amplified) DHFR gene resides on the long arm of chromosome 2 in Chinese hamster cells, the position of the HSR in the cell line we have studied (Nunberg et al, 1978). Thus we conclude that the chromosomally amplified genes are present at the site of the resident gene.

In unstably amplified cell lines the DHFR genes are present as extrachromosomal elements, called double minute chromosomes (DMs).

Double minute chromosomes are self-replicating chromosomal elements that do not contain centromers (Levan and Levan, 1978, Barker and Hsu, 1979) and have been reported in tumor cell lines of human origin (Balaban-Malenbaum and Gilbert, 1976, Barker and Hsu, 1979).

Double minute chromosomes (containing DHFR genes) can be lost from cells by two different mechanisms. Since DMs do not contain centromers, they have the potential for unequal segregation into daughter cells at the time of mitosis. We have shown in mouse S-180 cells that individual cells with lower DHFR gene copy number grow more rapidly over a number of cell doublings in the absence of MTX. Thus those cells with progressively fewer DHFR genes will become dominant in the population (Schimke et al, 1979). In addition, extrachromosomal elements can undergo micronucleation (the nuclear membrane can reassemble around a packet of DMs) and be lost from cells as a single step process (Levan et al, 1976). We have observed in the progeny of single cells undergoing gene loss cells which have lost virtually all of the amplified genes, as well as cells that show marked heterogeneity with respect to the gene copy number (Schimke et al, 1980).

<u>How common is gene amplification</u> ?

Gene amplification is considered to be a major mechanism for the increase in size and complexity of the genome during evolution. In addition selective gene amplification occurs in certain developmentally controlled cases (e.g. ribosomal genes in amphibian oocytes) and as compensation in instances where certain genes have been deleted (ribosomal genes in <u>Drosophila</u>). The gene amplification involving MTX resistance is a relatively infrequent event, but such a process is not limited to MTX and DHFR genes. Stark and his collegues (Wahl et al, 1979) have shown that resistance to a highly specific inhibitor of aspartyltranscarbamylase (PALA), generated by stepwise selection also involves gene amplification. In addition there are other examples of stepwise selection for drug resistance that is either stable or unstable and results from elevated levels of specific enzymes (Schimke et al, 1978). Certain reports of the properties of insecticide resistances also have these same characteristics. Most recently our laboratory has been studying several patients with tumors resistant to MTX, and we have preliminary evidence that this resistance results from elevated DHFR levels and that there is selective amplification of DHFR genes (Dower, Horns, Schimke, preliminary results). Thus we conclude that gene amplifications may be relatively common, and that it occurs in clinical circumstances as well as in the experimental cell culture systems we have been studying.

Possible mechanisms for amplification of DHFR genes.

Our studies raise a large number of questions. Does such gene amplification occur in normal cells? Are there some DNA sequences that can be amplified more readily than others? Do the biochemical events leading to amplifications have any relationship to alterations in chromosome structure observed in various malignant cells? We are currently examining the molecular structure of the DHFR gene using recombinant DNA techniques (Nunberg et al, 1980), and characterizing the DNA sequences present in DMs and their potential relationship to the amplified DNA sequences in HSRs.

We are currently considering three different possible means for generating amplified DHFR genes: (1) DNA uptake from killed cells. If DNA segments are engulfed by a few remaining cells, and if such DNA can replicate, it would constitute DMs. If they subsequently integrated into a specific region of a chromosome, they could generate HSRs. (2) Unequal mitotic sister chromatid exchange. This process would generate cells with progressively expanding chromosomally localized genes, and if excised to produce self-replicating elements, would constitute DMs. (3) Saltatory (disproportionate) replication. If there are origins of DNA replication where multiple initiations of replication occur within a given S phase ("hot spots") relative to adjacent replication forks, amplified DNA sequences would be generated, and they could be removed from the chromosome to constitute DMs, or could recombine into the chromosome to generate a HSR (see Schimke et al, 1980 for a discussion of these possible mechanisms and why mechanism # 3 most generally fits a single means for various types of gene amplification).

All three of these mechanisms may occur in cultured cells to generate various cell lines with differing properties of gene amplification. The mechanisms are not mutually exclusive. The hypotheses are amenable to experimental testing, and an understanding of the generation of HSRs and DMs may provide information concerning abnormal replication processes in malignancy, as well as provide information about how organisms (and cells) become resistant to various drugs by a gene amplification mechanism.

Acknowledgements

I would like to acknowledge the many collaborators who have assisted in these studies, including Dr. J. Bertino of Yale Univ., Dr. L. Chasin of Columbia Univ., Dr. S. Cohen of Stanford Univ., as well as members of my laboratory group, F. Alt, R. Kellems, R. Kaufman, J. Nunberg, P. Brown, M. McGrogan, D. Slate, G. Crouse, W. Dower, R. Horns, and C. Simonsen. This work is supported by research grants from the American Cancer Society, the National Institute of General Medical Sciences, and the National Cancer Institute.

References

Alt, F.W., R.E. Kellems, and R.T. Schimke 1976. Synthesis and degradation of folate reductase in sensitive and methotrexate-resistant lines of S-180 cells. J. Biol. Chem. 251: 3063-3074.

Alt, F.W., R.E. Kellems, J.R. Bertino, and R.T. Schimke 1978. Selective amplification of dihydrofolate reductase genes in methotrexate-resistant variants of cultured murine cells. J. Biol. Chem. 253: 1357-1370.

Balaban-Malenbaum, G., and F. Gilbert 1977. Double minute chromosomes and homogeneously staining regions in chromosomes of a human neuroblastoma cell line. Science 198: 739-742.

Barker, P.E., and T.C. Hsu. 1979. Double minutes in human carcinoma cell lines, with special reference to breast tumors. J. Natl. Cancer Inst. 62: 257-261.

Beidler, J.L., and B.A. Spengler 1976. Metaphase chromosome anomaly: association with drug resistance and cell-specific products. Science 191: 185-188.

Dolnick, B.J., R.J. Berenson, J.R. Bertino, R.J. Kaufman, J.H. Nunberg, and R.T. Schimke 1979. Correlation of dihydrofolate reductase elevation with gene amplification in a homogeneously staining chromosomal region in L5178Y cells. J. Cell Biol. 83: 394-402.

Kaufman, R.J., P.C. Brown, and R.T. Schimke 1979. Amplified dihydrofolate reductase genes in unstably methotrexate-resistant cells are associated with double minute chromosomes. Proc. Natl. Acad. Sci. USA 76: 5669-5673.

Levan, G., N. Mandahl, V. Bregula, G. Klein, and A. Levan 1976. Double minute chromosomes are not centromeric regions of host chromosomes. Hereditas 83: 83-90.

Levan, A., and G. Levan 1978. Have double minutes functioning centromers? Hereditas 88: 81-92.

Nunberg, J.M., R.J. Kaufman, R.T. Schimke, G. Urlaub, and L.A. Chasin 1978. Amplified dihydrofolate reductase genes are localized to a homogeneously staining region of a single chromosome in a methotrexate-resistant Chinese hamster ovary cell line. Proc. Natl. Acad. Sci. USA 75: 5553-5556.

Nunberg, J.H., R.J. Kaufman, A.C.Y. Chang, S.N. Cohen, and R.T. Schimke 1980. Structure and genomic organization of the mouse dihydrofolate reductase gene. Cell 19: 355-364.

Schimke, R.T., R.J. Kaufman, F.W. Alt, and R.E. Kellems 1978. Gene amplification and drug resistance in cultured murine cells. Science 202: 1051-1055.

Schimke, R.T., R.J. Kaufman, J.H. Nunberg, and S.L. Dana 1979. Studies on the amplification of dihydrofolate reductase genes in methotrexate-resistant cultured mouse cells. Cold Spring Harb. Symp. Quant. Biol.43: 1297-1303.

Schimke, R.T., P.C. Brown, R.J. Kaufman, M. McGrogan, and D.L. Slate 1980. Chromosomal and extrachromosomal localization of amplified dihydrofolate reductase genes in cultured mammalian cells. Cold Spring Harb. Symp. Quant. Biol. in press.

Wahl, G.M., R.A. Padgett, and G.R. Stark 1979. Gene amplification causes over-rpoduction of the first three enzymes of UMP synthesis in N-(phosphoacetyl l-aspartate)-resistant hamster cells. J. Biol. Chem. 254: 8679-8689.

Satellite DNA – change and stability

W. J. Peacock, E. S. Dennis and W. L. Gerlach

Division of Plant Industry, CSIRO, Canberra, Australia

Chromosomes of eukaryotes have several classes of DNA sequence with different properties of stability through development and evolution. For example, structural genes are conserved in their chromosome locations; the mammalian X chromosome appears to have had the same complement of genes throughout the evolutionary history of mammals including the marsupials (Cooper *et al*. 1975). In *Drosophila* species, the banding patterns of salivary gland chromosomes show that large segments of chromosomes are conserved, although sometimes being rearranged by inversions or whole arm translocations (Sturtevant and Novitski, 1941). G-banding analyses show a similar picture for many other groups of animals.

There are other components of chromosomal DNA which are labile over short periods of evolutionary time. In both *Drosophila* and yeast, some moderately repeated sequence elements are mobile in their chromosome locations and vary in number, even between strains of the same species (Rubin *et al*. 1980; Young 1979; Cameron *et al*. 1979). These elements, probably a general feature of eukaryote chromosomes, have properties similar to transposable elements of prokaryotes. In *Drosophila melanogaster* the presence of a *copia* sequence, one form of these mobile elements, has no visible effect on chromosome morphology or banding pattern (Rubin *et al*. 1980). Changes occurring in yet another class of chromosomal DNA, highly repeated DNA, can have a marked effect on chromosome morphology. A highly repeated, or satellite, DNA sequence may be present in 10^6 copies in one species and yet be represented by only 10^2-10^3 copies in a closely related species. Since the repeats are usually grouped in long tandem arrays in heterochromatin, and may account for several percent of the genome, such changes of frequency can result in marked differences in size of a heterochromatic segment at the cytological level.

Satellite DNA can change in repeat numbers

Initially, when satellite DNAs were identified only by buoyant density analysis, related species showed different complements of highly repeated sequences (Walker 1971). This led to the idea that these sequences were short-lived over evolutionary time. When techniques allowing direct comparison of nucleotide sequences were developed, hybridization data showed that related species usually contained the same complements of highly repeated DNAs, with the amounts of any one sequence often differing greatly between the species. Even in cases in which a major satellite DNA was present in such a low repetition frequency in another species that it could not be detected as a buoyant density satellite, the nucleotide sequence of the repeat units was maintained (Fry and Salser 1977, Gosden *et al.* 1977). Different satellites have different repetitive values in related species (Peacock *et al.* 1977), and where a particular repeated sequence is present over an extended range of taxa (e.g. the "garden of Eden" sequence on the sex chromosomes of many animals; Singh *et al.* 1978) its repeat number can vary widely from species to species. The population of repeat units of a satellite is generally distributed over a number of heterochromatic segments in a genome and the change in repeat numbers seen in a comparison of species may not be equal at all of these sites.

Satellite DNA consists of related arrays of repeat units

Analysis of the repeat units of a satellite in a genome shows that a number of amplification events are involved in the generation of the total population of repeats. The 1.672 g/cm^3 satellite of *D. melanogaster*, apparently homogeneous by a number of physical criteria, is composed of two sequence elements, $\genfrac{}{}{0pt}{}{\text{(AATAT)}}{\text{(TTATA)}}$ and $\genfrac{}{}{0pt}{}{\text{(AATATAT)}}{\text{(TTATATA)}}$, present in separate arrays (Brutlag and Peacock (1979), so at least two separate amplification events must have been involved.

Restriction enzyme analyses have shown that a similar organisation of sets of different homogeneous arrays applies in satellites with more complex repeating units. An example is the 1.708 g/cm^3 satellite of the red-necked wallaby (Dennis et al. 1980) where the recognition sites of the restriction enzymes, Bam and Pst, are regularly placed at 2500 bp intervals throughout all this satellite DNA. Other recognition sites, such as those for Hind III and Xma, occur in only a proportion of the population of 2500 bp repeat units. The repeats which contain these sites are not randomly distributed but are in contiguous arrays. By testing these different arrays with a battery of restriction enzymes, we have shown that a hierarchical pattern of subpopulations can be recognised within the satellite. These subpopulations reflect amplification events in each of which one 2500 bp unit, containing a mutation differentiating it from its neighbours, is multiplied into a tandem array of identical units. The subpopulation structure of the red-necked wallaby satellite was such that we could reconstruct the temporal order of the various segmental amplification events (Fig. 1).

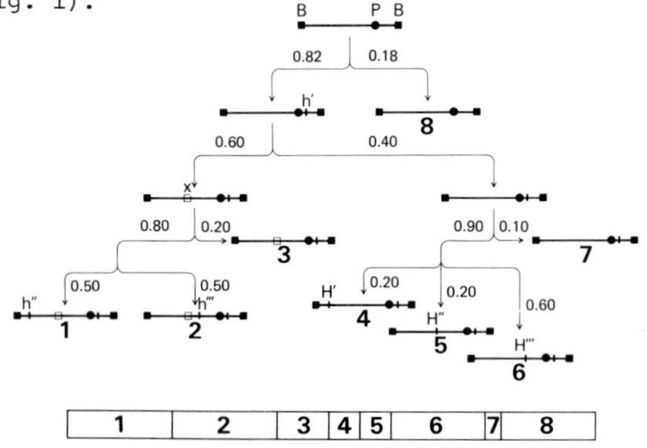

Fig. 1. The evolution of red-necked wallaby satellite DNA. Eight different subpopulations (1-8) are derived in a temporal order from one ancestral unit. The proportions of the new and unchanged units are shown for each amplification event. Recognition sites for enzymes: Bam(B), Pst(P), Hha I(h), Xma(X), Hind III (H).

Other examples of tandemly arrayed subpopulations are the 1.688 g/cm^3 satellite of D. melanogaster (Carlson and Brutlag 1977), and some highly repetitive components of mouse (Horz and Zachau 1977), rat (Pech et al. 1979a), and red crab (Christie and Skinner 1980) DNA.

Complex satellites are formed from shorter repeats

Just as the population of repeating units of a satellite is generated by a succession of amplification events, so too are long repeat units generated by amplification and union of preexisting shorter repeats. Restriction enzyme mapping and nucleotide sequencing of the bovine 1.706 g/cm^3 satellite (Pech et al. 1979b) has shown that the 2350 bp unit is composed of a series of smaller repeating segments all originally derived from 12 and 23 bp repeats (Fig. 2).

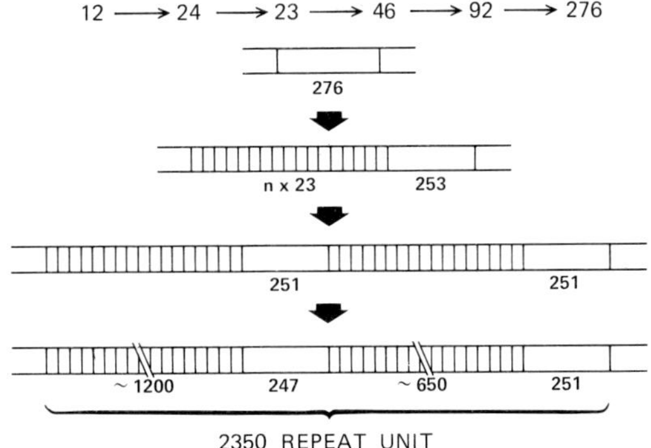

Fig. 2 The development of the 2350 bp repeating unit of a bovine satellite DNA from an ancestral 12 bp unit (Pech et al. 1979b).

This plausible schema involves some sequence divergence by base pair mutation and deletion, and amplification of diverged units, the unit of amplification changing at different stages in the evolution of the satellite.

Amplification units are not always unit repeats

Many puzzling observations on satellite DNAs are explicable in terms of localised amplification events - these events, which can be of several types, produce a wide variety of changes to the organisational patterns of this sequence class.

In the case of the red-necked wallaby satellite, the unit of amplification we detected was invariably the 2500 bp repeat, but in some satellites, a multiple length of the repeat unit can be the segment which is amplified. In the red-necked wallaby, the arithmetic segment series, resulting from site alterations, has a frequency distribution compatible with random inactivation of recognition sites, but in the red crab (Christie and Skinner 1980) the representation of segment lengths is markedly non-random. For example, octamers have been amplified to high frequency. These two classes of segment amplification can be represented as $n(u)$ and $n(ku)$ respectively, where u is the unit repeat of the satellite, n is the new number of copies of the unit amplified and k is the number of repeat units involved. The case where the amplified unit is the repeat unit *per se* depends for its detection on an initial sequence alteration to a restriction enzyme recognition site and should be represented as $n(u^*)$, the * denoting a mutational change.

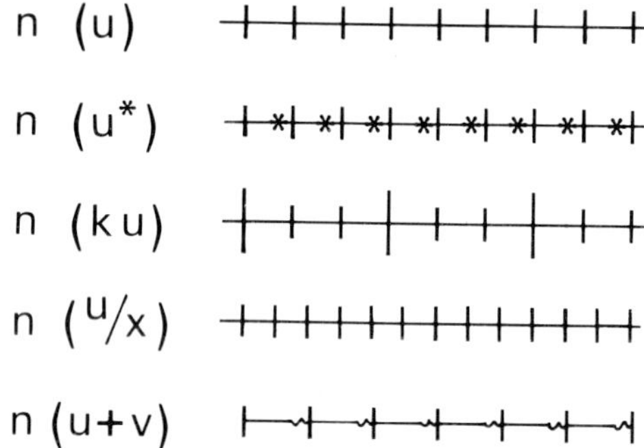

Fig. 3. A summary of the types of amplification events occurring in the formation of satellite DNAs. The nomenclature is explained in the text.

Figure 3 shows two other types of amplification which have been detected both within and between species. If a nonintegral length of an existing tandem array of units is amplified, $n(u/x)$, then a new repeat segment length, not fitting the arithmetic ladder pattern is generated. A well documented example is the 254 bp variant of the 359 bp unit in the 1.688 g/cm^3 satellite of *D. melanogaster* (Carlson and Brutlag 1979). Another type of amplification is where a change in repeat length is a consequence of amplification of an adjacent sequence together with the repeat unit, *n(u+v)*, as described in rye by Bedbrook *et al.* (1980).

Restriction enzymes can generate a continuous array of segment lengths in some satellites. In rye, Bedbrook *et al.* (1980) have interpreted such a case to mean that the satellite repeat is associated in "a myriad of complex arrangements with other sequences". However, in the major satellite of the euro, the smear of molecule lengths seen following digestion with Sau3A is not due to a heterogeneous composite of sequences. It is a consequence of the nucleotide sequence. Sequencing has shown that the predominant tetranucleotide is $\frac{\text{(GATG)}}{\text{(CTAC)}}$ which has given rise to Sau3A sites $\frac{\text{(GATC)}}{\text{(CTAG)}}$ by single base changes.

In those satellites which have short homogeneous repeating units (e.g. the *D. melanogaster* 1.672 g/cm^3 satellite, where the repeats are 5 and 7 bp, and the silver satellite of wheat in which a principal repeat is 3 bp) amplification events are not detectable.

There are several possible mechanisms of amplification

The mechanisms of generating *n*, the number of repeats in a homogeneous tandem array, have not been unequivocally established. We do know that satellite units are amplified in localised regional events and yet a particular repeat can occur in several different chromosomal sites. Recombination mechanisms have been implicated to explain both the generation of tandem arrays and the transposition of repeats from one chromosome to another. Various replication mechanisms can also be invoked to explain the same observations. Certainly, sister chromatid exchanges occur and although most observations rely on techniques which themselves generate exchanges, spontaneous exchanges are observable between the sister chromatids in ring chromosomes (McClintock 1938). Difficulties are that *unequal* sister chromatid exchanges have not been detected by these methods and furthermore these cytological analyses show an absence of sister chromatid exchanges in those very regions of the chromosomes which are the domains of the satellite sequences - heterochromatin (Gatti et al. 1979). Perhaps the levels of inequality in exchange can never be observed at a cytological level and perhaps very low frequencies of exchanges in heterochromatin may be sufficient over long periods of time to achieve the amplification of subpopulations in satellites. Unequal sister chromatid exchanges have been demonstrated in the tandem arrays of ribosomal RNA genes in yeast (Petes 1980). The tandem arrays of ribosomal genes also provide some indication of the possibilities of replicative mechanisms since it is for these sequences that extra chromosomal amplification events are known.

It is possible that there are no specific mechanisms of amplification and that the situations analysed are events which have been selected from a wide horizon of chromosomal mutations and rearrangements. Where there are sufficient selection pressures, as for example in the amplification of the dihydrofolate reductase genes in rodent cells, amplification of required gene sequences can occur by chromosomal rearrangements which would normally not be viable (Bostock and Clark 1980).

Some properties of satellite DNA may result from selection

In many organisms, there are several satellite DNAs which may be related in sequence. For the simple satellites in *D. melanogaster* and *D. virilis*, this is clearly the case (Peacock et al. 1977, Gall and Atherton 1974). Mutational change, coupled with amplification can generate new buoyant density satellites when the repeat is short. This also applies to more complex satellites such as those of calf and human. Within a satellite, random mutations occur and are readily shown in restriction enzyme digests by the multimer ladders. Even where, for different enzyme sites in the one satellite, the proportions of the different length classes fit random expectations, the probablity of mutation can vary markedly (Dennis et al. 1980). This may reflect a constraint on sequence divergence in some regions of the repeating unit (Altenburger et al. 1977). Direct nucleotide sequencing has produced data supporting this possibility. In the 1.688 g/cm^3 satellite of *D. melanogaster*, out of the 359 bp unit only a total of eleven positions show changes (Hseih and Brutlag 1979a). We too have found in a maize satellite that certain regions of the sequence are more likely to mutate and only a limited number of possible sequence alterations occur. A comparable situation has been described for the African green monkey satellite (Rosenberg *et al*. 1978). The regions of a satellite which are conserved may be important, for example, for binding of proteins. A protein binding specifically to the 1.688 g/cm^3 satellite of *D. melanogaster* has been isolated (Hseih and Brutlag 1979b).

It is also possible that selection pressures might operate to maintain some satellites as very short repeats rather than allowing them to develop as more complex satellites. Rather than assuming that the more complex 1.688 g/cm^3 satellite of *D. melanogaster* is older than the simpler 1.705, 1.672 and 1.686 satellites, their joint existence may be a consequence of intranuclear roles which are under positive selection.

Specific satellite sequences may be in specific heterochromatic sites

With few exceptions, satellite DNA sequences are restricted to blocks of heterochromatin rather than being distributed throughout the genome. In *D. melanogaster* the distribution of several satellites has been mapped; each heterochromatic block has a unique arrangement and content of the various satellite sequences. This may simply be a reflection of the properties of amplification and transposition of highly repeated sequences, or it may signal a differentiation of heterochromatin. Genetic differences are known for heterochromatic segments. For example, the heterochromatin on chromosome 2 contains several essential loci (Hilliker 1976). X heterochromatin contains the ribosomal genes and other genetic elements.

Maize provides the best examples of specific effects associated with classes of heterochromatin. There are well documented genetic and cytological effects attributable separately or jointly to B chromosome heterochromatin and knob heterochromatin

(Rhoades 1978). We have isolated a satellite sequence of repeat length 185 bp which is restricted to knob heterochromatin and is the major sequence constituent of all the knobs including the large knob on chromosome 10 (K10) (Fig. 4).

The presence of K10 in the maize genome has a spectacular effect on the course of meiosis. When it is present in either homozygous or heterozygous form, all knobs act as precocious centromeres (neocentromeres) in the two meiotic divisions. All knobs can be induced by K10 to function as neocentromeres and no other classes of heterochromatin respond. The property of neocentric activity is not a function of chromosome location but is inherent in knobs; if knob heterochromatin is moved in a chromosome neocentric activity is also moved; if centromeric heterochromatin is moved away from the centromeres to a position comparable to that occupied by knobs, neocentric activity is still not induced.

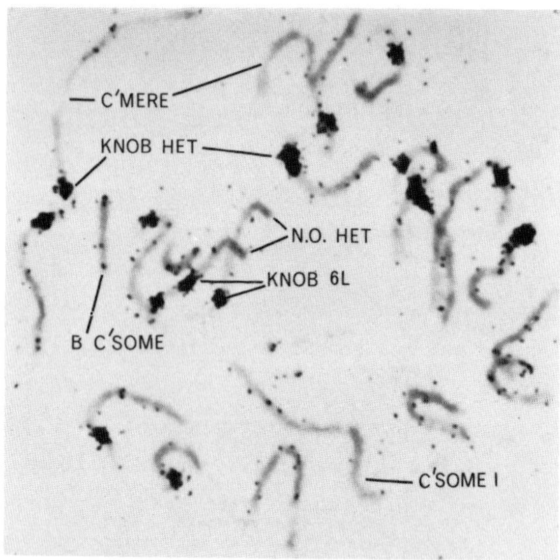

Fig. 4. _In situ_ hybridization of maize satellite DNA to metaphase chromosomes. The sequence occurs only in knob heterochromatin and not in any other classes of heterochromatin.

We conclude that the neocentric property is a function of the sequence composition of knobs, which we know to be chiefly composed of the 185 bp satellite DNA. The primitive relative of maize, teosinte, also has knobs with the same satellite sequence as their major constituent, and which show neocentric activity when introduced into maize containing K10. This is a case of conservation of satellite sequence and cytogenetic affect. However, other DNA sequences are present in knobs and until we can specifically manipulate the satellite DNA and show an effect on the cytogenetic property, it remains a correlation.

Conclusion

Amplification is a basic property of highly repeated DNA and explains many observations including the formation of complex units from shorter repeats, and the generation of tandemly arranged populations of repeats in the genome. However, it does not account for all properties of satellite DNA, at least some of which imply the existence of positive selection pressures.

REFERENCES

Altenburger, W., Horz, W. and H. G. Zachau, 1977.Comparative analysis of three guinea pig satellite DNAs by restriction nucleases. Eur. J. Biochem. 73, 393-400.

Bedbrook J., Jones, J. and R. Flavell, 1980.Evidence for the involvement of recombination and amplification events in evolution of *Secale* chromosomes. Cold Spr. Har. Symp. Quant. Biol. 45 (In Press).

Bostock, C. J. and E. M. Clark. 1980.Satellite DNA in large marker chromosomes of methotrexate resistant mouse cells. Cell 19, 709-716.

Brutlag, D. L. and W. J. Peacock, 1979.DNA sequences of the 1.672 g/cm^3 satellite of *Drosophila melanogaster*. J. Mol. Biol. 135, 565-580.

Cameron, J. R., Loh, E. Y. and R. W. Davis, 1979.Evidence for transposition of dispersed repetitive DNA families in yeast. Cell 16, 739-751.

Carlson, M. and D. Brutlag, 1977.Cloning and characterization of a complex satellite DNA from *Drosophila melanogaster*. Cell 11, 371-381.

Christie, N. T. and D. M. Skinner, 1980.Selective amplification of variants of a complex repeating unit in DNA of a crustacean. Proc. Natl. Acad. Sci. USA, 77, 2786-2790.

Cooper, D. W., Johnston, P. G., Murtagh, C. E. and J. L. VandeBerg, 1975. In The eukaryote chromosome. pp.381-391. Ed. W. J. Peacock and R. D. Brock. Canberra: ANU Press.

Dennis, E. S., Dunsmuir, P. and W. J. Peacock, 1980.Segmental amplification in a satellite DNA: Restriction enzyme analysis of the major satellite of *Macropus rufogriseus*. Chromosoma 79, 179-198.

Fry, K. and W. Salser, 1977.Nucleotide sequences of HS α satellite from kangaroo rat Dipodomys ordeii and characterization of similar sequences from other organisms. Cell 12, 1069-1074.

Gall, J. G. and D. D. Atherton, 1974.Satellite sequences in Drosophila virilis. J. Mol. Biol. 85, 633-664.

Gatti, M., Santini, G., Pimpinelli, S. and G. Oliveri, 1979.Lack of spontaneous sister chromatid exchange in somatic cells of Drosophila melanogaster. Genetics 91, 255-274.

Gosden, J. F., Mitchell, A. R., Sueanez, H. N. and C. M. Gosden, 1977.The distribution of sequences complementary to human satellite DNAs I, II and IV in the chromosomes of the chimpanzee (Pan troglodytes), gorilla (Gorilla gorilla) and orang-utan (Pongo pygmaeus). Chromosoma 63, 253-271.

Hilliker, A. J. 1976.Genetic analysis of the centromeric heterochromatin of chromosome 2 of Drosophila melanogaster: Deficiency mapping of EMS-induced lethal complementation groups. Genetics 83, 765-782.

Horz, W. and H. G. Zachau, 1977.Characterization of distinct segments in mouse satellite DNA by restriction nucleases. Eur. J. Biochem. 73, 383-392.

Hseih, T. and D. Brutlag, 1979a.Sequence and sequence variation within the 1.688 g/cm^3 satellite DNA of Drosophila melanogaster. J. Mol. Biol. 135, 465-481.

Hseih, T. and D. Brutlag, 1979b.A protein which preferentially binds Drosophila satellite DNA. Proc. Natl. Acad. Sci. USA 76, 726-730.

McClintock, B. 1938.The production of homozygous deficient tissues with mutant characteristics by means of the aberrant mitotic behaviour of ring-shaped chromosomes. Genetics 23, 315-376.

Peacock, W. J., Lohe, A. R., Gerlach, W. L., Dunsmuir, P., Dennis, E. S. and R. Appels, 1977.Fine structure and evolution of DNA in heterochromatin. Cold. Spr. Harb. Symp. Quant. Biol. 42, 1121-1135.

Pech, M., Igo-Kemenes, T. and H. G. Zachau, 1979a.Nucleotide sequence of a highly repetitive component of rat DNA. Nuc. Acid Res. 7, 418-432.

Pech, M., Streeck, R. E. and H. G. Zachau, 1979b.Patchwork structure of a bovine satellite DNA. Cell, 18, 883-893.

Petes, T. D. 1980.Unequal meiotic recombination within tandem arrays of yeast ribosomal DNA genes. Cell 19, 765-774.

Rhoades, M. M. 1978.Genetic effects of heterochromatin in maize. In Maize breeding and genetics. pp.641-672. Ed. D. B. Walden New York: Wiley and Sons.

Rosenberg, H., Singer, M. and M. Rosenberg, 1978.Highly reiterated sequences of SIMIANSIMIANSIMIANSIMIANSIMIAN. Science 200, 394-402.

Rubin, G. M., Brorein (Jr.) W. J., Dunsmuir, P. Flavell, A. J., Levis, R., Strobel, E., Toole, J. J. and E. Young, 1980."Copia-like" transposable elements in the Drosophila genome. Cold Spr. Harb. Symp. Quant. Biol. 45 (In Press).

Singh, L., Purdom, I. F. and K. W. Jones, 1976.Satellite DNA and evolution of sex chromosomes. Chromosoma 59, 43-62.

Sturtevant, A. H. and E. Novitski, 1941.The homologies of the chromosome elements in the genus Drosophila. Genetics 26, 517-541.

Walker, P. M. B. 1971.Origin of satellite DNA. Nature 229, 306-308.

Young, M. W. 1979.Middle repetitive DNA: a fluid component of the *Drosophila* genome. Proc. Natl. Acad. Sci. USA 76, 6274-6278.

Molecular changes in chromosomal DNA organisation and origins of phenotypic variation

R. B. Flavell

Plant Breeding Institute, Trumpington, Cambridge CB2 2LO

INTRODUCTION

The molecular changes that occur in the chromosomal DNA of higher organisms and the mechanisms producing them are of fundamental significance because they are the basis of chromosome evolution and phenotypic variation. Inferences about the molecular changes can be drawn from the kinds and arrangement of repeated and non-repeated sequences found in the chromosomes. However, the relationship of these changes, if any, to the origins of phenotypic variation is as yet not well defined. In this short paper I would therefore like to review how different kinds of nucleotide sequences are organised in chromosomes and how they change during evolution and then proceed to speculate on some of the ways in which these kinds of molecular changes might generate phenotypic variation. Most of the information on genome evolution I have drawn, in the interests of brevity, from our comparative sequence organisation studies on the cereal species wheat, rye, barley and oats, which have diverged from a common ancestor (Flavell, Rimpau and Smith, 1977).

THE EVOLUTION OF SEQUENCE VARIATION IN CEREAL CHROMOSOMES

To learn about the molecular changes which occur frequently in chromosomes during evolution, it is obviously desirable to focus attention on DNA fractions which are not under strong sequence-dependent selection and therefore tolerate changes at a high frequency. The cereal genomes, like many other relatively large genomes, have been particularly useful in teaching us about frequent molecular events because a major fraction of their DNA appears not to be highly conserved. The possible reason for this can be inferred from the following calculations.

The nuclear genomes of wheat, rye, barley and oats contain 5.4×10^9, 7.8×10^9, 5.3×10^9, and 4.2×10^9 nucleotide pairs per haploid genome respectively (Rimpau, Smith and Flavell 1978; 1980). The number of sequences which specify different messenger RNAs (mRNA) is not known precisely but 100,000 per haploid genome seems an over-estimate from studies on barley and tobacco (Kiper, Bolte and Herzfeld 1980; Goldberg, Hoschek and Kamalay 1978). Assuming each mRNA sequence is approximately 1000 nucleotides, then the coding sequences occupy approximately 10^8 nucleotide pairs. The amount of DNA in introns and DNA concerned directly with gene regulation, chromosome pairing, replication, recombination etc. that is not included in mRNA estimates, is unknown. However it is probably not more than 5×10^8 nucleotide pairs. Therefore, this "primary DNA", as it has been called by Hinegardner (1976) is likely to comprise approximately 6×10^8 nucleotide pairs or less, which is around 10% of the total DNA in cereal chromosomes. These calculations which are obviously only very approximate, suggest that 90% or more of the total DNA of cereal chromosomes is not carrying out sequence-specific functions. This is not to say, however, that this fraction of the DNA called "secondary" by Hinegardner (1976) has no function ! The calculations nevertheless do offer an explanation for why so much of each genome can change rapidly without causing immediate lethality.

The comparative studies on the organisation of related sequences within and between the four cereal species have clearly illustrated that the common molecular changes in chromosomes include sequence translocation, amplification, deletion and mutation. The evidence for each kind of event is briefly reviewed below.

(a) Sequence translocation

The following results imply that short pieces of DNA (100 to several thousand nucleotide pairs) are translocated frequently to new chromosomal sites: (1) short repeated and non-repeated DNA segments are found interspersed throughout a large proportion of higher eukaryotic genomes (Davidson *et al.* 1975; Flavell 1980); (2) short repeats belonging to different families are commonly interspersed with each other (Rimpau, Smith and Flavell 1978; Smith, Rimpau and Flavell 1976); (3) *in situ* hybridisation of purified repeats to metaphase chromosomes has shown that homologous sequences are commonly dispersed over many or all chromosomes (Bedbrook *et al.* 1980; Flavell, O'Dell and Hutchinson 1980; Gerlach and Peacock 1980; Appels, Driscoll and Peacock 1978); (4) analyses of restriction digests of families of repeats in rye have shown that members of most families are present on all chromosomes (Bedbrook, O'Dell and Flavell 1980); (5) related sequences are organised differently in related species (Rimpau, Smith and Flavell 1978, 1980; Flavell, O'Dell and Hutchinson 1980; Bedbrook, O'Dell and Flavell 1980).

The translocation of a DNA segment to a new site creates a new sequence(s) and destroys the sequence at the insertion site. Depending on the sequence and the mechanism of translocation, it may also alter the site from which it was translocated. Because most cereal chromosomal DNA segments a few thousand base pairs long show evidence of sequence translocation in their evolutionary history (Rimpau, Smith and Flavell 1978; 1980; Flavell, O'Dell and Hutchinson 1980; Bedbrook *et al.* 1980; Bedbrook, O'Dell and Flavell 1980) translocation clearly contributes substantially to new sequence construction during evolution.

(b) Amplification and deletion

Because more than 75% of the DNA in the cereal genomes consists of families of repeated sequences most cereal DNA is created by amplification. Several different amplification mechanisms are probably involved. For example, unequal crossing over types of events (Smith 1973, 1976) may be responsible for sequence duplications and more extensive amplifications while rolling circle type mechanisms (Hourcade, Dressler and Wolfson 1973), or others producing very extensive replication over short time periods, seem more attractive candidates for the rapid production and dispersion of very large numbers of repeats. Whatever the mechanism(s) of amplification, the resulting repeats are probably initially organised in tandem arrays and therefore suitable substrates for subsequent quantitative modification by unequal crossing over.

Quantitative changes in DNA do not involve only amplification. Deletion must also be a common event, as a consequence of unequal crossing over as well as other molecular processes. Comparative studies between related species have provided evidence for the loss of single copy as well as repeated DNA during evolution (Flavell, Rimpau and Smith 1977; Flavell, O'Dell and Hutchinson 1980; Belford and Thompson 1980).

Once a piece of DNA has been amplified it is not immune from further amplification. Indeed, it is possible that certain sequences are predisposed to being amplified. Evidence for the re-amplification of repeats is now extensive, e.g. the presence of (i) variant tandem arrays within families of high copy repeats and (ii) related repeats, amplified to different copy numbers in different sequence permutations (Rimpau, Smith and Flavell 1978,1980; Flavell et al. 1979, 1980; Bedbrook, O'Dell and Flavell 1980; Bedbrook et al. 1980). These different sequence permutations are created by sequence translocation or rearrangement and thus amplification of such segments propagates the sequence variation created by the recombination of sequences into new sites.

How often do amplification and deletion events occur in evolution ? The number of ribosomal RNA genes clustered in homologous nucleolus organisers in wheat differs considerably in different individuals (Flavell and Smith 1974; Miller, Gerlach and Flavell 1980). This is also true for highly repeated sequences found in rye heterochromatin (Jones and Flavell, unpublished). This suggests that amplification and/or deletion events occur frequently in populations. Comparisons of the DNAs of wheat, rye, barley and oats also provide relevant information. The percentages of the wheat, rye, barley and oats genomes consisting of species-specific repeated sequences are 16, 22, 28 and 58% respectively (Rimpau, Smith and Flavell 1978, 1980). Some of these species-specific sequences are part of larger repeating units which also contain sequences shared between species. Estimates of the percentages of each genome consisting of repeating units which possess some species-specific DNA are as follows: wheat 27%, rye 34%, barley 44%, oats 66% (calculated from data in Rimpau, Smith and Flavell 1978 and 1980). These estimates are inevitably underestimates of the amount of DNA modified by amplification or deletion since species divergence because they do not include the amplification and/or deletion of sequences common to two or more species. This must occur because related sequences are commonly found in different copy numbers in related species (Flavell, O'Dell and Hutchinson 1980; Bedbrook *et al.* 1980). When all these quantitative changes are summed, it can be concluded that probably more than half if not most of the DNA in wheat and rye (the two most closely related species) has changed since the two species diverged from a common ancestor. It also appears that almost all the DNA of oats is unrelated to that in the other three cereals. The extent of these changes illustrates how little of the chromosomal DNA is highly conserved during evolution.

(c) Mutation

Families of repeated sequences do not consist of identical sequences but usually include a wide spectrum of variant but related sequences. Point mutations or small additions and deletions which create these variants therefore appear to be tolerated at a high frequency in many families. This family heterogeneity is recognised when the sequences are compared by (1) studying the thermal stability of hybrid molecules formed *in vitro* between different members (Smith and Flavell 1974; Flavell, Rimpau and Smith 1977), (2) direct sequencing (unpublished), or (3) the complement of restriction endonuclease cutting sites (Bedbrook *et al.* 1980). Thus mutation contributes considerable sequence variation to evolving plant chromosomes.

In summary then, there is strong evidence to conclude that during evolution (1) new sequences are created by translocation and mutation and (2) amplification and deletion together "turn over" major fractions of the genome in relatively short evolutionary time periods. A model of genome evolution based on these conclusions has been described elsewhere (Flavell *et al.* 1979, 1980; Flavell 1980; Thompson and Murray 1980). The obvious and extremely important question which follows these conclusions is what is the relevance of sequence translocation, amplification, deletion and mutation to gene control mechanisms, phenotypic variation and speciation ? In the remainder of this paper I want to use the available space to speculate briefly on selected aspects of this issue. I have chosen to omit the role of base change mutation from the discussions, not because it is unimportant - it clearly is an extremely important source of phenotype variation - but because its role is better appreciated compared with sequence translocation, amplification and deletion.

POSSIBLE CONTRIBUTIONS OF SEQUENCE TRANSPOSITION, AMPLIFICATION AND DELETION TO VARIATION IN GENE EXPRESSION

Any discussion on the molecular control of gene activity in higher organisms is constrained by how little is known about it and the molecular basis of variation affecting it. Furthermore, there are likely to be many different mechanisms of gene control. However, two assumptions regarding the control of gene expression seem acceptable and have some experimental support. First, there are sequences (regulatory) in the vicinity of each coding sequence (gene) that regulate whether the gene forms a messenger RNA or not and that related, i.e. repeated, sequences occur close to genes which are coordinately expressed at some time in the life cycle. Second, there are other regions containing DNA sequences (regulatory) whose products, RNA or protein, are specifically involved in the control of gene expression and these different regulatory regions must similarly have some sequences in common to facilitate the integrated control of different genes during development. Detailed models of gene control based on these assumptions and a review of the evidence supporting them have been developed by Britten and Davidson (1969) and Davidson and Britten (1979) to which the reader should refer.

If these assumptions are correct, then repeated sequences, dispersed into different sites, are key components of gene regulation systems. This means sequence amplification and translocation have been vital mechanisms in the evolution of gene control systems. Therefore the translocation, amplification and deletion events which occur at high frequency in chromosomes during evolution are likely to be continuing sources of variation affecting gene expression. For example, if a piece of DNA were translocated into either kind of region of regulatory DNA then the activities of individual genes or groups of genes would be abolished or occasionally modulated. Alterations in the extent and timing of gene expression by the translocation of DNA elements into specific loci are well-known in maize (reviewed in Fincham and Sastry 1974; Peterson 1978).

Modulation of gene expression could result from (a) altering the affinities of the DNA regions for RNA polymerase, regulatory RNA or regulatory protein molecules or (b) modification of the structure of the RNA transcripts to alter their processing into regulatory or mRNAs (Davidson and Britten 1979). Because such a vast number of different DNA sequences are generated in large genomes during evolution, presumably at random, but from pre-existing sequences, and many may be "tested" in the large number of postulated regulatory systems, it would be very surprising indeed if new phenotypic variation were not created, albeit rarely, in this way.

If a regulatory sequence of one gene control system were translocated into that of a different gene system then the donor and recipient gene systems might become coordinated to produce major new phenotypic variation.

Creation of variation in gene activity can also be envisaged by changes in copy number of sequences other than the coding sequences themselves. Gene control is likely to be highly dependent upon (1) the concentration of the regulatory molecules (RNA or protein) responsible for activating gene expression, (2) the number of sequences in the nucleus with affinity for the regulatory molecules, and (3) the dissociation constants of the regulatory molecules for their various binding sites.

The concentration of the regulatory RNA or protein molecules in the nucleus will depend upon their rates of synthesis, breakdown and presumably the volume of the nucleus (Cavalier-Smith 1978). Their rates of synthesis will depend not only upon the regulation of their transcription etc. but also on the copy number of the DNA sequences giving rise to them. Their concentration at the sites where they are required to regulate gene activity will also depend upon factors (2) and (3) i.e. the concentration of other "decoy" sequences in the nucleus with some affinity for the regulatory molecules and the relative affinities of the regulatory molecules for the "decoy" sequences and the specific regulatory sites. It seems inevitable that the translocation/amplification/deletion cycles will occasionally generate DNA sequences that have some affinity for some of the many RNA or protein regulatory molecules, or change the copy number of sequences that produce the regulatory molecules in the cell. Such events could alter the concentration of regulatory molecules at the specific sites of gene control. This would be particularly likely if a large family of repeated sequences evolved with reasonable affinity for a regulatory molecule. On many, probably most, occasions such nuclear changes would be deleterious or lethal but occasionally they could be neutral or advantageous and be positively selected. Therefore some variation in gene expression may result from modulation of the copy number of regulatory sequences (Davidson and Britten 1979) and the evolution of families of repeated sequences which indirectly affect gene control because of their affinities for regulatory molecules. This is a possible explanation for the diverse heritable phenotypic changes induced during plant development in some genotypes of flax (reviewed by Cullis 1977).

Members of individual families of repeated sequences are often dispersed on some or all chromosomes, sometimes in clusters. If this were true for any family with affinity for an RNA or protein regulatory molecule then a genetic analysis of the sites regulating the relevent phenotypic character would indicate that many chromosomal sites were involved, some of bigger effect than others. The phenotypic character would appear polygenically controlled, the segregating variation being of the 'continuous' kind (reviewed in Thompson and Thoday 1979). The finding that developmental characters are frequently polygenically controlled by loci which have different magnitudes of effect and which show pleiotropic effects on several characters (see Thompson and Thoday 1979) is consistent with (but of course does not prove) the sorts of regulatory gene models discussed here and by Davidson and Britten (1979).

The potential for sequence translocation, amplification and deletion to generate phenotypic variation briefly outlined in this section has been developed from some basic assumptions about gene control mechanisms and the knowledge that these molecular processes occur frequently in chromosomes. Where sequences from the pool of "secondary" DNA evolve to become part of regulatory systems, then the frequency of new variation from this source would presumably be related to the amount of "secondary" DNA undergoing continual change; the smaller the amount of "secondary" DNA (i.e. in small genomes) the smaller the chance that "useful" sequences will emerge. The general observation that higher organisms often become more specialised and less adaptable when their excess DNA is reduced has been discussed by Hinegardner (1976) in the light of a reduced probability of "useful" sequences arising in the "secondary" DNA.

VARIATION IN GENE EXPRESSION AND SPECIATION

The idea that large changes in both morphology and speciation may evolve over short periods of time owing to changes in gene regulatory systems is currently receiving much attention and the reader is referred to other papers on the topic (e.g. King and Wilson 1975; Wilson 1976; White 1977; Gould 1980; Bush *et al.* 1977; Dover 1979, 1980; Dover, Strachen and Brown 1980; Hedrick and McDonald 1980). This viewpoint contrasts with the traditional Darwinian one that major phenotypic changes and speciation emerge over a long time period from the summation of a large number of changes, each of relatively small effect. There are undoubtedly many routes to speciation, as reviewed by White (1977) and it is foolish to attempt to explain all speciation events and dramatic changes in morphology by a single mechanism. However, because changes in copy number of repeated sequences can occur rapidly and may in specific cases have major consequences on integrated gene regulation systems, it is interesting to consider the possible role of sequence amplification in speciation.

Let us assume that the regulation of fertile offspring production after mating can become modified in an individual by the evolution of a family of repeats dispersed at many chromosomal sites. If the initial amplification with concomitant phenotypic change were small, production of fertile offspring from a cross with an organism lacking the family would not necessarily be prevented. However, because the repeats are at many sites, essentially all the progeny of the cross would carry some of the repeats and therefore the enhanced potential to generate more. Subsequent breeding of the progeny would result in a rapid spread of the repeats and hence the modified phenotype through the population, albeit to quantitatively varying extents. In this way extreme forms of the new phenotype, which would prevent successful mating with organisms lacking the regulatory repeated sequences, could become established rapidly in the population to achieve speciation. This kind of route to speciation would not only be rapid but could also occur without physical isolation of populations, a major change in environment or the need to involve strong adaptive selection. It therefore merits consideration where these features are relevant and other molecular explanations for speciation are inappropriate (see White 1977). A similar proposal for speciation, being provoked by the rapid spread of new repeated sequences through a population has been made recently by Dover, Strachan and Brown (1980). Their proposal focussed more on the modification of specific features of chromosome structure than the control of specific sets of genes active in reproduction. In the context of considering chromosome structure and speciation it is clearly worth noting that during evolution, sequence translocation, mutation, amplification and deletion reduce chromosome structural homology between separated populations or species. Thus even when speciation has not abolished the ability for fertilisation and zygote formation, as is the case between wheat and rye, chromosome pairing and recombination are expected to be absent or rare, as is observed.

In this short paper I have attempted in a superficial way to draw attention to the fact that the molecular events now known to be occurring in chromosomes at high frequency during evolution and the emerging models of gene regulation suggest that sequence rearrangement and modulation in copy number might be common sources of phenotypic variation affecting gene expression in higher organisms. The implications of this conclusion, if correct, are very far-reaching in our attempts to understand and manipulate gene activity in higher organisms.

ACKNOWLEDGEMENTS

I am grateful to Gabriel Dover and Jonathan Jones for stimulating discussions and to Colin Law for useful comments on an earlier version of the manuscript.

REFERENCES

Appels, R., C. Driscoll and W. J. Peacock. 1978. Heterochromatin and highly repeated DNA sequences in rye (*Secale cereale*). Chromosoma 70, 67-89.

Bedbrook, J. R., J. Jones, M. O'Dell, R. Thompson and R. B. Flavell. 1980. A molecular description of telomeric heterochromatin in *Secale* species. Cell 19, 545-560.

Bedbrook, J. R., M. O'Dell and R. B. Flavell. 1980. Amplification of rearranged sequences in cereal plants. Nature, in press.

Belford, H. S. and W. F. Thompson. 1979. Single copy DNA homologies and the phylogeny of *Atriplex*. Carnegie Institution Year Book 78, 217-223.

Britten, R. J. and E. H. Davidson. 1969. Gene regulation for higher cells: a theory. Science 165, 349-357.

Bush, G. L., S. M. Case, A. C. Wilson and J. L. Patton. 1977. Rapid speciation and chromosomal evolution in mammals. Proc. Nat. Acad. Sci. 74, 3942-3946.

Cavalier-Smith, T. 1978. Nuclear volume control by nucleoskeletal DNA, selection for cell volume and cell growth rate and the solution of the DNA C-value paradox. J. Cell Science 34, 247-278.

Cullis, C. A. 1977. Molecular aspects of the environmental induction of heritable changes in flax. Heredity 38, 129-154.

Davidson, E. H. and R. J. Britten. 1979. Regulation of gene expression. Possible role of repetitive sequences. Science 204, 1052-1059.

Davidson, E. H., G. A. Galau, R. C. Angerer and R. J. Britten. 1975. Comparative aspects of DNA organisation in *Metazoa*. Chromosoma 51, 253-259.

Dover, G. A. 1979. Problems in the use of DNA for the study of species relationships and the evolutionary significance of genomic differences. In *Chemosystematics: Principals and Practice*. Syst. Abs. Series. F.A. Bisbey, J.G. Vaughan and C.A. Wright, eds., Academic Press, in press.

Dover, G. A. 1980. The evolution of DNA sequences common to closely-related insect genomes. In *Insect Cytogenetics*, R.L. Blackman, G.M. Hewitt, M. Ashburner, eds., Roy. Ent. Sci. (Lond.) Symp. 10. Oxford: Blackwell.

Dover, G. A., T. Strachan and S. Brown. 1980. The evolution of genomes in closely-related species. In *Proc. 2nd International Congress of Systematics and Evolutionary Biology*, G.O. Scudder, ed., in press.

Fincham, J. R. S. and G. R. K. Sastry. 1974. Controlling elements in maize. Ann. Rev. Genet. 8, 12-50.

Flavell, R. B. 1980. The molecular characterisation and organisation of plant chromosomal DNA sequences. Annual Review of Plant Physiology 31, 569-596.

Flavell, R. B., J. R. Bedbrook, J. Jones, M. O'Dell, W. Gerlach, T. A. Dyer and R. D. Thompson. 1980. Molecular events in cereal genome evolution. In The 4th John Innes Symposium D.R. Davies and D.A. Hopwood, eds. John Innes Charity, 15-30.

Flavell, R. B., M. O'Dell and J. Hutchinson. 1980. Nucleotide sequence organisation in plant chromosomes and evidence for sequence translocation during evolution. Cold Spring Harbor Symposium Quant. Biol. Vol 45, in press.

Flavell, R. B., J. Rimpau and D. B. Smith. 1977. Repeated sequence DNA relationships in four cereal genomes. Chromosoma 63, 205-222.

Flavell, R. B., J. Rimpau, D. B. Smith, M. O'Dell and J. R. Bedbrook. 1979. The evolution of plant genome structure. In Plant Genome Organisation and Expression, C.J. Leaver, ed. Plenum Press, 35-47.

Flavell, R. B. and D. B. Smith. 1974. Variation in nucleolar organiser and RNA gene multiplicity in wheat and rye. Chromosoma 47, 327-334.

Gerlach, W. L. and W. J. Peacock. 1980. Chromosomal locations of highly repeated DNA sequences in wheat. Heredity 44, 269-276.

Goldberg, R. B., G. Hoschek and J. C. Kamalay. 1978. Sequence complexity of nuclear and polysomal RNA in leaves of the tobacco plant. Cell 14, 123-131.

Gould, S.J. 1980. Is a new theory of evolution emerging ? Paleobiol. 6, 119-130.

Hedrick, P. W. and J. F. McDonald. 1980. Regulatory gene adaptation: an evolutionary model. Heredity 45, 83-97.

Hinegardner, R. 1976. Evolution of genome size. In Molecular Evolution, G. J. Ayala, ed., Sinauer Associates Inc. Mass. USA, 179-199.

Hourcade, D., P. Dressler and J. Wolfson. 1973. The amplification of ribosomal RNA genes involves a rolling circle intermediate. Proc. Nat. Acad. Sci. 70, 2926-2930.

King, M. C. and A. C. Wilson. 1975. Evolution at two levels in humans and chipmanzees. Science 188, 107-188.

Kiper, M., M. Bolte and F. Herzfeld. 1980. Reiteration frequency of genes coding for abundant and rare messenger RNA in greened barley seedlings. Heredity, in press.

Miller, T. E., W. L. Gerlach and R. B. Flavell. 1980. Nucleolus organiser variation in wheat and rye revealed by in situ hybridisation. Heredity, in press.

Peterson, P. A. 1978. Controlling Elements: the induction of mutability at the A2 and C loci in maize. In Maize Breeding and Genetics. D. B. Walden, ed. New York: Wiley. 601-631.

Rimpau, J., D. B. Smith and R. B. Flavell. 1978. Sequence organisation analysis of the wheat and rye genomes by inter-species DNA/DNA hybridisation. J. Molec. Biol. 123, 327-359.

Rimpau, J., D. B. Smith and R. B. Flavell. 1980. Sequence organisation in barley and oats chromosomes revealed by interspecies DNA/DNA hybridisation. Heredity 44, 131-149.

Smith, G. P. 1973. Unequal crossover and the evolution of multi-gene families. Cold Spr. Harb. Quant. Biol. 38, 507-514.

Smith, G. P. 1976. Evolution of repeated DNA sequences by unequal crossover. Science 191, 528-535.

Smith, D. B. and R. B. Flavell. 1974. The relatedness and evolution of repeated nucleotide sequences in the DNA of some Gramineae species. Biochem. Genetics 12, 243-256.

Smith, D. B., J. Rimpau and R. B. Flavell. 1976. Interspersion of different repeated sequences in the wheat genome revealed by interspecies DNA/DNA hybridisation. Nucleic Acid Res. 3, 2811-2825.

Thompson, W. F. and M. G. Murray. 1980. Sequence organisation in pea and mung bean DNA and a model for genome evolution. In Fourth John Innes Symposium, D.R. Davies and D.A. Hopwood, eds. John Innes Charity, Norwich UK, 31-45.

Thompson, J. N. and J. M. Thoday, 1979. Quantitative Genetic Variation. Academic Press.

White, M. J. D. 1977. Modes of Speciation. Freeman & Co. San Francisco.

Wilson, A. C. 1976. Gene regulation in evolution. In Molecular Evolution, F. J. Ayala, ed. Sinauer Press, Mass. USA, 255-284.

Mapping the human genome by analysing the DNA

E. M. Southern

MRC Mammalian Genome Unit, King's Buildings, West Mains Road, Edinburgh

This paper discusses an approach to building a map of the human genome which uses newly developed methods of analysing the DNA. The current map of the genome (see McKusick and Ruddle, 1977) has two different forms derived by quite different methods. On the one hand the physical map, seen in the banding patterns is derived by direct observation of the metaphase chromosomes. On the other, the genetic map of phenotypic characters has been assembled indirectly, by inferences from linkage analysis. These two maps are of course colinear. The projected map discussed in this paper has in common with the cytological map of the chromosomes the feature that it is a physical map based on the DNA sequence, and does not require gene expression. Although the method of in situ hybridisation can be used to locate the map position of DNA sequences directly, in this paper we discuss the potential of less direct but more sensitive methods made possible by recently developed procedures for cloning and analysing DNA.

Three aspects of building the maps are considered: the choice of DNA markers, the method of analysis which enables the DNA sequences to be used as markers, and two approaches to determining their position in the map.

Choice of DNA sequences for use as markers

It is not necessary that the features used to build a map of the genome have a biological function: the bands which form the maps seen in insects polytene chromosomes or mammalian metaphase chromosomes have no known function, but they are convenient, readily recognisable features. Similarly, the choice of DNA sequences used as markers need not be limited to those which have known functions. It is necessary however that each sequence used as a marker should identify a unique position in the genome, and this need rules out the use of repeated sequences. In addition, the DNA sequences used as markers should be scattered through the entire genome; and since we aim to produce a comprehensive physical map of all the DNA rather than a genetic map this requirement may not be met by choosing sequences in the DNA which correspond to expressed genes. The Y-chromosome, for example, might be poorly represented in any population of mRNAs.

These arguments suggest that the best starting point for preparing a set of DNA markers for mapping the human genome is genomic DNA. Only from this starting material can we be reasonably sure of representing all parts of the genome. Unlimited numbers of individual sequences, selected at random from the genome can be produced by so-called "shot-gun" cloning in a suitable host-vector, and a library of human DNA sequences cloned in λ-phage has already been produced by Maniatis and his colleagues (1978). However, such libraries include repeated sequences, which are not useful for mapping; Bottstein et al (1980), estimate that only 1-3% of clones in the human sequence library with inserts of 15-20 kb contain no repeated sequence. From analyses of the pattern of interspersion of repeated sequences in human DNA it is predicted that about half of the fragments 1kb in length will contain no repeated sequence, and a library of clones made from fragments in this smaller size range may be a better starting point for the production of unique sequence probes. Clones which do contain repeated sequences are readily identified by molecular hybridisation (Grunstein and Hogness, 1975; Benton and Davis 1977). The cloned DNA is denatured and attached to a piece of paper, which is then immersed in a solution of radioactively-labelled, denatured human DNA, in conditions which allow DNA reassociation. Those clones which contain repeated sequences pick up sufficient radioactivity to be detected by radioautography, while those which contain only a unique sequence will pick up an undetectable amount of the complementary sequence.

By these methods, it is easy to produce many thousands of individual DNA sequences suitable for use as markers. Indeed it is possible to produce the million or so clones needed to include all the unique sequences of the human genome. However, the method of analysing the clones, described below, limits the number that can be used to build the map of the genome.

Detection of marker sequences in human DNAs

Linkage between the DNA sequences used as markers will be determined by following their segregation in human-rodent somatic cell hybrids, or in pedigrees. When DNA prepared from say a human-rodent hybrid cell is digested with a restriction endonuclease the product is a mixture of around a million fragments; but as a result of the specificity of the restriction endonuclease for a particular sequence of bases, each unique sequence within this mixture forms a fragment with a characteristic size. Thus, when the fragments are separated according to size, by gel electrophoresis, each unique sequence forms a sharp band in the gel; but this band is buried in a smear formed by the rest of the DNA. The position of a particular sequence can be marked by molecular hybridisation: the DNA fragments in the gel are first denatured and then transferred to a sheet of cellulose nitrate paper (Southern 1975), or of chemically activated cellulose (Alwine et al 1977). Specific bands can then be detected by molecular hybridisation using a radioactive "probe" made from a cloned sequence.

Note that the specificity of this method of analysis is provided in two quite different ways. First, molecular hybridisation distinguishes the sequence from unrelated sequences. Second, the restriction endonuclease gives a fragment of characteristic length, and thus a band which moves with characteristic mobility in the gel. As we shall see, the first criterion for specificity provides a method of detection but does not discern fine detail in the sequence. The second provides the fine detail that can allow distinction to be made between two copies of a sequence which are similar but not identical.

Forming the map

Two independent methods can be used to determine the position of a DNA sequence in the genome: the analysis of somatic cell hybrids which contain limited portions of the genome, and linkage analysis by family studies.

A. By analysing human-rodent somatic cell hybrids.

Hybrids between human and rodent cells lose human chromosomes preferentially, and a set or panel of hybrid cells can be chosen which permits each chromosome to be distinguished from all others (Ruddle and Creagan, 1975). A minimum of eight somatic cell hybrids, with appropriate chromosome contents, is needed to single out each of the twenty-four human chromosomes. This ideal has not yet been met, and more typical panels are composed of about twelve to fifteen cell hybrids.

To allocate a particular DNA sequence to a chromosome, DNAs from each cell line in the panel are compared by a gel-transfer with rodent and human DNAs. Lines which contain the relevant human chromosome show human characteristic bands; those which do not, may show no bands at all, if the conditions used for hybridisation or washing are stringent enough to prevent formation of hybrids between human and rodent sequences. The major part of human and rodent DNA forms very unstable duplexes, but coding sequences, which make up probably less than 10% of the single copy DNA, form relatively stable duplexes. However, any band due to a rodent sequence, should be distinguishable from the human sequence by its mobility in the gel, because although the rodent and human sequences may be similar enough to cross-reassociate they will usually differ in the restriction sites they contain. On the other hand, we must be able to identify the human bands as human, and problems could arise if there were a high degree of variation in sequence in the DNA of humans. As we shall see later, there is variation in human DNA, but it is unlikely to present many problems for this approach to mapping.

This analysis which has already been applied successfully to specific genes takes us to the point of allocating DNA sequences to chromosomes; to take the analysis further and place the markers in order along the chromosomes we need a method of segregating fragments of chromosomes. To build a map, the method should be applicable to all sequences in the genome, a requirement that rules out methods which rely on selection of markers, such as transformation of $HPRT^-$ rodent cells with fragments of human chromosomes (Willecke and Ruddle, 1975). A more universal approach described by Goss and Harris (1977), is similar in principle to the method used to assign markers to chromosomes. They produced a "panel" of somatic cell hybrids which contain sets of fragmented chromosomes by fusing irradiated human cells to rodent cells. Syntenic DNA markers could obviously be placed in order along the chromosome by this approach, using the method of analysis described above.

B. By analysing human pedigrees.

If variation in human DNA presents an obstacle to mapping sequences in somatic cell hybrids, it is the basis for plans to map the genome by analysing pedigrees; for this approach, it is necessary to distinguish homologous human sequences from each other rather than from the homologous rodent sequence.

The general strategy is too complex to be considered here but has been dealt with in a thorough review by Bottstein _et al_ (1980). Briefly, the analysis starts with a library of clones of human DNA sequences which are single-copy, and which also show polymorphism in human populations. Using the method of analysis described above, polymorphism would be seen as differences in the length of a fragment produced from the sequence by a particular restriction enzyme when the sequence was detected using the cloned DNA as a radioactive probe. Although there is little available information on the degree of polymorphism, variation in human DNA sequences has been shown to give rise to variation in the length of restriction fragments. For example; Kan and Dozy (1978) showed that a HpaI fragment containing the β-globin gene can have three different lengths; Jeffreys (1979) compared restriction fragments of the DNAs corresponding to the ${}^{G}\gamma$, ${}^{A}\gamma$, δ and β-globin genes in 60 individuals and found a small degree of variation which, extrapolated to the whole genome, would suggest that around 1 in 100 base pairs along the genome may vary polymorphically; Wyman and White (1980) selected 20 single-copy probes from a library of human genomic DNA that had been cloned in λ-phage. Of these 20, one was highly polymorphic, and showed at least 8 different fragment lengths in restriction digests of DNAs from 43 individuals. Linkage between such polymorphic markers can be determined by following their segregation in human families. However, Bottstein _et al_ (1980) estimate that around 150 polymorphic probes would be needed to provide detectable linkage between markers, and that to produce a linkage map it would be necessary to analyse tens to hundreds of individuals, depending on the structure of the pedigree. Thus, thousands of analyses will be needed to produce the map in this way, and while it is feasible to perform such a large number of analyses, it would clearly simplify the analysis if the markers were first grouped into syntenic sets as described above.

Location of other genetic markers in the DNA map

Linkage between DNA markers and any other marker can be determined either using either of the two approaches used to establish the DNA map.

But of the two approaches, pedigree analysis is far the more informative. Somatic cell hybrids express a very limited range of characters that can be analysed and adding these biochemical markers to the DNA markers will increase the detail in the map, but will have limited application to analysing biological problems. Pedigree analysis, on the other hand could be used to determine linkage between any inherited trait detectable in the pedigree and a polymorphic DNA marker, and this will have many applications. Following the lead set by Kan and Dozy (1978) an important example will be the application to prenatal diagnosis of genetic diseases. By analysing families which carry a particular disease, it should be possible to identify a closely linked polymorphic DNA marker and once such a marker has been identified, to use it to determine the genotype of a foetus by analysing DNA prepared from amniotic cells.

Conclusion

In a recent article, Conneally and Rivas considered the properties of genetic markers which make them useful for pedigree analysis:

"Not all of the 50,000 plus loci in man are suitable for mapping by the family study method. Those which meet the following criteria can be used in linkage studies:

(1) the mode of inheritance is known: (2) the phenotypic expression(s) of each genotype is well defined: (3) allelic frequencies are sufficiently high to ensure a 'reasonable' level of heterzygosity in the population, and (4) phenotypic expression is detectable in tissues amenable to study."

Points (1), (2) and (4) are readily met by DNA markers since they should be inherited as Mendelian codominant markers, require no gene expression, and are detectable in any cell containing DNA. The extent of variation in DNA sequences and allelic frequencies have yet to be determined, but are unlikely to cause more difficulties than other markers such as proteins. Thus DNA sequences are almost ideal by the criteria of Conneally and Rivas, and we may add other advantages: (1) the DNA can be analysed by a single method, applicable to every cloned DNA sequence and to almost every cell type (including amniotic cells); (2) cloned libraries provide an unlimited number of markers, which are not confined to a single location as for example the HLA markers, but scattered throughout the gene.

REFERENCES

Alwine, J.C., D. J. Kemp and G. R. Start 1977. Proc. Natl. Acad. Sci. U.S.A. 74, 5350-5354.

Benton, W. D. and R. W. Davis 1977. Screening λgt recombinant clones by hybridisation to single plaques in situ. Science 196, 180-182.

Botstein, D., R. L. White, M. Skolnick and R. W. Davis 1980. Construction of a genetic linkage map in Man using restriction fragment length polymorphisms. Am. J. Hum. Genet. 32, 314-331.

Goss, S. J. and H. Harris 1977. Gene transfer by means of cell fusion. I Statistical mapping of the human X chromosome by analysis of radiation induced gene segregation. J. Cell. Sci. 25, 17-38.

Grunstein, M. and D. S. Hogness 1975. Colony hybridisation: A method for the isolation of cloned DNAs that contain a specific gene. Proc. Nat. Acad. Sci. U.S.A. 72, 3961-3965.

Jeffreys, A. F. 1979. Sequence variants in the $^{G}\gamma$, $^{A}\gamma$, δ and β - globin genes of man. Cell 18, 1-10.

Kan, Y. and A. Dozy 1978. Antenatal diagnosis of sickle-cell anaemia by DNA analysis of amniotic-fluid cells. Lancet 2, 910-912.

McKusick, V. A. and F. H. Ruddle 1977. The status of the gene map of the human chromosomes. Science 196, 390-405.

Maniatis, T., R. C. Hardison, E. Lacy, J. Lauer, C. O'Connell, D. Quon, G. K. Sim and A. Efstratiadis 1978. The isolation of structural genes from libraries of eukaryotic DNA. Cell 15, 687-701.

Ruddle, F. H. and R. P. Creagan 1975. Parasexual approaches to the genetics of man. Ann. Rev. Genet. 9, 405-486.

Southern, E. M. 1975. Detection of specific sequences amount DNA fragments separated by gel electrophoresis. J. Mol. Biol. 98, 503-517.

Willecke, K. and F. H. Ruddle 1975. Transfer of the human gene for hypoxanthine-guanine phosphoribosyltransferase via isolated human metaphase chromosomes into mouse L-cells. Proc. Nat. Acad. Sci. 72, 1792-1796.

Wyman, A. R. and R. L. White 1980. A highly polymorphic locus in human DNA. Proc. Natl. Acad. Sci. U.S.A. in press.

In situ hybridization to lampbrush chromosomes

H. G. Callan

Department of Zoology, University of St. Andrews, St. Andrews, KY16 9TS, Scotland

Denatured ^{3}H-labelled DNA probes prepared by nick-translating cloned echinoderm histone genes were found to hybridize with RNA transcripts on some 12 pairs of lateral loops of newt (*Triturus cristatus carnifex*) lampbrush chromosomes, and the hybridization patterns revealed some individual variation between newts (see Old, Callan and Gross, 1977).

Denatured ^{3}H-labelled DNA probes containing *Xenopus* or human globin sequences were found to hybridize to a single pair of lateral loops on chromosome IX, and to no other loops on this chromosome or elsewhere in the complement. However they have been shown to do so, not because of the globin sequences in the probes, but rather because the plasmids from which the probes were prepared were constructed with G.C homopolymer tails. Simple sequence poly d $(C/G)_n$ probes also hybridize with RNA transcripts on this same pair of loops, and with no others (see Callan and Old, 1980).

The histone probes used in the original experiments were later found to include repetitive $(CT/GA)_n$ sequences present in spacer(s) alongside histone genes. In a second series of experiments involving other probes and other newts, probes which included repetitive $(CT/GA)_n$ sequences labelled some 20 pairs of loops, including most of those labelled in the first experiment, and again demonstrated some individual variation between newts; synthetic $(CT/GA)_n$ probes formed hybrids with RNA transcripts on these same loops, and exposed the same variation. 2 probes nick-translated from cloned echinoderm histone sequences which lack repetitive $(CT/GA)_n$, Strongylocentrotus H2A in pML21 and H2B in pGM16 (for both of these clones the entire sequences are known) were found to hybridize with a small subset of the loops which reacted with all the other probes, including synthetic, and with one major site that is common to all the newts examined. This major site (I_{24}) lies within the heteromorphic region of bivalent I of T.c. carnifex, and is regularly present on one chromosome but not on its partner. In the 4 newts used for the earlier hybridizations with histone probes, the labelled region of I_{24} extended over some 100 to 150 μm length of loop, followed by a 50 to 100 μm unlabelled (but nevertheless transcribed) region, before re-entry of the loop into the main chromosome axis. In both newts used for the later hybridizations with histone probes, all the probes (i.e. both with and without the CT/GA repeat) labelled I_{24} throughout its length of 100 to 150 μm. Evidently in these latter individuals there is an untranscribed region intervening between I_{24} and an adjacent loop, and this untranscribed region lies compacted in an axial chromomere. In the individuals used for the earlier hybridizations with histone probes, this untranscribed region is missing, and transcription proceeds without interruption beyond the limit where those transcripts which include histone RNA sequences are released.

A further conclusion revelled by these experiments is that repetitive sequences similar to those present in the spacers between echinoderm histone sequences are also present in newt histone gene complexes; they occur elsewhere in newt genomes too, unaccompanied by histone sequences.

REFERENCES

Old, R.W., H.G. Callan and K.W. Gross. 1976. Localisation of gene transcripts in Newt Lampbrush chromosomes by *in situ* hybridisation. *J. Cell Sci.* 27, 57-79.

Callan, H.G. and R.W. Old. 1980. *In situ* hybridization to lampbrush chromosomes : A potential source of error exposed. *J. Cell Sci.* 41, 115-123.

Nucleolar organisers in mammalian cells

O. J. Miller

Columbia University, New York, NY 10032

NATURE OF NUCLEOLAR ORGANISERS

The nucleolus is the site of transcription and processing of 18S and 28S ribosomal RNA (rRNA). It contains long tandem arrays of actively transcribing rRNA genes, each separated from the next by a non-transcribed spacer region. Miller spreads of nucleoli viewed by electron microscopy show a characteristic repetitive pine tree appearance, with nascent rRNA chains of progressively greater length attached at successive growing points along the DNA of each transcribing unit (Beyer et al., 1979). Each nucleolus arises at telophase (rRNA transcription ceases throughout prophase, metaphase and anaphase) in close association with a specific chromosome segment called the nucleolar organiser or nucleolar organiser region (NOR). This region stains poorly with Feulgen, orcein or Giemsa and is sometimes visible at metaphase as a faintly stained secondary constriction, whose size is directly proportional to the size of the nucleolus it organises. NORs have a characteristic appearance by electron microscopy, with an ultrastructure different from that of the fully condensed chromosome arms.

Nucleolar organisers contain rRNA genes (rDNA). These genes are present in multiple, sometimes hundreds, of copies in diploid mammalian cells. Several methods have been used to identify the rDNA sites on the metaphase chromosomes (Figure 1). In situ hybridization of radioactively labeled rRNA or cDNA to fixed metaphase chromosomes can localize the gene clusters (Henderson et al., 1973;

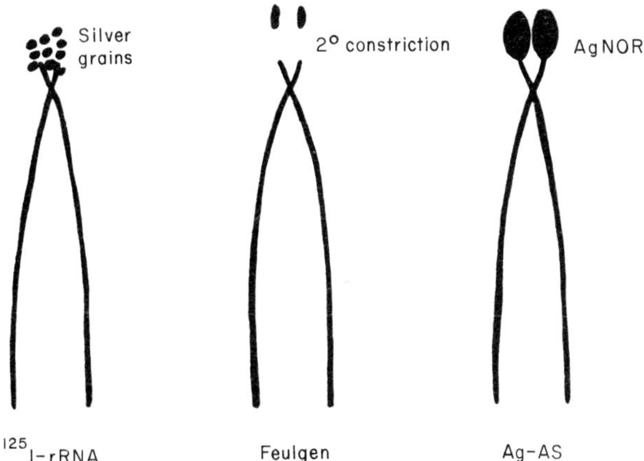

FIGURE 1. Methods for detecting rRNA gene sites. In situ hybridization with ^{125}I-rRNA, followed by autoradiography, detects all sites with sufficient numbers of gene copies. A secondary constriction and AgNOR staining detect only transcriptionally active rRNA gene sites.

Hsu et al., 1975), and grain counts can provide an estimate of the relative number of gene copies on different chromosomes. NORs whose rDNA was actively transcribed in the preceding interphase can be detected by a silver staining technique and, sometimes, by the presence of secondary constrictions. However, silver stained NORs (AgNORs) are often present in the absence of a secondary constriction, as in the guinea pig, where AgNORs are present on up to five pairs of chromosomes but a clear secondary constriction is seen only on chromosome 1 (Zenzes et al., 1977). Similarly, the NORs at the distal end of the long arm of chromosomes in such animals as the Chinese hamster and the cow are readily detectable by silver staining but are not marked by a clear secondary constriction because of the absence of a satellite distal to the NOR.

Location, size and number of NORs

Ribosomal RNA genes are concentrated on a single chromosome pair in some mammals, such as the lower primates, but are distributed over a number of chromosomes in others, such as many rodents, higher primates and humans. In both the mouse (Winking et al., 1980) and the orangutan (Tantravahi et al., 1976), AgNORs are visible on up to eight pairs of chromosomes. When the rDNA is concentrated on a single chromosome pair, it can be present far from either end of the chromosome, even near the centromere of a metacentric chromosome, as it is in the gibbon and various monkeys. However, when rDNA is present on multiple chromosomes, it is usually located very close to one or the other end, usually on the short arm. This nearly telomeric location minimizes the harmful effects of interchange (by crossing over or translocation) between rRNA genes on nonhomologous chromosomes, a phenomenon that is facilitated by nucleolar fusion.

The number of AgNORs per diploid cell can be as many as 10 in the human or 16 in the mouse (Tantravahi et al., 1976; Winking et al., 1980). The number of nucleoli is much lower, only 1-3 in most cells, because of a marked tendency for nucleoli to fuse. This maintains NOR chromosomes in proximity to one another, and is presumably responsible for the NOR (satellite) associations seen at metaphase. Chromosomes with larger AgNORs are more frequently involved in NOR associations (D. A. Miller et al., 1977). The chromosomes in such associations appear, at a light microscope level of resolution, to be attached to one another by rDNA connectives (Henderson et al., 1973). Nucleolar fusion may thus predispose NOR chromosomes to Robertsonian translocation. Furthermore, in many species the nucleolus tends to be surrounded by centromeric heterochromatin from various chromosomes. This could lead to preferential occurrence of Robertsonian translocations involving one NOR chromosome and one other chromosome, as seen in the mouse (O. J. Miller et al., 1978b).

In species whose rDNA is distributed over several chromosomes, there is a marked inter-individual variability in the location, size and number of NORs; these features are constant within an individual (Dev et al., 1976; D. A. Miller et al., 1977). For example, in the mouse, NORs can be present on three to eight different chromosomes, with a characteristic distribution in each animal or inbred strain. The location is usually on the long arm near the centromere, distal to the satellite DNA in the C-band heterochromatin. In some mice, however, NORs can also occur terminally, at the distal end of the long arm, and interstitially, near the centromere of Robertsonian translocation chromosomes

(Winking et al., 1980). The occurrence of telomeric NORs in addition to those in the locations characteristic of a particular species has also been noted in the gorilla (Tantravahi et al., 1976) and the guinea pig (Zenzes et al., 1977), indicating how widespread is the underlying (and unknown) mechanism responsible for variation in the location of NORs. It should be noted that the presence of NORs at opposite ends of a homologous chromosome pair can lead, by regular crossing over, to loss of both NORs.

The amount of rDNA on a given chromosome varies markedly. This has been studied most extensively in the human and the mouse, using in situ hybridization and silver staining. The size of each AgNOR, which usually reflects the amount of rDNA at the site (Goodpasture and Bloom, 1975; Hsu et al., 1975; Warburton et al., 1976), is characteristic for an individual, and does not often change from generation to generation. This suggests that unequal crossing over is not as common in mammals as it is in yeast, where it may occur in 10% of meiotic divisions (Petes, 1980). Nevertheless, the marked variability in the amount of rDNA on each NOR chromosome in most populations is probably due to unequal crossing over, which is facilitated by the organization of rRNA genes in long tandem arrays.

Gene amplification

We have studied one family in which seven phenotypically normal individuals have a 14p+ chromosome with about eight times as many rRNA gene copies in the GC-rich (and thus differentially staining) DNA of its long short arm as the average NOR chromosome (D. A. Miller et al., 1978a). Other examples of such highly amplified rRNA gene clusters appear to be fairly common (Tantravahi et al., 1980), and most of these probably arise by unequal crossing over. However, some other mechanism may have been involved in their origin, just as in the case of the even more highly amplified rDNA clusters seen in certain tumor cell lines. We have found a three-fold increase in cellular rRNA gene multiplicity in the XC rat Rous sarcoma virus-induced tumor cell line (U. Tantravahi and O. J. Miller, unpublished) and a ten-fold increase in the H4-IIE-C3 rat hepatoma cell line (Miller et al., 1979). In the latter, despite a low frequency of sister chromatid exchanges (R. Tantravahi, unpublished), there is a high frequency of unequal interchanges between sister chromatids within the amplified rDNA (Miller, 1980). It is possible that such a mechanism also led to the initial amplification of rDNA in this line. In the rat, rDNA is present on chromosomes 3, 11 and 12 (Tantravahi et al., 1979). In H4 cells, amplified rDNA is present on several chromosomes, including both 3 and 11, raising the possibility that amplification may have occurred at more than one primary site.

REGULATION OF NUCLEOLAR ORGANISER ACTIVITY

Nucleolar dominance in hybrids

In a variety of interspecific hybrid plants and animals, a nucleolus is organized by the NOR chromosomes of only one species; the hybrid cells have fewer nucleoli than expected and the chromosomes of only one species have a secondary constriction marking each active nucleolar organiser. In hybrids between two species, the same species always dominates, and in hybrids among a group of species, there is an orderly hierarchy of nucleolar dominance. The molecular mechanism underlying nucleolar dominance is not well understood, but in *Xenopus laevis* x *X. mulleri* hybrids it is associated with repression of transcription of the *X. mulleri* rRNA genes (Honjo and Reeder, 1973), confirming the importance of rRNA synthesis for the formation of the nucleolus.

Species-specific regulation of rRNA synthesis has also been observed in interspecific somatic cell hybrids. Eliceiri and Green reported the absence of human 28S rRNA in a number of mouse-human hybrids, with a greatly reduced number of human chromosomes, and this was confirmed in a larger series by Marshall, Handmaker and Bramwell. Definitive evidence that human NOR chromosomes were indeed present in mouse-human hybrid cells not expressing human rRNA genes has been obtained using Q-banding. A subsequent analysis of the same cells by the silver-staining technique shows that only the mouse, and not the human, nucleolar organisers are stained (D. A. Miller et al., 1976). Since such hybrid cells have human rRNA genes (Arnheim and Southern, 1978) which are not transcribed to form the 45S precursor of 18S and 28S rRNA (Perry et al., 1979), silver staining must be restricted to NORs which are capable of transcriptional activity. This finding has been confirmed in several other systems, e.g., early embryos and germ line cells. Nucleolar dominance in both organismic and cell hybrids is thus due to species-specific suppression of transcription of the 45S precursor of 18S and 28S rRNA.

In somatic cell hybrids, nucleolar dominance appears to be closely related to chromosome loss. Nucleolar organising activity declines within days of hybridization, and the most rapid loss of activity occurs in hybrid cells with the greatest disparity between the number of mouse and human chromosomes (Dev et al., 1979). Furthermore, when the direction of chromosome loss in somatic cell hybrids is reversed, so is that of nucleolar dominance, in both mouse-human and rat-human hybrids (O. J. Miller et al., 1976; Tantravahi et al., 1979). Finally nucleolar dominance is not present in all interspecific somatic cell hybrids. For example, in mouse-Syrian hamster hybrids, both mouse and hamster NORs are Ag-stained in each hybrid cell, in keeping with Eliceiri's earlier observation in such hybrids that 28S rRNA of both species is produced in amounts proportional to the number of chromosomes of each species (O. J. Miller et al., 1978a).

Regulation in amplified rDNA

When a chromosome has a much increased rRNA gene multiplicity (amplification), there can be a marked discrepancy between the number of gene copies and the level of gene activity, with only a fraction of the amplified genes active. In every case in which there is amplification of rDNA, most of the extra copies appear to be inactive; the small number of active genes are clustered at small sites along the amplified segment, with each site marked by silver staining and sometimes by a secondary constriction (D. A. Miller et al., 1978a; Miller et al., 1979). The nature of this regulation is unclear, but it is not simply due to the increased number of rRNA genes per cell. In one human tumor cell line with a near-diploid modal number of chromosomes but a range extending to more than three times this number, the number of AgNORs was proportional to the total number of chromosomes. In mouse-human reverse hybrids made with this cell line, the number of human chromosomes ranged from 50 to 300, and again the number of AgNORs paralleled the number of chromosomes (D. A. Miller et al., 1978b).

DNA methylation and rRNA gene regulation

DNA methylation appears to play a role in some aspects of cell differentiation and gene regulation in various systems. We have shown that it plays a similar role in the regulation of amplified rRNA genes. However, this system differs from others in that, within a single cell (even a single chromosome), some copies of this gene are active and unmethylated while others are inactive and methylated. In two unrelated families, a 14p+ chromosome containing amplified rDNA shows restricted sites of gene activity, marked by silver-stained secondary constrictions. The DNA in the differentially staining region containing inactive rRNA genes is especially rich in 5-methylcytosine, as shown by extensive binding of antibodies to this minor constituent of DNA (Tantravahi et al., 1980). Similarly, there is hypermethylation of the long differentially staining regions (DSRs, or HSRs) containing inactive amplified rDNA in rat XC sarcoma and H4 hepatoma cell lines (Tantravahi et al., 1980). The striking enrichment of 5-methylcytosine in regions containing inactive rRNA genes suggests that DNA methylation may play a role in the inactivation of these genes. However, the amplified regions also contain an indeterminate but possibly large amount of non-rDNA. The nature of the methylated DNA has been clarified by molecular studies.

In order to find out whether the 5-methylcytosine residues are within the 18S plus 28S rRNA genes (including transcribed and nontranscribed spacers), H4 cells have been grown in [^{14}C-methyl] methionine to label the methyl group of 5-methylcytosine, the DNA isolated and cut with one or a combination of restriction enzymes. The fragments have been separated on agarose gel, denatured, transferred to nitrocellulose filters by Southern blotting, and the location of the amplified rDNA correlated with the location of the C^{14}-methyl label. The results indicate that the fragments containing both the 18S and 28S rDNA are highly methylated. The location of the 5-methylcytosine residues has been defined more precisely by using restriction enzymes that do not cut DNA if the

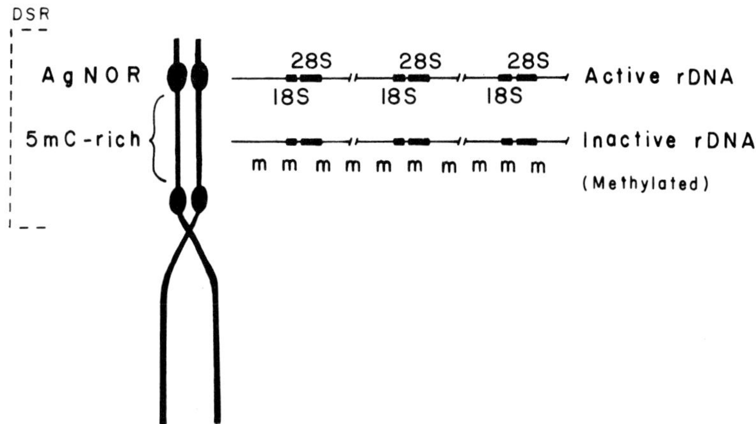

FIGURE 2. Model of amplified rDNA, illustrating the proposed role of DNA methylation in the regulation of rRNA gene expression.

internal cytosine in the recognition sequence has been converted to 5-methylcytosine. Neither HpaII nor HhaI cuts the H4 rDNA (they do cut control rDNA) indicating that the internal C in their recogition sequence, CCGG and GCGC, respectively, are methylated in H4 rDNA. CCGG sequences are present in the H4 rDNA because the DNA is cut by MspI, which recognizes this sequence whether or not its internal C is methylated (Tantravahi et al., 1980).

These results are summarized in a model of amplified rDNA (Figure 2), indicating the proposed role of DNA methylation in the regulation of rRNA gene expression. Is DNA methylation associated with suppression of nucleolar organiser activity in interspecific hybrids, in early embryos or in terminal differentiation of many types of cells? The answers to such questions should soon be available.

Acknowledgements: This work was supported by research grants from the American Cancer Society (CD-66A), the March of Dimes Birth Defects Foundation (I-361) and the National Institutes of Health (CA 27655 and GM 25193).

REFERENCES

Arnheim, N. and E. M. Southern 1977.Heterogeneity of the ribosomal genes in mice and men. *Cell* 11, 363-70.

Beyer, A. L., S. L. McKnight and O. L. Miller, Jr. 1979.Transcriptional units in eukaryotic chromosomes. In *Molecular genetics, part III.Chromosome structure*, J. H. Taylor, ed., 117-75. New York: Academic Press.

Dev, V. G., R. Tantravahi, D. A. Miller and O. J. Miller 1977. Nucleolus organizers in Mus musculus subspecies and in the RAG mouse cell line. *Genetics* 86, 389-98.

Dev, V. G., D. A. Miller, M. Rechsteiner and O. J. Miller 1979. Time of suppression of human rRNA genes in mouse-human hybrid cells. *Exp. Cell Res.* 123, 47-54.

Goodpasture, C. and S. E. Bloom 1975.Visualization of nucleolar organizer regions in mammalian chromosomes using silver staining. *Chromosoma* 53, 37-50.

Henderson, A. S., D. Warburton and K. C. Atwood 1973.Ribosomal DNA connectives between human acrocentric chromosomes. *Nature* 245 96-97.

Honjo, E. and R. H. Reeder 1973.Preferential transcription of Xenopus laevis ribosomal RNA in interspecies hybrids between Xenopus laevis and Xenopus mulleri. *J. Mol. Biol.* 80, 217-28.

Hsu, T. C., S. E. Spirito and M. L. Pardue 1975.Distribution of 18+28S ribosomal genes in mammalian genomes. *Chromosoma* 53, 25-36.

Miller, D. A., V. G. Dev, R. Tantravahi and O. J. Miller 1976. Suppression of human nucleolus organizer activity in mouse-human somatic hybrid cells. *Exp. Cell Res.* 101, 235-43.

Miller, D. A., R. Tantravahi, V. G. Dev and O. J. Miller 1977. Frequency of satellite association of human chromosomes is correlated with amount of Ag-staining of the nucleolus organizer region. *Am. J. Hum. Genet.* 29, 490-502.

Miller, D. A., W. R. Breg, D. Warburton, V. G. Dev and O. J. Miller 1978a.Regulation of rRNA gene expression in a human familial 14p+ marker chromosome. *Hum. Genet.* 43, 289-97.

Miller, D. A., V. G. Dev, R. Tantravahi, C. M. Croce and O. J. Miller, 1978b.Human tumor and rodent-human hybrid cells with an increased number of active human NORs. *Cytogenet. Cell Genet.* 21, 33-41.

Miller, O. J., D. A. Miller, V. G. Dev, R. Tantravahi and C. M. Croce 1976.Expression of human and suppression of mouse nucleolus organizer activity in mouse-human somatic cell hybrids. *Proc. Natl. Acad. Sci. USA* 73, 4531-35.

Miller, O. J., V. G. Dev, D. A. Miller, R. Tantravahi and G. L. Eliceiri 1978a.Transcription and processing of both mouse and Syrian hamster ribosomal RNA genes in individual somatic hybrid cells. *Exp. Cell Res.* 115, 457-60.

Miller, O. J., D. A. Miller, R. Tantravahi and V. G. Dev 1978b. Nucleolus organizer activity and the origin of Robertsonian translocations. *Cytogenet. Cell Genet.* 20, 40-50.

Miller, O. J., R. Tantravahi, D. A. Miller, L.-C. Yu, P. Szabo and W. Prensky 1979.Marked increase in ribosomal RNA gene multiplicity in a rat hepatoma cell line. *Chromosoma* 71, 183-95.

Miller, O. J., U. Tantravahi, R. Katz, B. F. Erlanger and R. V. Guntaka 1980.Amplification of mammalian ribosomal RNA genes and their regulation by methylation. In _Genes, chromosomes and neoplasia_, T. E. Stubblefield, P. N. Rao and F. E. Arrighi, eds, Baltimore: Williams and Wilkins Co., in press.

Perry, R. P., D. E. Kelley, U. Schibler, K. Huebner and C. M. Croce 1979.Selective suppression of the transcription of ribosomal genes in mouse-human hybrid cells. _J. Cell.Physiol._ 98, 553-59.

Petes, T. D. 1980.Unequal meiotic recombination within tandem arrays of yeast ribosomal DNA genes. _Cell_ 19, 765-75.

Tantravahi, R., D. A. Miller, V. G. Dev and O. J. Miller 1976. Detection of nucleolus organizer regions in chromosomes of human, chimpanzee, gorilla, orangutan and gibbon. _Chromosoma_ 56, 15-27.

Tantravahi, R., D. A. Miller, G. D'Ancona, C. M. Croce and O. J. Miller 1979.Location of rRNA genes in three inbred strains of rat and suppression of rat rRNA gene activity in rat-human somatic cell hybrids. _Exp. Cell Res._ 119, 387-92.

Tantravahi, U., R. V. Guntaka, B. F. Erlanger and O. J. Miller 1980.Amplified mammalian ribosomal RNA genes are enriched in 5-methylcytosine. _Proc. Natl. Acad. Sci. USA_, in press.

Tantravahi, U., W. R. Breg, V. Wertelecki, B. F. Erlanger and O. J. Miller 1980.Evidence for methylation of inactive human rRNA genes in amplified regions. _Hum. Genet._, in press.

Warburton, D., K. C. Atwood and A. S. Henderson 1976.Variation in the number of genes for rRNA among human acrocentric chromosomes: correlation with frequency of satellite association. _Cytogenet. Cell Genet._ 17, 221-30.

Winking, H., K. Nielsen and A. Gropp 1980.Variable positions of NORs in Mus musculus. _Cytogenet. Cell Genet._ 26, 158-64.

Zenzes, M. R., M. Schmid and W. Engel 1977.Silver-stained nucleolus organizers in the guinea pig, Cavia cobaya. _Cytogenet. Cell Genet._ 19, 368-72.

Proposed structural principles of polytene chromosomes

C. Laird, L. Wilkinson, D. Johnson* and C. Sandström

*Department of Zoology and *Center for Bioengineering, University of Washington, Seattle, Washington 98195*

Polytene chromosomes are useful for cytogenetic and molecular analyses. Their large sizes and their reproducible patterns of bands result in unusually good resolution at the light (Bridges, 1935) and electron microscopic (Sorsa and Sorsa, 1968) levels. Knowledge of the structural basis of these chromosomes is therefore likely to be especially illuminating.

The large size of polytene chromosomes arises from DNA replication without cell division, resulting in cells with up to several thousand times the haploid DNA content (Swift, 1962; Rudkin, 1969; see Beermann, 1972). The assembly of this large amount of DNA into chromatin, and the three-dimensional organization of this chromatin, are thought to provide the structural basis of the chromosome morphology.

The reproducible appearance and size of individual bands, as well as their pattern, suggest that the three-dimensional structure of polytene chromosomes is highly controlled. What information would be sufficient to provide the reproducibility and specificity of band structure? For example, in applying this question to the "folded-fibre" model of polytene chromosomes (DuPraw and Rae, 1966), we can ask what information would lead to chromatin folding in bands but not in interbands? What difference in chromatin folding would lead to specific band lengths, widths, and densities? Is this information used specifically in polytene cells? Although these are general questions that apply to the morphology of most chromosomes, they are perhaps easiest to formulate for polytene chromosomes.

We suggest here that two structural principles are sufficient to explain the morphology of polytene chromosomes. These principles are the local control of the DNA replication and the formation of chromatin loops. In particular, we propose that the width of each band is determined by the level of polyteny of sequences in that region; the length of each band is determined by the size of the chromatin loop at that region; heterogeneity in band structure arises from differences in linear spacing in DNA of a small number of informational sequences; these sequences may also be functional in non-polytene cells (Fig. 1).

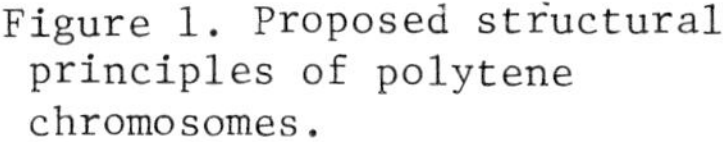
Figure 1. Proposed structural principles of polytene chromosomes.

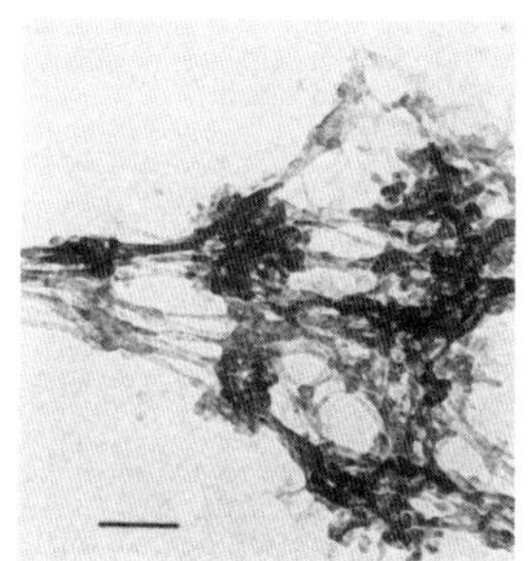

A. High-voltage electron micrograph of a region of a fat body chromosome from D. melanogaster. Scale bar represents 0.2 μm.

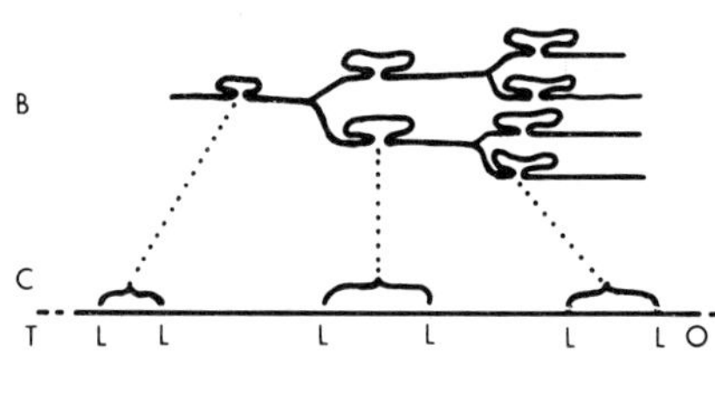

B. Interpretation of the relative polyteny in the three bands in A, estimated from dry mass data (see Laird, 1980).

C. An origin and a terminus of DNA replication are proposed for the widest band and the narrowest band, respectively. Loop-determining sequences L are proposed for the base of each loop. Polarity and spacing of one such sequence would suffice to encode specific loops.

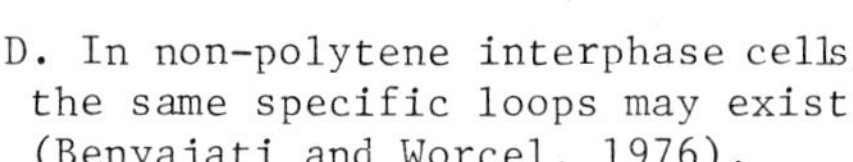

D. In non-polytene interphase cells the same specific loops may exist (Benyajati and Worcel, 1976).

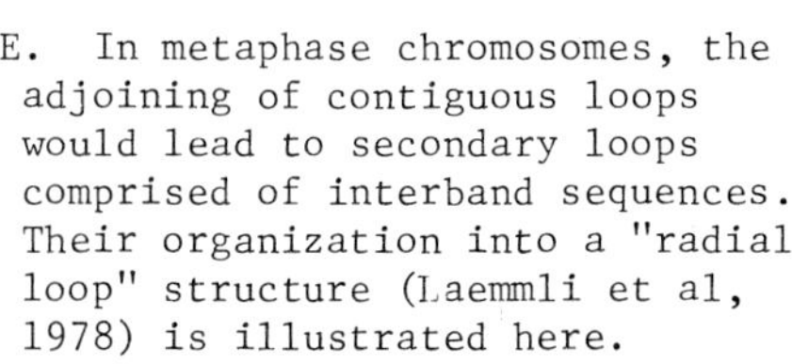
E. In metaphase chromosomes, the adjoining of contiguous loops would lead to secondary loops comprised of interband sequences. Their organization into a "radial loop" structure (Laemmli et al, 1978) is illustrated here.

Appendix:

In this section we summarize some of the data that led to the model of polytene chromosomes illustrated in Fig. 1.

1. The cross-sectional area of bands

By measuring from electron micrographs the average width of bands in chromosomes of known polyteny, we calculated the maximum cross-sectional area of chromatin that could be contributed by each chromatid. This area is equivalent to the cross-sectional area of three chromatin fibers, each with a maximum diameter of 33 nm (Laird, Ashburner, and Wilkinson, 1980). The actual diameter of three such fibers is likely to be considerably less than 33 nm - 20 to 30 nm - because the assumptions were designed to establish maximum estimates for area and fiber diameter. (The cross-sectional geometry of whole mounted chromosomes is thought to be elliptical rather than circular; cylindrical fibers can not be completely space-filling.)

A cross-sectional count of three fibers from each chromatid in a band can be depicted most simply by either two folds of chromatin (Fig. 2a), or by one flattened chromatin loop (Fig. 2b). Chromatin loops have been reported previously for polytene chromosomes (Derksen and Sorsa, 1972). Chromatin and DNA loops are also postulated to be important in the structure of other chromosomes, both condensed and interphase (cf. Keyl, 1975; Cook and Brazell, 1975; Benyajati and Worcel, 1976; Laemmli et al, 1978; Ratner, Goldsmith and Hamkalo, 1980).

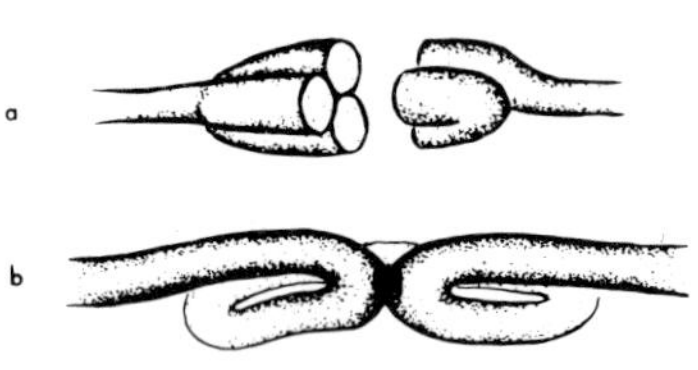

Figure 2. Arrangement of thick chromatin fibers contributed by each chromatid to an average band. A cross-sectional count of three thick fibers (maximum diameter of 33 nm - see Laird et al, 1980) is consistent with two folds (a) as well as with one flattened loop (b).

What would be the DNA content of a single chromatin loop contributed by each chromatid to band structure? The length of chromatin in a flattened loop would be twice the length of the band (where length refers to the long axis of the chromosome arm). Electron micrographs of sectioned polytene chromosomes indicate an average band length of about 0.1 µm in salivary gland chromosomes of D. melanogaster (see Beermann, 1972). Therefore, at least twice this length, or 0.2 um of chromatin fiber, would be expected for the loop size if single flattened loops are the structural basis of bands. With an estimated 20 to 50 um DNA per um of thick chromatin fiber (Green and Bahr, 1975; Worcel and Benyajati, 1977; Finch and Klug, 1976), one flattened loop would correspond to 4 to 10 um (12 to 30 kb) of DNA per band per chromatid. This would not be an unusually large DNA loop. An average size of 80 kb has been reported for super-coiled domains in DNA from tissue culture cells of Drosophila (Benyajati and Worcel, 1976). Somewhat smaller loops - 45 kb - are reported for Hela cell metaphase chromosomes (Laemmli et al, 1978).

2. Relative cross-sectional mass and phosphorus of bands and interbands

It was suggested by Rae (1966) and DuPraw and Rae (1966) that a thick (25 nm) chromatin fiber from each chromatid is oriented parallel to the long axis of the chromosome in interbands, and that this fiber is folded in bands. The relative cross-sectional dry mass of chromatin is, on the average, three to four times higher in bands than in interbands (Laird, 1980). If Rae's (1966) conclusion about interband fibers is correct, this is the ratio that would be expected from the maximum number of thick fibers calculated above for bands (Fig. 2.)

Similar ratios have been obtained with X-ray microanalysis of mass and phosphorus in whole mounted polytene chromosomes (Fig. 3). The distribution of phosphorus is especially useful because it reflects the distribution of nucleic acids in chromosomes. (More than 90% of phosphorus in acid-fixed chromosomes is expected to be in nucleic acids (Kleinsmith and Allfrey, 1969; Chen et al, 1974; de Morales et al, 1974).)

3. Differences in polyteny as the basis for variation between individual bands in cross-sectional width and mass

It has been accepted that interbands contain such low concentrations of DNA that chromatin in interbands must be in a very extended form (Swift, 1962; Mulder, van Duijn and Gloor, 1968; see Beermann, 1972). This is, however, at odds with predictions from

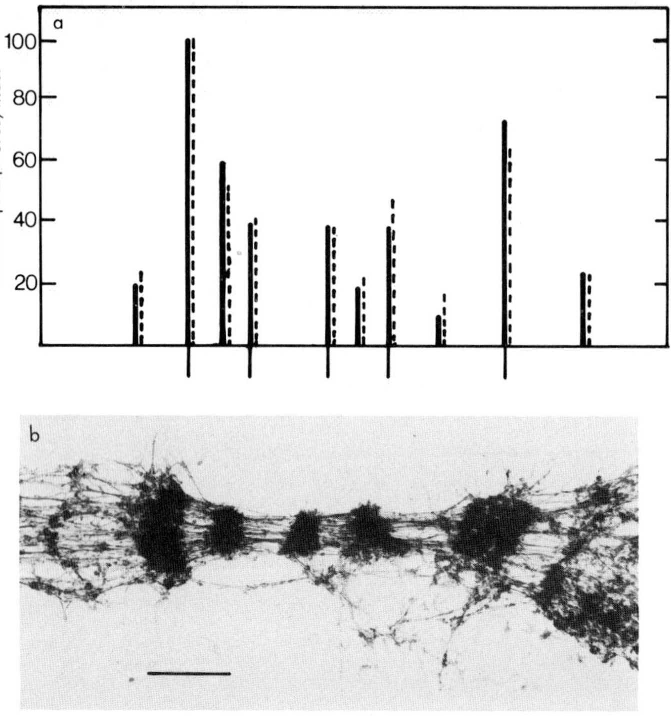

Figure 3. Relative cross-sectional mass (dashed line) and phosphorus (solid line) in a region of a polytene chromosome from larval fat body of D. melanogaster. X-ray microanalysis of this whole-mounted chromosome was carried out on a JEOL 100C with scanning attachment and a KEVEX 7000 computer-based energy-dispersive spectrometer (see Shuman et al, 1976; Hutchinson, 1978). Scanning dimension parallel to the long axis of the chromosome was 0.1 μm. Scanning dimension across the chromosome width was set to be slightly greater than the widest band. Scale bar represents 1.0 μm. Lines extending below the graph indicate regions designated as bands. For this chromosome region the relative cross-sectional phosphorus was 3.3 times higher in bands than in interbands.

electron microscopic observations of thick chromatin fibers in interbands (Laird, 1980). On the basis of dry mass measurements, it was concluded that prominent interbands - the ones most likely to have been measured by Feulgen-DNA cytophotometry - do have relatively low cross-sectional mass values. However, prominent interbands are usually adjacent to bands whose cross-sectional mass is also low. To accommodate the data, it was proposed that two- to four-fold variations sometimes exist in the polyteny of euchromatic sequences, and that regions containing such variation comprise replication domains similar to those described by Plaut, Nash, and Fanning (1966).

The idea that gradients of DNA replication extend over several bands and interbands was reinforced by examples of regions where adjacent bands formed a doubling series of increasing size. Fig. 4 illustrates a region where this is especially marked. A sixteen fold range in cross-sectional phosphorus, and a four fold variation in band width, is interpreted as being indicative of a sixteen fold range in polyteny of sequences in these bands (Fig. 4c).

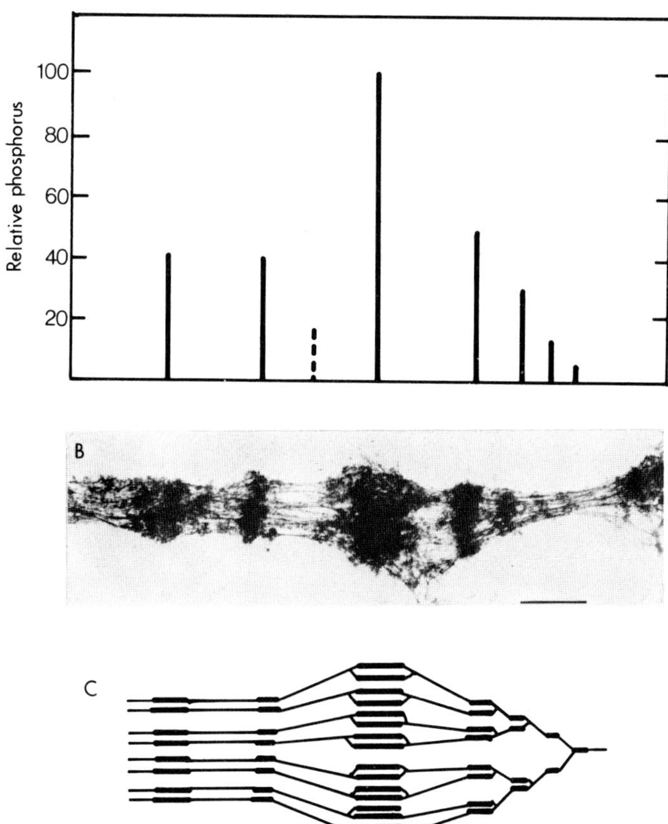

Figure 4. X-ray microanalysis of a region of a larval fat body chromosome. Conditions of microanalysis were as described in the legend to Fig. 3, except for the scanning dimension of 0.12 μm. In (c), thick and thin regions of each line represent bands and interbands, respectively. Proposed relative levels of polyteny are indicated by the number of lines at each region. Branch points could represent dormant replication forks (Laird et al, 1973), but no evidence for such forks has been presented.

It is also of interest that the cross-sectional dry mass of the measured interband is higher than the dry mass of two of the bands illustrated in Fig. 4. This result indicates that a systematic under-replication of interband sequences relative to all band sequences (Sorsa, 1974) cannot explain the low Feulgen-DNA values reported for interband DNA.

The suggestion that replication of some regions of polytene chromosomes is reinitiated before completion of replication of other regions was originally made by Heitz (1934). This was confirmed biochemically by comparing heterochromatic and euchromatic DNA (Gall, Cohen and Polan, 1971; see Laird et al, 1973). Moreover Breuer and Pavan (1955) report that extra replication of DNA in some bands occurs in *Rhynchosciara*. Thus there is evidence that Dipteran polytene cells are able to replicate differentially both euchromatic and heterochromatic sequences.

One key assumption in our previous work (Laird, 1980) was that dry mass values are proportional to DNA content. Although this was demonstrated to be true over long chromosome regions (Laird et al, 1980), no data were available to test whether chromatin in bands and interbands contained equivalent proportions of DNA to chromatin mass.

To test this assumption, polytene chromosomes were treated with ribonuclease, which removed more than 90% of nascent RNA associated with nucleoli and heat induced puffs. The distribution of phosphorus in these chromosomes was similar to that in untreated chromosomes (Fig. 5), suggesting that the data derived from dry mass measurements also reflect accurately the distribution of DNA.

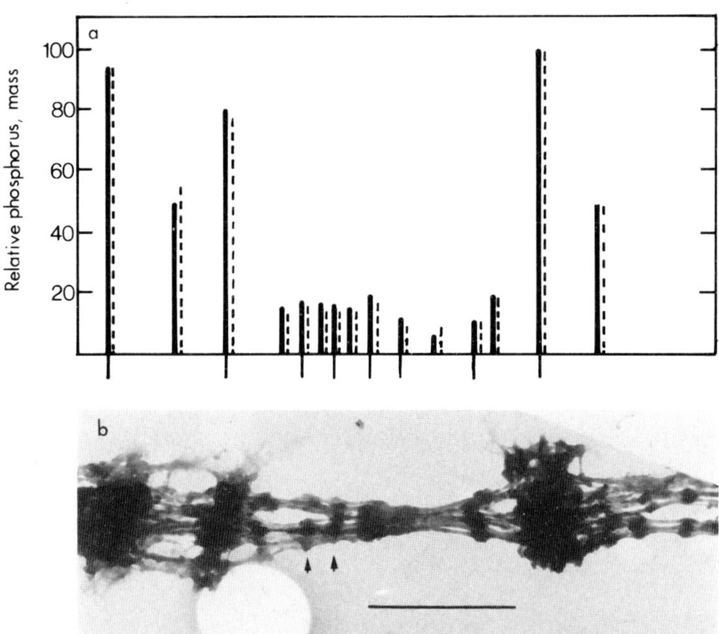

Figure 5. X-ray microanalysis of a region of a ribonuclease-treated polytene chromosome from D. melanogaster. Whole-mounted chromosomes from larval fat bodies were prepared as described elsewhere (Laird et al, 1980) except that slides with acid-fixed chromosomes were incubated in 10 μg/ml Ribonuclease A (0.1 M NaCl, 10 min). Autoradiography of control slides with chromosomes from salivary glands labeled with ^{3}H-uridine demonstrated that this ribonuclease treatment was sufficient to remove more than 90% of the nascent RNA. Conditions of microanalysis, graph conventions, and scale bar are as described in the legend to Fig. 3, except for a scanning dimension of 0.06 μm. For this region the band to interband ratio of cross-sectional phosphorus was 2.5. This ratio was calculated excluding the two very thin bands (arrows), which were below the limit of spatial resolution.

4. Conclusions

We have used two electron microscopic approaches to analyze the structure of polytene chromosomes. We conclude that: (i) The reason for the previous low estimates of interband DNA is that prominent interbands were selectively measured. Prominent interbands are often in chromosome regions where both bands and interbands have low cross-sectional mass. (ii) These regions may be delayed in DNA replication, leading to at least three levels of polyteny within replication domains. The control of replication is therefore proposed to be a major source of variation in chromosome width. (iii) The other dimension of morphological variation - that of band length - is proposed to result from variations in the size of the chromatin loops. (iv) The control signals for band width and band length can thus be encoded with the same basic information that is necessary to replicate DNA and to organize chromatin loops in other cells.

The major variables in determining the structure of polytene chromosomes are therefore proposed to be the distance between a small number of replication and loop-forming sites in DNA. Tests of this model are in progress.

Acknowledgements: We thank M. Hammond and S. Henikoff for their stimulating comments.

REFERENCES

Beermann, W. 1972. In Results and Problems - Cell Differentiation, Vol. 4, W. Beermann, J. Reinert, H. Ursprung, ed., 1-34. Berlin: Springer-Verlag.

Benyajati, C. and A. Worcel 1976. Cell 9, 393-407.

Bridges, C.B. 1935. J. Heredity 26, 60-64.

Breuer, M.E. and C. Pavan 1955. Chromosoma 7, 371-386.

Chen, C.C., D.L. Smith, B.B. Bruegger, R.M. Halpern and R.A. Smith 1974. Biochemistry 13, 3785-3789.

Cook, P.R. and I.A. Brazell 1975. J. Cell Sci. 19, 261-279.

Derksen, J. and V. Sorsa 1972. Exptl. Cell Res. 70, 246-248.

DuPraw, E.J. and P.M.M. Rae 1966. Nature 212, 598-600.

Finch, J.T. and A. Klug 1976. Proc. Natl. Acad. Sci. USA 73, 1897-1901.

Gall, J.G., E.H. Cohen and M.L. Polan 1971. Chromsoma 33, 319-344.

Green, R.J. and G.F. Bahr 1975. Chromosoma 50, 53-67.
Hartmann-Goldstein, I. and D.J. Goldstein 1980. Chromosoma 71, 333-346.
Heitz, E. 1934. Biologisches Zentralblatt 54, 588-609.
Hutchinson, T.E. 1978.Internat. Rev. Cytol. 58, 115-158.
Keyl, H.G. 1975. Chromosoma 51, 75-92.
Kleinsmith, L.J. and V.G. Allfrey 1969. Biochem. Biophys. Acta 175, 123-135.
Laemmli, U.K., S.M. Cheng, K.W. Adolf, J.R. Paulson, J.A. Brown and W.R. Baumbach 1978. Cold Spring Harbor Symp. Quant. Biol. 42, 351-360.
Laird, C.D. 1980. Submitted to Cell.
Laird, C.D., W.Y. Chooi, E.H. Cohen, E. Dickson, N. Hutchinson and S. Turner 1973. Cold Spring Harbor Symp. Quant. Biol. 38, 311-327.
Laird, C.D., M. Ashburner, and L. Wilkinson 1980. Chromosoma 76, 175-189.
de Morales, M.M., C. Blat and L.Harel 1974. Exptl. Cell Res. 86, 111-119.
Mulder, M.P., P. van Duijn and H.J. Gloor 1968. Genetica 39, 358-428.
Plaut,W., D. Nash, T. Fanning 1966. J. Molecular Biol. 16, 85-93.
Rae, P.M.M. 1966. Nature 212, 139-142.
Rattner, J.B., M. Goldsmith and B.A. Hamkalo 1980. Chromosoma 79, 215-224.
Rudkin, G.T. 1969. Genetics 61, No.1 Suppl. 227-238.
Shuman, H., A.V. Somlyo and A.P. Somlyo 1976. Ultramicroscopy 1, 317-339.
Sorsa, V. 1974. Hereditas 78, 298-302.
Sorsa, M. and V. Sorsa 1968. Annales Academiae Scientiarum Fennicae, Series A 127, 1-8.
Swift, H. 1962. In Molecular Control of Cellular Activity, John M. Allen, ed., 73-125.
Worcel, A. and C. Benyajati 1977. Cell 12, 83-100.

Mobile DNA sequence in *Drosphila*

D. J. Finnegan

Department of Molecular Biology, University of Edinburgh, Edinburgh EH9 3JR

A number of transposable DNA elements have been identified in the genome of *Drosophila melanogaster*. These sequences are usually repeated about 30-50 times per haploid genome and are often referred to as 'repeated genes' since many of them are complementary to polyA$^+$ RNA from *D.melanogaster* tissue culture cells (Finnegan *et al*, 1978; Ilyin *et al*, 1978). Two of the most extensively studied families have been called '412' and 'copia' after the first member of each to be characterised and I shall refer to them as such here (Finnegan *et al*, 1978). There is evidence for a further 15-20 such families and Rubin has estimated that perhaps as much as 5% of the *D.melanogaster* genome may be comprised of these sequences (Rubin *et al*, 1980). This would account for about one third of the moderately repetitive DNA in this species.

Each member of the 412 family is about 7 kb long (1 kb = 1000 base pairs) with a direct repeat sequence of 500 base pairs at each end (Fig. 1). *In situ* hybridisation to polytene salivary gland chromosomes indicates that the 412 genes are distributed at sites on all five major chromosome arms (Finnegan *et al*, 1978). The number of members of the family is not known exactly. DNA renaturation experiments suggest that it is about 40 (Potter *et al*, 1979) while the number of chromosomal sites containing 412 sequences is about 30 (Strobel *et al*, 1979). There is a high degree of sequence conservation between members of the 412 family at least in so far as they all have the *Eco*RI and *Hind*III

Chromosomes today, volume 7   George Allen & Unwin 1981

restriction map shown in Figure 1 (Finnegan et al, 1978).

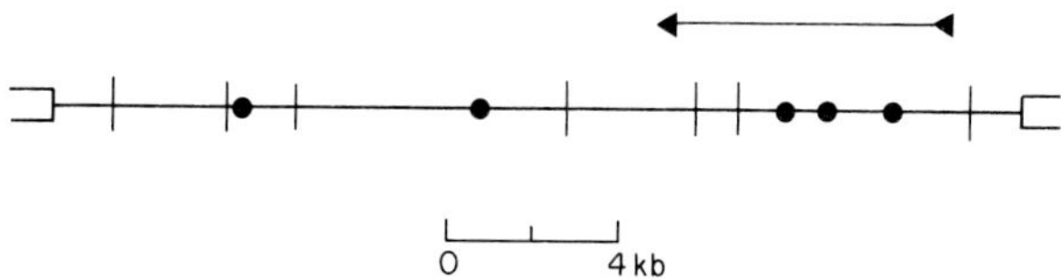

Fig. 1. Map showing the positions of EcoRI (-o-) and HindIII (+) restriction sites in the ColE1/D.melanogaster hybrid plasmid cDm412. The thin line represents D.melanogaster DNA and the open blocks ColE1 DNA. The horizontal line above the map indicates the position of sequences complementary to RNA (the '412 gene') and the arrow heads represent the terminal repeats described in the text.

The copia gene family has properties very similar to those of 412. In this case the genes are about 5 kb long and have a terminal redundancy of about 300 base pairs which does not cross hybridise with that of the 412 family (Finnegan et al, 1978). There are about 30 sites containing copia sequences and again these are distributed on all chromosome arms (Strobel et al, 1979).

Strobel et al (1979) have used in situ hybridisation to analyse sites containing 412 and copia sequences in four different strains of D.melanogaster and have found considerable variation in their number and location. This suggests that these sequences can move around the genome or in other words that they are transposable elements.

The general properties described above, and in particular the apparent ability to transpose, are not confined to the 412 and copia families. Strobel et al (1979) have found them to apply to another repeated gene family, 297, and Georgiev's group have reported similar results for other sequences which they refer to as mobile disperse genes (mdg) (Ilyin et al, 1978; Tchurikov et al, 1978; Bayev et al, 1980).

Nothing is known about the rate of transposition but it is clearly very rapid in evolutionary terms. Strobel et al (1979) not only noticed variation in the location of copia elements between strains of D.melanogaster but also within their stock of Oregon R. There is no evidence to indicate whether or not transposition occurs during the life of the individual.

MECHANISM OF TRANSPOSITION

The direct repeats found at the ends of transposable elements in D.melanogaster suggest a possible mechanism for their movement. Figure 2 shows how a single crossover event could lead to insertion of a gene consisting of a circular DNA with one copy of the repeat at an 'empty' chromosomal site containing a second copy. This yields a 'filled' site that has a terminal redundancy Deletion of a gene from a filled site could occur by the reverse reaction giving a circular DNA and an empty site.

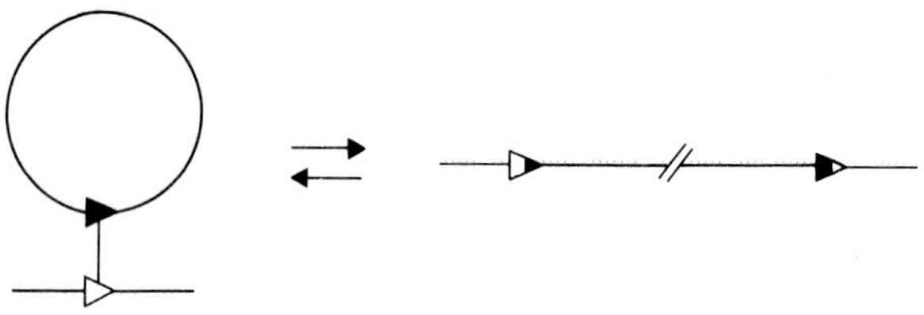

Fig. 2. A model for gene transposition by reciprocal recombination

The extensive strain differences in the chromosomal locations of 412 and copia sequences (for copia only one common site was found in four strains (Strobel et al, 1979)) suggests that there must be many potential integration sites for members of both families. The recombination model above predicts that at each potential site there must be a complete copy of the terminal repeat. This has been tested for the 412 family by screening a library of λ/D.melanogaster recombinant phage for those containing fragments with homology only to the terminal repeat. Sufficient recombinants to cover the entire genome with 99% probability yielded only 11 such phages (unpublished data). We do not know as yet whether they contain complete copies of the terminal repeat but even if they do the number is far too low to account for all potential integration sites. Levis et al (1980) have obtained similar results for the copia family by different methods and we therefore believe that transposition does not involve reciprocal recombination between terminal repeats.

Transposable DNA sequences have been known in bacteria for

some time. One class of such elements, the transposons, have a sequence organisation resembling that of 412 and copia genes in that they are composed of a few thousand base pairs of DNA with terminal repeats. These are usually inverted repeats which vary in length from a few tens to a few hundreds of base pairs (Calos and Miller, 1980).

Transposons can move from place to place in the bacterial genome almost at random by a mechanism which does not involve homologous recombination. Transposition to a particular site results in duplication of a few base pairs originally present once at the site of insertion. After insertion they are found repeated immediately before and after the transposon. The number of bases duplicated is characteristic of a particular element but their sequence may vary from transposition to transposition.

The structural similarity between transposons and transposable elements in *D.melanogaster* suggests that they may move by a related mechanism. Recent data lend weight to this idea. Levis *et al* (1980) have shown that the copia terminal repeat is 276 base pairs long and has an inexact inverted repeat of 17 base pairs at each end. In addition Dunsmuir *et al* (1980) have determined the sequence of DNA immediately adjacent to a particularly copy of copia and have compared this with that of the same region of the genome from a strain of *D.melanogaster* without copia at this position. In three such comparisons they found that five base pairs repeated immediately before and after the copia elements occurred only once at the sites of insertion. The sequence of bases was different in each case and there was no detectable homology between copia elements and their sites of insertion. Bayev *et al* (1980) have preliminary evidence to suggest that the same may be true of mdg 3 another transposable element in *D.melanogaster*. Insertion of the 297 element is associated with duplication of 4 base pairs (Young and Rubin, quoted in Dunsmuir *et al*, 1980).

TRANSPOSABLE ELEMENTS IN OTHER EUKARYOTES

Transposable DNA elements are not confined to *D.melanogaster*. Cameron *et al* (1979) have identified a similar sequence, Ty1, in the yeast *Saccharomyces cerevisiae*. Ty1 elements are 5.6 kb long and have direct repeats of about 330 base pairs (known as 'δ') at each end. There are about 35 copies of Ty1 per genome and their chromosomal distribution differs between strains (Cameron *et al*, 1979). Unlike the terminal repeats of copia and 412 there are many copies of δ in the yeast genome separate from the rest of Ty1 (Cameron *et al*, 1979). Despite this, integration of Ty1 can occur by a mechanism which does not involve recombination between δ elements.

Farabaugh and Fink (1980) have sequenced homologous regions of the yeast genome with and without a copy of Ty1. As with copia elements Ty1 was flanked by a direct repeat of 5 base pairs which were present only once in its absence. There was no sequence homology between Ty1 and the site of insertion. Gafner and Philippsen (1980) have results suggesting that the same is true of 3 other copies of Ty1.

Transposable DNA sequences have not as yet been identified in vertebrates but there are similarities between proviruses of RNA retroviruses and copia and Ty1. When retroviruses infect cells they are copied into linear and circular double stranded DNAs one or both of which may integrate into many sites in the host chromosomes (Bishop, 1978; Hughes *et al*, 1978). These integrated copies of the viral genome resemble transposable elements in *D.melanogaster* and yeast in that they are bounded by direct repeats a few hundred base pairs long. In the two cases studied so far integration is associated with duplication of 4 (Moloney murine leukemia virus) or 5 (chicken spleen necrosis virus) base pairs (Dhar *et al*, 1980; Shimotohno *et al*, 1980).

GENETIC CONSEQUENCES OF TRANSPOSITION

Each transposition event involving a 412 or copia element is a mutation which may or may not have a detectable genetic effect. Bacterial transposons inactivate genes into which they insert and can cause deletion or translocation of adjacent DNA. The same may well be true of transposable elements in eukaryotes. It is certainly the case in yeast as Farabaugh and Fink (1980) have shown that an unstable mutation of the *his4* locus is due to insertion of a Ty1 element at or near the start of the gene.

This mutation is associated with deletions and translocations which have one end point in the Ty1 element (Roeder and Fink, 1980).

Transposable genetic elements have been known in D.melanogaster for some time. The best studied of these carries the white eye (w) and roughest (rst) genes (Ising and Ramel, 1976). It also contains at least part of a copia element but there is no evidence as yet to indicate that this is responsible for transposition (Gehring and Paro, 1980). Similarly a number of mutations in D.melanogaster have high reversion frequencies or result in variable gene expression (Engles, 1979; Green, 1976) and Rubin et al (1980) are investigating the possibility that these are caused by insertion of transposable elements at or near the genes in question.

It is not difficult to imagine how transposable element might be responsible for a proportion of mutations in all species. These could be the immediate result of an element inserting into or next to a gene or the consequence of recombination between scattered copies of an element on the same or different chromosomes. The latter would lead to inversion or deletion of adjacent DNA depending on the relative orientation of the elements involved, or to its translocation.

ACKNOWLEDGEMENTS

This work has been supported by the Jane Coffin Childs Memorial Fund for Medical Research and the Medical Research Council. Experiments were carried out with the assistance of Mrs Susanna Dunbar.

REFERENCES

Bayev, A.A., Krayev, A.S., Lyubamirskaya, N.V., Ilyin, Y.V., Skryabin, K.G. and Georgiev, G.P. (1980). The transposable element mdg 3 in Drosophila melanogaster is flanked with the perfect direct and mismatched inverted repeats. Nucleic Acid Research, 8, 3263-3273

Bishop, J.M. (1978) Retroviruses. Ann.Rev.Biochem. 47, 35-88

Calos, M.P. and Miller, J.H. (1980) Transposable elements. Cell, 20, 579-595

Cameron, J.R., Loh, E.Y. and Davis, R.W. (1979) Evidence for transposition of dispersed repetitive DNA families in yeast. Cell, 16, 739-751

Dhar, R., McClements, W.L., Enquist, L.W. and van de Woude, G.F. (1980) Terminally repeated sequences (TRS) of integrated Maloney sarcoma proviruses: nucleotide sequence of TRS and its host and viral junctions. Proc.Nat.Acad.Sci.USA, in press.

Dunsmuir, P., Brorien, W.J., Simon, M.A. and Rubin, G.M. (1980) Insertion of the Drosophila transposable element copia generates a 5 base pair duplication. Cell, in press.

Engles, W.R. (1979) Extrachromosomal control of mutability in Drosophila melanogaster. Proc.Nat.Acad.Sci.USA 76, 4011-4015

Farabaugh, P.J. and Fink, G. (1980) Insertion of the eukaryotic transposable element Ty1 creates a 5-base pair duplication. Nature, 286, 352-356

Finnegan, D.J., Rubin, G.M., Young, M.W. and Hogness, D.S. (1978) Repeated gene families in Drosophila melanogaster. Cold Spring Harbor Symp.Quant.Biol. 42, 1053-1063

Gafner, J. and Philippsen, P. (1980) The yeast transposon Ty1 generates duplications of target DNA on insertion. Nature 286, 414-418

Gehring, W.J. and Paro, R. (1980) Isolation of a hybrid plasmid with homologous sequences to a transposing element of Drosophila melanogaster. Cell, in press.

Green, M.M. (1976) Mutable and Mutator Loci. In The Genetics and Biology of Drosophila. ed. M. Ashburner and E. Novitski.

Hughes, S.H., Shank, P.R., Spector, D.H., Kung, H., Bishop, J.M., Varmus, H.E., Vogt, P.K. and Breitman, M.L. (1978) Proviruses of avian sarcoma virus are terminally redundant, co-extensive with unintegrated linear DNA and integrated at many sites. Cell, 15, 1397-1410

Ilyin, Y.V., Tchurikov, N.A., Ananiev, E.V., Ryskov, A.P., Yenikolopov, G.N., Limborska, S.A., Maleva, N.E., Gvozdev, V.A. and Georgiev, G.P. (1978) Studies on the DNA fragments of mammals and Drosophila containing structural genes and adjacent sequences. Cold Spring Harbor Symp.Quant.Biol. 42, 959-969

Ising, G. and Ramel, C. (1976) The behaviour of a transposing element in *Drosophila melanogaster*. In *The Genetics and Biology of Drosophila*. ed. M. Ashburner and E. Novitski, Academic Press (London).

Levis, R., Dunsmuir, P. and Rubin, G.M. (1980) Terminal repeats of the Drosophila transposable element *copia*: nucleotide sequence and genomic organisation. *Cell*, in press.

Potter, S.S., Brorein, W.J., Dunsmuir, P. and Rubin, G.M. (1979) Transposition of elements of the 412, copia and 297 dispersed repeated gene families in *Drosophila*. *Cell*, *17*, 415-427

Roeder, G.S. and Fink, G.R. (1980) DNA rearrangements associated with a transposable element in yeast. *Cell*, *21*, 239-249

Rubin, G.M., Brorien, W.J., Dunsmuir, P. Flavell, A.J., Levis, R., Strobel, E., Toole, J.J. and Young, E. (1980) '*copia*-like' transposable elements in the *Drosophila* genome. *Cold Spring Harbor Symp.Quant.Biol.* *45*, in press.

Shimotohno, K., Mizutani, S. and Temin, H.M. (1980) Sequence of retrovirus provirus resembles that of bacterial transposable elements. *Nature*, *285*, 550-554

Strobel, E., Dunsmuir, P. and Rubin, G.M. (1979) Polymorphisms in the chromosomal locations of elements of the 412, copia and 297 dispersed repeated gene families in *Drosophila*. *Cell*, *17*, 429-439

Tchurikov, N.A., Ilyin, Y.V., Ananiev, E.V. and Georgiev, G.P. (1978) The properties of gene Dm225, a representative of dispersed repetitive genes in *Drosophila melanogaster*. Nucleic Acid Research *5*, 2169-2187

CHROMOSOMES IN MEIOSIS

Chromosome organization and DNA metabolism in meiotic cells

Herbert Stern

Department of Biology, UCSD, La Jolla, CA 92093

Meiotic cells of species as phylogenetically distant as lilies and mice share a common pattern of DNA metabolism during the prophase interval. The distinctive features of that pattern include an activation of several meiotic-specific proteins and an occurrence of site-specific DNA syntheses. Three proteins have thus far been identified, all of which act on DNA and achieve peak activities during zygotene and pachytene. During these stages, DNA is synthesized at specific chromosomal sites, their accessibility to required enzymes being dependent on localized changes in chromatin structure. Meiotic prophase encompasses a significant level of DNA synthesis, and although such synthesis is considered to be related to chromosome pairing and crossing-over (Stern and Hotta 1980), the information available is insufficient to account for the relationship in molecular terms. Despite the large gap in understanding, it is significant that the meiotic program of molecular events has been conserved during evolution. An immediate aim is to fit these events into a scheme that is consistent with cytogenetic data. In so doing, the characteristics of specificity and accessibility become prominent issues. The issue of specificity centers on the distinctive sequence organization of DNA synthesized during prophase. The issue of accessibility centers on the regulation of interactions between the DNA synthesized and the meiotic-specific proteins.

Chromosomes today, volume 7 George Allen & Unwin 1981

THE MOLECULAR PROGRAM AT MEIOTIC PROPHASE

A. Protein Activities

Among the many proteins acting on DNA that are present in meiocytes at least three may be considered to have unique meiotic functions. The proteins each catalyze a specific change in DNA structure and, as illustrated in Figure 1, their activities follow a common cyclic course during meiosis. They rise during leptotene, reach a peak at some time between late zygotene and early pachytene, and return to the original base level by the end of pachytene. We consider these proteins to be meiotic-specific because of their lack, or near lack, of activity in somatic tissues and in the mitotically dividing precursors of meiocytes (Stern and Hotta 1980). Activities of a similar, but nevertheless different, nature have been observed in somatic tissues, but how the differences might account for tissue-specific functions remains undetermined.

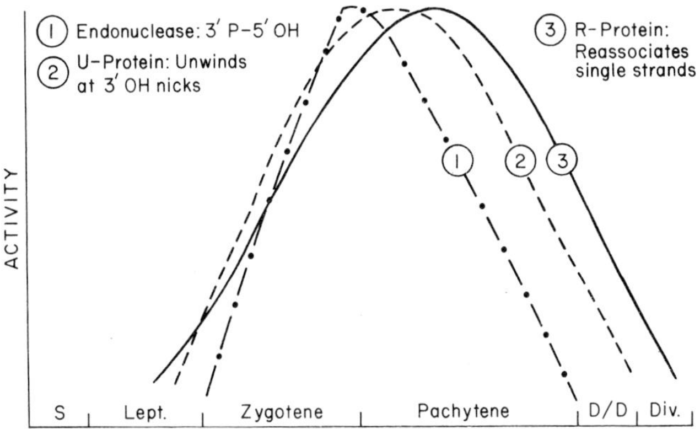

FIGURE 1. Meiotic-specific proteins acting on DNA.

Based on their _in vitro_ characteristics the proteins can be assigned hypothetical functions leading to crossing-over (Figure 2). The endonuclease introduces single strand nicks into DNA thus serving to initiate a process with potential for recombination. The nicked sites are targets for the U-protein which unwinds several hundred base pairs of DNA, making single strands available for duplex formation with DNA from homologous chromosomes. Reassociation of the single strands into duplex forms is facilitated by the R-protein. No direct evidence in support of this model is available but it does tie together the coordinated induction of the three protein activities with those events in chromosomal DNA that may initiate crossing-over. The three proteins cannot account for recombination at the molecular level, let alone for crossing-over at the chromosomal level. Proteins required for repair synthesis are also essential to recombination, but since they show no striking correlation with meiotic stage they are unlikely to regulate the timing of meiotic events. An important question is the mechanism by which the meiotic-specific proteins act at restricted times on specific DNA sequences.

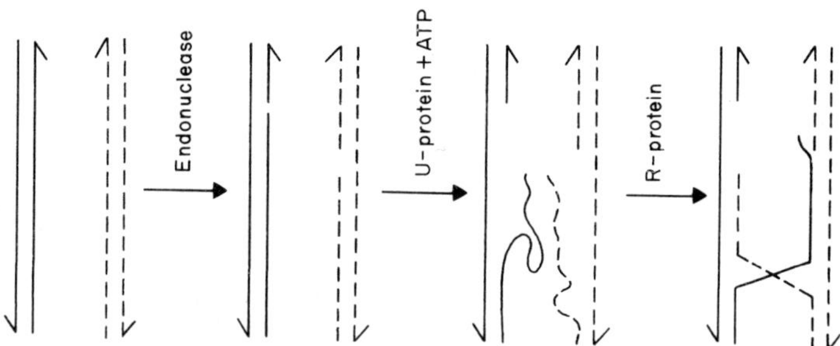

FIGURE 2. Action of meiotic specific proteins on DNA.

The R-protein merits special mention. It is the only one of the three proteins that is tightly bound to chromatin, most of the binding being in association with nuclear lipoprotein. In male meiocytes of lily, mouse, rat, bull, and man, the fraction of nuclear lipoprotein containing the R-protein undergoes substantial increase with the onset of meiosis. It is significant that this fraction including the R-protein increases only slightly in an achiasmatic lily hybrid ("Black Beauty"). By contrast, the endonuclease and U-protein undergo normal prophase cycles of activity in the achiasmatic cells. The distinctive behavior of the R-protein is in some way due to insufficient pairing homology.

Tetraploid and chiasmatic microsporocytes that have been formed by treatment of premeiotic flower buds with colchicine achieve a peak level of R-protein per genome that is at least as high as in the chiasmatic parental species (Hotta et al. 1979). We do not know how the level of R-protein is regulated, but it is probably significant that the protein has internal phosphorylated sites, probably two per molecule, which regulate its activity. If the phosphates are removed, or if additional sites are phosphorylated, several properties of the protein change including its capacity to facilitate DNA reassociation, its specificity for single strand DNA, and its stimulatory effect on the chromatin-bound DNA polymerase (Hotta and Stern 1979).

B. DNA metabolism

Compared with the mitotic cell cycle, DNA behavior in meiocytes is distinctive in at least two respects, the timing of DNA syntheses and the programmed introduction of discontinuities (Stern and Hotta 1980). In microsporocytes of lily, and probably also in spermatocytes of mouse, there are four intervals of DNA synthesis. The first of these occurs at S-phase which, apart from its attenuated duration (Callan 1972), is similar to the S-phase in mitotic cell cycles. A second synthesis, which represents a delayed replication of about 0.3% of the lily genome (Stern and Hotta 1980), occurs at zygotene in apparent coordination with chromosome pairing. The regions replicated are referred to as "Z-DNA". They consist of 5-10 kpb segments and are distributed generally, but not necessarily uniformly, among all the chromosomes. Replication of these regions is unusual not only because of the initial delay but also because the process is incomplete even by termination of zygotene, completion occurring after diplotene during the fourth and final period of DNA synthesis. Preceding the latter is a third interval which begins at the transition from zygotene to pachytene and differs from the other syntheses in that it is entirely of the repair kind. The process is caused by endonuclease nicking accompanied by gap formation, thus providing sites for DNA repair synthesis during pachytene.

Although nick-repair activities at pachytene have been considered as part of the crossing-over process, their actual relationship has been difficult to resolve. In both lily and mouse the modal distance between nicks is about 150,000 bases (Hotta et al. 1977). However, the number of nicks generated over the number required for the chiasmata ultimately formed is very large, about 10^4 in the case of Lilium. There is, nevertheless, a strong correlation between chiasmata and nicking. The achiasmate hybrid, Black Beauty, has about 10% of normal chiasma frequency and a similar proportion of nick-repair activity. The latter can be further reduced by lowering the residual chiasma frequency with colchicine. Cochicine may also be used to generate the opposite effect by inducing formation of chiasmatic tetraploid microsporocytes. Such cells have a level of nick-repair activity that is similar to other chiasmatic forms (Hotta et al. 1979). Regions undergoing nick-repair during pachytene are referred to as "P-DNA".

DNA SEQUENCE ORGANIZATION AND DNA ACCESSIBILITY

A. Meiotic DNA sequences

Z-DNA and P-DNA have different sequence characteristics. Z-DNA consists of sequences with a low or single copy number, whereas P-DNA sequences belong to the middle repeat class. Progress in clarifying the function of Z-DNA sequences has been minimal. Kurata and Ito (1978), using EM radioautography, have found Z-DNA label in the region of the synaptonemal complex and have speculated on its role in chromosome pairing. Recent analyses of mouse spermatocytes have uncovered a class of single copy sequences which, like Z-DNA in lilies, are not ligated until after pachytene (Hotta and Stubbs, unpublished). The unusual replicative behavior of Z-DNA in lily, its low copy number, and its probable presence in mouse spermatocytes strongly argue for a distinctive meiotic role of this genomic component. However, the actual nature of that role has yet to be revealed.

P-DNA sequences were originally identified by their preferential labelling during pachytene. Since then, it has become increasingly apparent that pachytene repair synthesis is strongly selective in at least two respects, one involving an exclusion of certain sequence classes from repair activity and the other involving a restricted subclass of sequences in which most of the activity occurs. Highly repeated DNA is excluded from the nick-repair process. Satellite DNA sequences from neither mouse nor human become significantly labelled during pachytene (Hotta and Stern 1978). Even in the case of the large mammal, <u>Oryx lencoryx</u>, whose satellite DNA represents at least 40% of the genome, no endogenously programmed repair synthesis was found in satellite DNA by pulse labelling pachytene spermatocytes (Stern and Hotta 1980). In both lilies and mice, a major fraction of P-DNA synthesis occurs in middle repeat sequences. In lily the repeat number is about 1000, and in mouse it is about 400 (Hotta et al. 1977). Recently, a more detailed analysis has been made of the P-DNA sequences in lily (Bouchard and Stern 1980). Synthesis does not occur uniformly among middle repeat sequences, but rather within a special subclass of such sequences. This subclass is, from an evolutionary standpoint, a highly conserved grouping. Sequence divergence within each of the estimated 600 families is no greater than 1% and is probably less than that. The sequences have a modal length of about 1500-2000 bp, a value considerably greater than the 200 bp estimated to have undergone repair synthesis in any one region. The feature of evolutionary conservation suggests a general importance of the sequences to meiotic physiology. If, as supposed, P-DNA is part of the recombination process, it is very likely that the families of repeated sequences containing P-DNA function as highly preferred sites for its initiation.

<u>B. DNA accessibility</u>

It is conceivable that sequence specificity and coordinated activation of meiotic-specific proteins during zygotene and pachytene are sufficient to regulate the timing and sites of DNA synthesis. However, no sequence-specific affinities have yet been found for the proteins, and even if such were found, it is already clear that prophase DNA syntheses are correlated with localized alterations in chromatin structure. One source of evidence on this point has been the differential susceptibility of meiotically active DNA sequences in isolated nuclei to nuclease digestion. In all cases, the differential susceptibility is observed only with intact chromatin; no differences are observed in the absence of protein. During prophase, 55% of Z-DNA remains acid-insoluble after more than 80% of the total DNA has been rendered acid-soluble by treatment of isolated zygotene or pachytene nuclei with DNase I (Stern and Hotta 1977). The Z-DNA-like sequences in mouse spermatocytes would appear to be similarly resistant to the nuclease (Hotta and Stubbs, unpublished). A simple interpretation of this result is that the chromatin component protecting Z-DNA from digestion also functions in regulating its synthesis.

Studies of P-DNA regions have provided a profounder view of localized chromatin organization in meiotic physiology. In the achiasmatic lily hybrid, Black Beauty, the absence of DNA nicking cannot be attributed to an absence of endonuclease because chiasmate and achiasmate cultivars have similar levels of enzyme (Hotta et al. 1979). Colchicine-induced chiasmate tetraploid microsporocytes of Black Beauty are unaltered in endonuclease activity but, as previously noted, achieve a high level of DNA nicking accompanied by repair synthesis. Inaccessibility of P-DNA to nuclease action seems to be a critical factor in the achiasmate meiocyte. This observation is particularly significant because it also implies a direct relationship between homologous chromosome pairing and accessibility of key DNA regions to interaction with protein. Localized differences in accessibility were noted earlier on treating isolated pachytene nuclei with micrococcal nuclease which quickly released labelled P-DNA as subnucleosomal fragments (Stern and Hotta 1977). Such preferential release did not occur if repair synthesis was induced by irradiation, or if nuclei containing labelled P-DNA were isolated from post-pachytene cells. Accessibility of micrococcal nuclease is a transient condition of chromatin associated with P-DNA sequences during pachytene and not beyond that stage.

C. The regulation of accessibility:Current studies

Current studies by Y. Hotta (unpublished) on the factors associated with changes in accessibility to DNase II of P-DNA in isolated nuclei may throw considerable light on the mechanism governing chromatin structure in P-DNA regions. A number of investigators have demonstrated that chromatin released by treating isolated nuclei with DNase II may be separated into transcribed and non-transcribed fractions by adding Mg^{2+} to the suspension medium. Under these conditions, transcribed chromatin remains soluble whereas the non-transcribed chromatin precipitates (Gottesfeld and Butler 1977). The presence of RNA in transcribed chromatin presumably prevents precipitation and, if treated with RNase, such chromatin precipitates. When isolated nuclei from pachytene cells are treated with DNase II as much as 90% of labelled P-DNA may be present in the Mg^{2+}-soluble fraction, the percentage varying with the duration of the labelling period. In this respect, chromatin containing P-DNA behaves like chromatin containing transcribed DNA. However, the two types of chromatin are separable by the RNase treatment which precipitates the transcribed DNA but has no effect on the solubility of at least 60% of the P-DNA.

P-DNA chromatin does not precipitate after exposure to RNase because the RNA present in the chromatin fragments is resistant to enzyme hydrolysis. This RNA has a number of distinguishing characteristics. It is first observed at zygotene and reaches its highest concentration during pachytene. The molecule is approximately 120 nucleotides long and may be classified as "snRNA". Labelled pachytene snRNA (PsnRNA) and P-DNA show identical kinetics of reassociation in a reaction driven by the DNA isolated from the P-DNA chromatin fragments. No significant reassociation has been observed between the same DNA and labelled snRNA isolated from interphase-leptotene microsporocytes. It may be inferred that PsnRNA is complementary in its nucleotide sequence to at least part of the labelled P-DNA sequences. Its physical association with those sequences points to a functional interaction. The nature of that interaction is a central question. PsnRNA might determine the sequence specificity of endonuclease nicking analogous to the role proposed for snRNA in mRNA processing (Lerner et al. 1980). Or, by interacting with a structural protein, it might modify chromatin organization. It is significant that pachytene microsporocytes of the achiasmatic hybrid Black Beauty have a very low concentration of PsnRNA. Hotta investigated the possibility that PsnRNA is essential to render P-DNA chromatin regions accessible to nuclease action. Since P-DNA sites are separated by about 150 kb, limited digestion of isolated pachytene nuclei with DNase II which cuts through P-DNA sites should release DNA of that modal size. This does not occur with the achiasmatic nuclei. If, however, such nuclei are first treated with PsnRNA, a 150 kb component is released by DNase II, but only with pachytene nuclei. Thus, PsnRNA is essential for modifying chromatin structure, but some nuclear factor present at pachytene but not at other stages enables it to do so. The *in vitro* modification of chromatin in isolated achiasmatic nuclei is highly specific. DNA in the Mg^{2+}-soluble and RNase resistant chromatin displays reassociation kinetics that are virtually identical with those of P-DNA. Thus, the sites of PsnRNA action are predetermined by DNA sequence and by meiotic stage. Whether PsnRNA interacts directly with meiotic endonuclease to effect a specificity of nicking and whether homologous pairing directly induces PsnRNA synthesis are two important questions that are still unanswered.

PERSPECTIVES

The studies described in this review turn on two aspects of DNA behavior in meiocytes, sequence-specific synthesis during prophase and accessibility of those sequences to the action of essential meiotic proteins. Sequence-specific regions may play a role in aligning homologous chromosomes, and homologous pairing, in turn, may regulate the localized metabolic activities that initiate events ultimately leading to crossing-over. It is significant that at least one set of activities, pachytene DNA nicking, is dependent upon structural changes in the chromatin. Simple, though limited, evidence for localized changes in chromatin structure is provided by the different stage-related susceptibilities of Z-DNA and P-DNA regions to nuclease digestion. The dependence of P-DNA accessibility on homologous chromosome pairing indicates that the functions of such pairing extend beyond a physical juxtapositioning of homologous sites. The snRNA synthesized during pachytene, its stage-specific effect on DNA accessibility to nuclease, and its complementarity to the DNA sequences rendered accessible provide pointers to the mechanisms governing localized structural change. The possibility that a critical factor regulating P-DNA metabolism is a product of P-DNA transcription raises the question of how homologous pairing might induce specific transcriptional activity. Whether or not such a relationship exists, the mechanism by which homologous pairing regulates P-DNA metabolism remains to be clarified. A broad question addressing itself to the behavior of meiotically active DNA sequences is their intra- and inter-chromosomal distribution, and also the nature of associated proteins that are likely to provide for the localized structural modifications of the chromatin. This applies not only to P- and Z-DNA regions but also to other regions whose modification contributes to the distinctive and dynamic organization of meiotic chromosomes. A significant beginning toward answering that question has been achieved in our laboratory by R. Appels (CSIRO, Canberra) and co-workers who obtained about 5000 cDNA clones by reverse transcription of mRNA prepared from *Lilium* microsporocytes. A comparison of *in vitro* translated products from premeiotic and meiotic stages reveals a relatively small number of proteins that are synthesized by microsporocytes prior to or during meiotic prophase but not by the archesporial or somatic cells. An effective approach is thus available for identifying and characterizing some of the proteins that modify chromatin organization during meiosis. Moreover, by hybridizing the clones to labelled stage-specific cDNA, it has also been possible to identify at least 49 meiotic-specific clones. Since some of these are repeated about 1000 times in the genome, their chromosomal localization is feasible. Yet another outcome of Appels' efforts is the possibility, if not probability, that the evolutionary conservation of meiotic cytology and physiology has its counterpart in a conservation of meiotic-specific DNA sequences. If so, the information obtained from lily microsporocytes and mouse spermatocytes may be advantageously extended to meiotic systems that have been characterized genetically.

I wish to acknowledge the rich stimulation afforded by my association with Drs. R. Appels, R. Bouchard, and Y. Hotta, an association indispensable to the writing of this article. I also wish to acknowledge the continuing financial support of the National Science Foundation and the National Institutes of Health in maintaining the research programs on meiosis.

REFERENCES

Bouchard, R. A. and H. Stern 1980. DNA synthesized at pachytene in Lilium: A non-divergent subclass of moderately repetitive sequences. Chromosoma (in press)

Callan, H. C. 1972. Replication of DNA in the chromosomes of eukaryotes. Proc. Roy. Soc. Lond. B. 181, 19-41.

Bottesfeld, J. M. and P. J. G. Butler 1977. Structure of transcriptionally-active chromatin subunits. Nucleic Acids Research 4, 3155-3173.

Hotta, Y., Chandley, A. C. and H. Stern 1977. Meiotic crossing-over in lily and mouse. Nature 269, 240-242.

Hotta, Y., Bennett, M. D., Toledo, L. A. and H. Stern 1979. Regulation of R-protein and endonuclease activities in meiocytes by homologous chromosome pairing. Chromosoma 72, 191-201.

Hotta, Y. and H. Stern 1978. Absence of satellite DNA synthesis during meiotic prophase in mouse and human spermatocytes. Chromosoma 69, 323-330.

Hotta, Y. and H. Stern 1979. The effect of dephosphorylation on the properties of a helix-destabilizing protein from meiotic cells and its partial reversal by a protein kinase. Europ. J. Biochem. 95, 31-38.

Kurata, N. and M, Ito 1978. Electron microscope autoradiography of ^{3}H-thymidine incorporation during the zygotene stage in microsporocytes of lily. Cell Structure & Function 3, 349-356.

Lerner, M. R., Boyle, J. A., Mount, S. M., Wolin, S. L., and J. A. Steitz 1980. Are snRNP's involved in splicing? Nature 283, 220-224.

Stern, H. and Y. Hotta 1977. Biochemistry of meiosis. Phil. Trans. R. Soc. Lond. B. 277, 277-293.

Stern, H. and Y. Hotta 1980. The organization of DNA metabolism during the recombinational phase of meiosis with special reference to humans. Molecular and Cellular Biochemistry 29, 145-158.

Synaptonemal complexes – origin and fate

J. Wahrman

Department of Genetics, The Hebrew University of Jerusalem, Israel

ABSTRACT

Electron microscopic and immunofluorescence observations of male first meiotic prophase suggest the following: 1. the chromosomes have a *double* scaffold from which DNA loops project outwards; 2. exchange is accompanied by chiasmata of the scaffolding-chromatid axes; 3. myosin is found along the length of the pachytene bivalents. The lateral elements of synaptonemal complexes are considered to be the meiotic equivalents of mitotic scaffolds, and as such are unlikely to be eliminated as long as the chromosomes are condensed. On the other hand, the centrally located fiber system, joining the four axes of the bivalent, is a transient meiotic device for drawing the homologous chromosomes together and maintaining synapsis until the onset of diplotene. It is suggested that the central element of the synaptonemal complex consists of one or more contractile proteins.

Since synaptonemal complexes were first described, almost 30 years ago, a considerable volume of work, both observational and experimental, has been dedicated to the origin, structure and function of this germ-line specific configuration (reviewed in Moses 1968, Westergaard and von Wettstein 1972, Gillies 1975). Synaptonemal complexes (henceforth called synaptons) are structures peculiar, but not confined to, meiotic bivalents, that are fully developed at pachytene when chromosome pairing is complete. Synaptons consist of two longitudinal, *lateral elements* (LE) about 100 nm apart, bound by a *central element* (CE) located

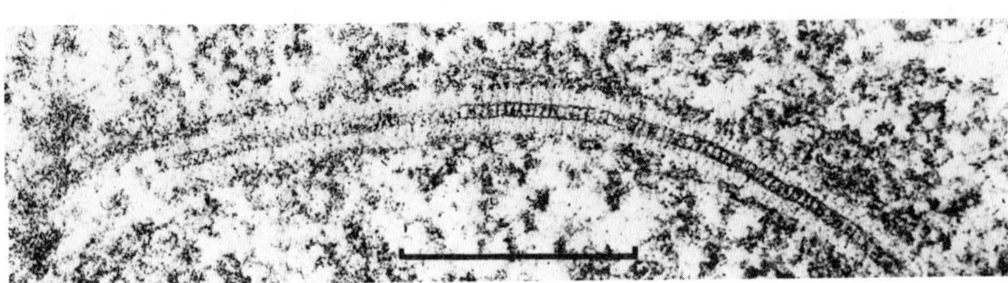

FIGURE 1. Part of a synapton of the beetle *Blaps cribrosa*. The lateral elements are not very conspicuous, but the parallel fibers of the central element, with a periodicity of about 15 nm, are very distinct. Thin section, uranyl acetate and lead citrate. The bar in this and all other figures equals 0.5 μm.

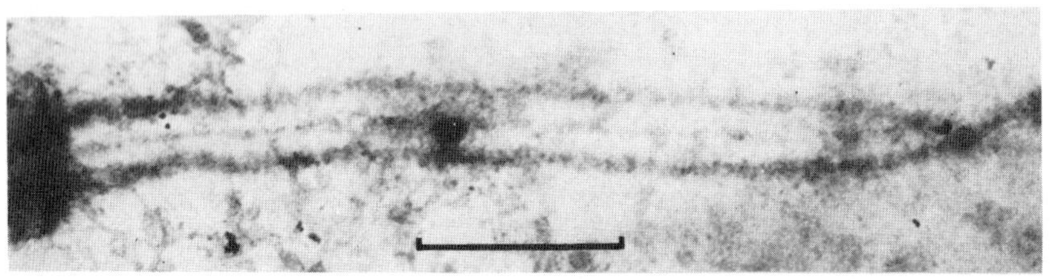

FIGURE 2. Part of a synapton of the rodent *Gerbillus gerbillus*. The lateral elements are well-defined; the central element differs structurally from that characteristic of the insect in Fig. 1. Microspread, ethanolic phosphotungstic acid. Figs. 2-7 are from preparations made by the technique of Counce and Meyer (1973).

between them. The fine structure of this region displays some variation which results in part from different techniques of preparation. The CE, for example, appears either as a longitudinal, sometimes periodically interrupted, fiber, or as a system of short, periodically spaced, fibers perpendicular to the LEs (compare Figs. 1 and 2). Groups of organisms are often characterized by a typical ultrastructure of their synaptons.

Functionally, synaptons have been implicated, by different investigators, in any, all or none of the major meiotic events, namely pairing, exchange, and disjunction. The development of bivalent-incorporated synaptons usually starts with the pairing of homologous chromosomes. At pairing, CE material appears between the partners, while each homologue contributes one lateral element. At diplotene, separation of chromosomes is associated with synapton disappearance, except at places where crossing over has previously occured. Chiasmata are thus marked by short stretches of synapton, which may persist until chromosome disjunction.

From this necessarily brief description, synaptons emerge as relatively short-lived synapsis-exchange related organelles. Interest in the behaviour of meiotic chromosomes led me to reexamine some of the current observations and interpretations. I was especially puzzled by claims that each chromosome, although consisting of two chromatids at pairing, is associated with only one lateral element, and that all synapton components are often shed at diplotene. I was also intrigued by the relative constancy in dimensions and appearance of the region between paired chromosomes, and particularly by the regularity of the fibrillar structure of the central element which can be observed so clearly in many insects. I have, therefore, begun a series of ultrastructural studies, using both spreading and sectioning of meiotic cells, in several species of rodents, as well as in chiasmate and achiasmate insects.

In this contribution, I discuss progress made relative to three of the more controversial issues. I suggest that:

1. Each bivalent has four axes, presumably corresponding to the protein scaffolds of mitotic chromosomes (Paulson and Laemmli 1977), grouped into two lateral elements. Thus LEs are not single but double structures.
2. The chromatid axes participate in exchange and are responsible for the chiasmatic aspect of diplotene bivalents. It is possible that the scaffold-axes are instrumental in determining crossover positions and chiasma interference.
3. Contractile protein(s) are present in bivalents. Myosin has already been identified along the bivalent, probably as a CE component.

Lateral elements are double

During pachytene the association between the two parallel scaffolds which comprise one lateral element is intimate. However, the double nature of the lateral elements is discernable under certain, not yet fully controllable, conditions of spreading, fixation or staining (Figs. 3-4). Moreover, in unpaired chromosome regions, such as the differential segments of the X and Y chromosomes in mammals, the two axes of the chromosome become strikingly clear (Fig. 5).

Two tentative rules of doubleness may perhaps be formulated. First, from the beginning of pachytene onwards, the ease with which the two sister scaffolds can be resolved is related to the intensity of homologue pairing; the more intimate the pairing, the more difficult it is to detect the duality. This may be related to the presence of contractile proteins at the paired stages (see below). On the other hand, in unpaired chromosome segments, as in those found in sex bivalents or when pairing relaxes, as in diplotene, doubleness is conspicuous (Figs. 5-7). Second, the factor which masks doubleness is not evenly distributed along the bivalent; chromosome ends have less of it than their central parts (Fig. 4).

Doubleness of lateral elements has occasionally been recorded in the past. However recently it was consistently observed in extensively spread bivalents of the moth, *Ephestia kuehniella,* (Weith and Traut 1980), and in silver-stained microspread cells of the Chinese Hamster, *Cricetulus griseus* (Dresser and Moses 1980). In the latter, two axes are discernable at mid-pachytene, but at late pachytene doubleness is restricted to chromosome ends.

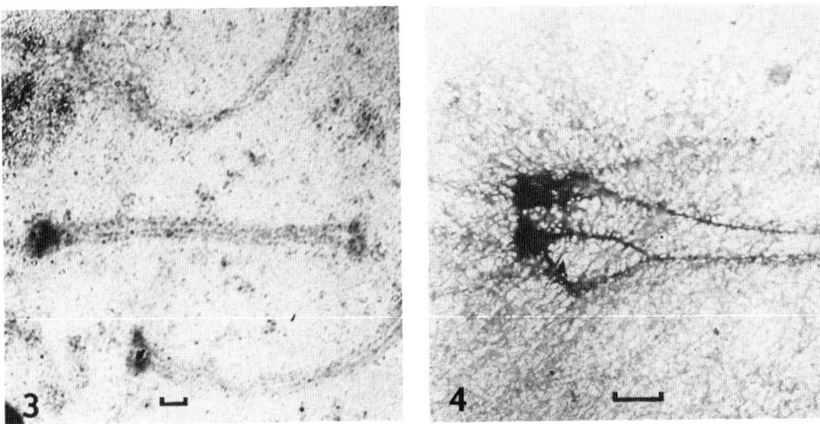

FIGURE 3. Several synaptons of the rodent *Apodemus mystacinus* showing doubleness of the lateral elements at pachytene.

FIGURE 4. End of a distorted pachytene bivalent of the mouse *Mus musculus*. The doubleness of the lateral elements is especially clear near the attachment plaques (telomeres) of the bivalent. The DNA networks surrounding each scaffold resemble those of mitotic chromosomes (Paulson and Laemmli 1977).

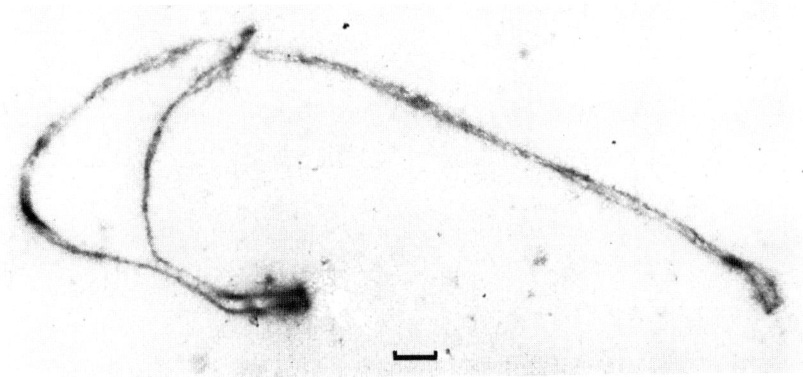

FIGURE 5. The XY bivalent of the mouse *Mus musculus*. The differential segments of the X and Y chromosomes display their double axes. The doubleness is conspicuous at the tip of the X chromosome.

Chromatid axes are involved in exchange

At diplotene, central-element material detaches from the bivalent but chromatid axes, contrary to most descriptions, are maintained in situ producing classical chiasmata (Figs. 6-7). It is possible that chromosome scaffolds play a fundamental role in the mechanism of eukaryotic genetic exchange and are responsible for its nonrandom distribution. The protein axes may not only provide for stabilization of the exchange that occurs at the level of DNA molecules, but they may also determine where crossovers will occur. A previous suggestion that lateral elements are themselves involved in the recombination (Moens 1978) is not easily reconciled with their double nature.

Two further findings are of interest. Reassociation kinetics indicate that segments of DNA directly associated with mitotic scaffolds are enriched for rapidly reassociating sequences (Jeppesen and Bankier 1979).

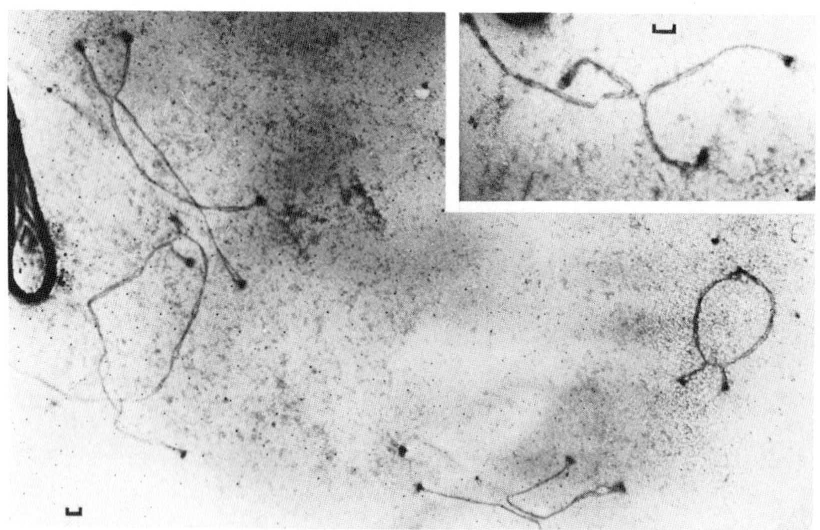

FIGURES 6-7. Bivalents at diplotene from two different cells of the rodent *Apodemus mystacinus*. The bivalents pictured have no, one or two chiasmata. Doubleness of lateral elements becomes conspicuous once pairing and sister chromatid cohesion are relaxed.

I have occasionally observed an achiasmatic bivalent among chiasmatic ones in the rodent *Apodemus mystacinus* (Fig. 6). This suggests that genetic crossing over and the accompanying protein-axis exchange is not essential for bivalent integrity. This, of course, must obtain in achiasmatic organisms.

Contractile proteins are found in bivalents

Considering both the presumptive function of the central element (drawing together the two homologues) and its fibrous nature, I have been trying for some time to find out whether myosin or other contractile proteins are found in bivalents. Together with E. Shashar, suspensions of mouse, *Mus musculus,* meiotic cells were exposed to anti-human uterine myosin, with appropriate controls, and the reaction was visualized by indirect immunofluorescence methods. We found that myosin is indeed present along all bivalents. We are now attempting to localize the myosin molecules within the fine structure of the bivalent.

According to our working hypothesis, myosin, perhaps in cooperation with other contractile proteins, acts, in a muscle-like fashion, to pull the two homologues together and to maintain pairing throughout pachytene. The part of the bivalent most likely involved in such a mechanism is the CE whose temporal appearance and disappearance corresponds with the requirements of this hypothesis. If this is true, the only component of the synapton which can be disposed of, once synapsis is relaxed, would be the central element.

Comparable results on myosin localization in bivalents of various vertebrate species, including the mouse, were convincingly presented at this Conference by Capanna et al. (1980). This group also reported that actin is present at one end of each autosomal bivalent. Karsenti et al. (1978) have found actin along the condensed chromatin of amphibian lampbrush bivalents.

Before concluding, I wish to say again that our findings were obtained in several different species and not all in one system. The possibility should therefore be borne in mind that some of the discrepancies which exist between our observations and those of others may be explained by interspecific variation in the origin and fate of synaptons. We are now endeavouring to document a complete series of meiotic ultrastructural stages in one species.

In conclusion, the pachytene bivalent can be portrayed as a bilateral symmetrical body basically consisting of two looped DNA-histone fibers emanating from two DNA-binding protein scaffolds which are separated from the other, similar, half-bivalent by a zone of contractile protein(s) inbetween. Not only is this molecular and fine structure picture not far removed from the classical findings of light microscopy, but it brings the structure of meiotic chromosomes into line with that of mitotic chromosomes.

ACKNOWLEDGEMENTS

The microscopical and immunochemical results were obtained in cooperation with A. Friedmann, R. Nezer, C. Richler and E. Shashar. Anti-myosin was generously prepared by B. Geiger. L. Sandler kindly commented on the manuscript. This work was supported by the Israel Commission for Basic Research.

REFERENCES

Capanna, E., C. de Martino and P. G. Natali 1980. Contractile proteins in the synaptonemal complex of vertebrates. Abstracts, 7th Intern. Chromosome Conference, Oxford, 58.

Counce, S. J. and G. F. Meyer 1973. Differentiation of the synaptonemal complex and the kinetochore in Locusta spermatocytes studied by whole mount electron microscopy. Chromosoma (Berl.), 44, 231-253.

Dresser, M. E. and M. J. Moses 1980. Synaptonemal complex karyotyping in spermatocytes of the Chinese Hamster *(Cricetulus griseus)*. Chromosoma (Berl.), 76, 1-22.

Gillies, C. B. 1975. Synaptonemal complex and chromosome structure. Ann. Rev. Genet. 9, 91-109.

Jeppesen, P. G. N. and A. T. Bankier 1979. A partial characterization of DNA fragments protected from nuclease degradation in histone depleted metaphase chromosomes of the Chinese Hamster. Nucl. Acids Res. 7, 49-67.

Karsenti, E., P. Gounon and M. Bornens 1978. Immunocytochemical study of lampbrush chromosomes: presence of tubulin and actin. Biol. Cellulaire, 31, 219-224.

Moens, P. B. 1978. Lateral element cross connections of the synaptonemal complex and their relationship to chiasmata in rat spermatocytes. Can. J. Genet. Cytol. 20, 567-579.
Moses, M. J. 1968. Synaptinemal complex. Ann. Rev. Genet. 2, 363-412.
Paulson, J. R. and U. K. Laemmli 1977. The structure of histone-depleted metaphase chromosomes. Cell, 12, 817-828.
Weith, A. and W. Traut 1980. Synaptonemal complexes with associated chromatin in a moth, *Ephestia kuehniella* Z. Chromosoma (Berl.) 78, 275-291.
Westergaard, M. and D. von Wettstein 1972. The synaptinemal complex. Ann. Rev. Genet. 6, 71-110.

Meiotic exchange analysis by molecular labelling

G. H. Jones and C. Tease*

Department of Genetics, University of Birmingham, Birmingham B15 2TT

The detection and analysis of meiotic exchange events depends upon having some means of differentially labelling or marking the chromosomes involved in exchange. Thus, meiotic crossover exchanges can be studied with great precision by genetical methods, provided suitable genetical markers are available. At the cytological level, gross structural differences between homologous chromosomes, such as heterochromatic segments or inversions, have served as markers to detect crossover exchanges and also to demonstrate a general though imprecise correspondence between physical exchanges and chiasmata (e.g. Brown & Zohary, 1955). The development of molecular labelling techniques has created a new approach to the cytological study of chromosomal exchanges, offering much greater precision in the indentification of exchange points. These techniques involve supplying particular molecular 'tags' or labels which are sufficiently similar to DNA precursors to be utilized in DNA replication and incorporated into the structure of the replicating chromosomes, and also possess characteristics which enable their detection by cytological means in chromosomes.

In principle, two quite different labelling strategies could be applied to the study of meiotic exchanges, although in practise only one of these has been used. The first of these (scheme 1) involves labelling both chromatids of one homologue while both chromatids of the other homologue remain unlabelled (Figure 1).

---

*Present address: MRC Radiobiology Unit, Harwell, Didcot, OXON.

This procedure would permit the detection of all crossover exchanges between non-sister chromatids, but sister chromatid exchanges would be undetectable. This labelling strategy is limited in its possible applications to certain lower eukaryotes which display 'zygotic' meiosis (Wilson, 1925), in which the diploid fusion nucleus undergoes meiosis directly, without intervening mitotic divisions. The small size and poor cytological quality of lower eukaryote chromosomes further limit the possible exploitation of this labelling scheme for meiotic exchange analysis and to our knowledge this approach has not been applied in practise.

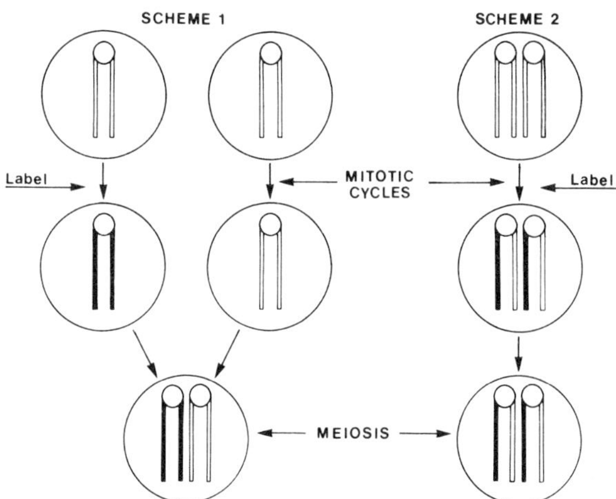

FIGURE 1. Two different labelling schemes for the analysis of meiotic exchanges. See text and FIGURE 2 for details of labelling procedures.

The alternative labelling strategy (scheme 2) involves differentially labelling the sister chromatids of both homologous chromosomes (FIGURE 1). The semi-conservative replication of chromosomal DNA combined with a labelling regime which introduces label at the penultimate DNA replication phase preceding meiosis generates precisely this labelling pattern (FIGURE 2) and scheme 2 is therefore applicable to the analysis of meiotic exchanges in higher eukaryotes, which are characterised by 'gametic' meiosis. The consequences of this scheme differ from scheme 1 in that only half the crossover exchanges between non-sister chromatids will be detected, while all sister chromatid exchanges will generate

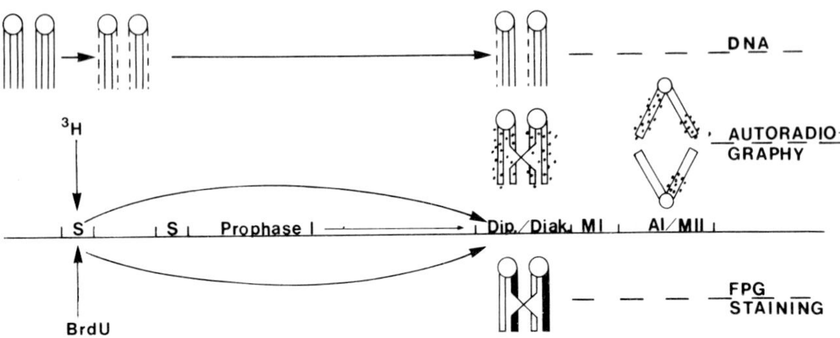

FIGURE 2. The experimental procedures employed for differential sister-chromatid labelling of meiotic chromosomes using tritiated-thymidine (3H-Tdr) and bromodeoxyuridine (BrdU). See text for details.

visible label exchanges.

Two different molecular labels have been applied to the study of meiotic exchanges, namely tritiated-thymidine combined with autoradiography, and bromodeoxyuridine (BrdU) combined with fluorescent staining or fluorescent plus Giemsa (FPG) staining (FIGURE 2). Chromosomes labelled by tritiated thymidine in the penultimate S-phase before meiosis, which subsequently pass through the meiotic S-phase in the absence of label, will show label segregation and enter meiosis having one labelled and one unlabelled chromatid (Taylor, 1965). Chromosomal exchanges during meiosis will modify this labelling pattern, producing label exchanges. However, the relatively low resolution of tritium-autoradiography, resulting from the spread of silver grains around the sources of radio-activity, prevents the analysis of labelling patterns in bivalents at diplotene, diakinesis and metaphase I, and label exchanges must be examined in post-metaphase I stages (i.e. anaphase I/metaphase II) which have a more favourable morphology for the analysis of labelling, but lack chiasmata (FIGURE 3). One obvious consequence of this limitation is that autoradiographic label exchanges can be only indirectly related to chiasmata. A further, less obvious, limitation is that label exchanges due to non-sister crossovers cannot be readily distinguished from sister chromatid exchanges. Despite these limitations autoradiographic studies established a clear, albeit indirect, correspondence between chiasmata and label exchanges (Taylor, 1965; Peacock, 1968, 1970; Church & Wimber, 1969; Craig-Cameron & Jones, 1970) and in one study a very clear and direct relationship was found between localised chiasmata in the grasshopper Stethophyma grossum and similarly localised label exchanges (Jones, 1971). These autoradiographic studies also noted, or inferred, the occurrence of meiotic sister chromatid exchanges, which in general appeared to be similar to those of somatic chromosomes.

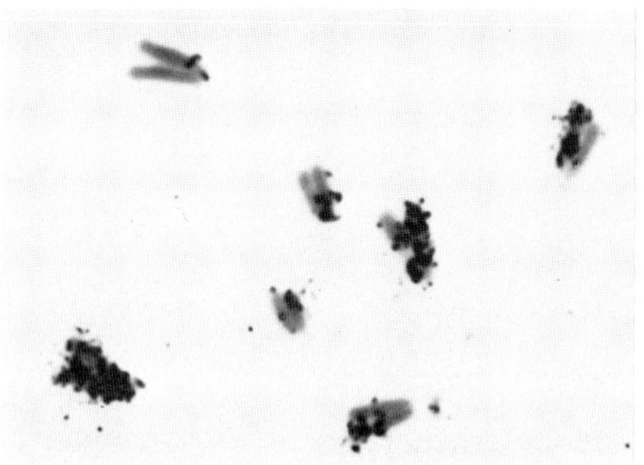

FIGURE 3. An autoradiograph of anaphase I chromosomes from Stethophyma grossum following tritiated-thymidine incorporation at the last spermatogonial interphase. Label segregation and exchanges of labelled and unlabelled chromatid segments can be clearly seen.

The subsequent development of a technique for differentially staining the chromosomes of somatic cells, based upon BrdU incorporation into chromosomal DNA (Latt, 1973; Perry & Wolf, 1974), offered the exciting prospect of a much greater precision and directness in the analysis of meiotic exchanges, reflecting the much higher resolving power of this method compared to tritium autoradiography. In principle the application of this technique to meiotic exchange analysis is relatively straightforward. Studies on somatic cells have established that differential staining of sister chromatids can be achieved following BrdU incorporation during the penultimate S-phase before division, or during both S-phases preceding division (Kato, 1974). In practise considerable difficulties were experienced in applying this technique to meiotic chromosomes. The failure of long-term in vitro cultures of germ cells to sustain normal meiotic development, and the very efficient *in vivo* degradation of BrdU were jointly responsible for these technical difficulties. Eventually, however, successful *in vivo* BrdU labelling was achieved in a variety of tissue and cell types, including meiocytes by a variety of procedures including massive and repeated BrdU injections (Allen & Latt, 1976; Tease, 1978), subcutaneous implantation of BrdU tablets (Allen, 1979; Tease & Jones, 1978) continuous infusions of BrdU into mammalian tail veins (Kanda & Kato, 1980) and *in vitro* labelling of foetal ovaries followed by implantation into spayed female mice (Polani *et al*. 1979). Clear differential staining of meiotic chromosomes has been achieved by one or more of these methods in the locust (Tease, 1978; Tease & Jones, 1978), the Armenian hamster (Allen, 1979), the female mouse (Polani *et al*. 1979) and most recently in the male mouse (Kanda & Kato, 1980).

Spermatocytes of the locust (*Locusta migratoria*) fixed 10 days after BrdU treatment showed clear differential staining of sister chromatids (Tease, 1978; Tease & Jones, 1978). From the pattern of labelling seen in occasional X_3 cells, it was deduced that BrdU incorporation was confined to spermatogonial S-phases. The timing of meiotic development at 30°C was not apparently affected by the treatment and the labelled meiocytes appeared completely normal in all respects, including the frequency and distribution of chiasmata.

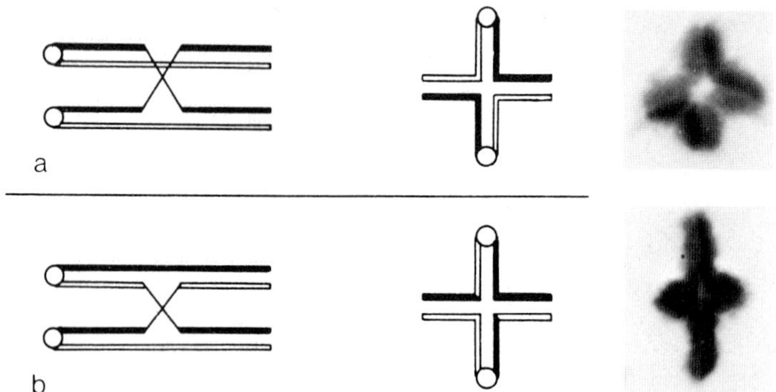

FIGURE 4. The origins of hidden (a) and visible (b) crossover exchanges in monochiasmate bivalents, with examples of both types from *Locusta migratoria* bivalents showing differential sister chromatid staining following BrdU incorporation.

Many aspects of meiotic exchange analysis are most easily

TABLE 1. Numbers of hidden (H) and visible (V) crossover exchanges in bivalents of locusts, hamsters and mice, tested for agreement with a 1:1 ratio. Numbers in parentheses refer to the numbers of animals studied.

Species	Reference	Exchange type H	Exchange type V	χ^2_1	P
Locust (1)	Tease & Jones (1980)	159	136	1.792	>0.1
Locust (4)	Tease (unpublished)	124	106	1.408	>0.2
		125	101	2.548	>0.1
		122	123	0.004	>0.9
		115	110	0.110	>0.7
Young hamsters (2)	Allen (1979)	52	47	0.252	>0.1
		65	61	0.126	>0.2
Old hamsters (2)		79	31	20.944	<0.001
		91	37	22.780	<0.001
♂ Mouse (5)	Kanda & Kato (1980)	143	92	11.068	<0.001
♀ Mouse (many)	Polani *et al* (in press)	47	49	0.040	>0.8

studied in monochiasmate bivalents (i.e. bivalents with a single chiasma), because of their topological simplicity and clarity. These bivalents cannot be considered unrepresentative because most bivalents in *Locusta* (>70%) are monochiasmate. FIGURE 4 shows the two possible consequences, in terms of labelling pattern, resulting from non-sister chromatid crossover exchanges. Exchanges between similarly stained non-sister chromatids (light-light or dark-dark) produce so-called 'hidden' crossover exchanges, whereas exchanges between differently stained non-sister chromatids produce 'visible' crossover exchanges (Taylor, 1965). Crossover exchanges occurring between two randomly selected non-sister chromatids are expected to result in equal numbers of hidden and visible crossover exchanges; the numbers observed in 5 different locusts show good agreement individually with a 1:1 ratio (TABLE 1). Polani *et al.* (in press) also observed closely similar numbers of hidden and visible crossover exchanges in mouse oocytes. Other investigators have reported deviations from a 1:1 ratio of hidden and visible exchanges (TABLE 1). Allen (1979) observed similar numbers of the two types of exchange in the XY bivalents of young

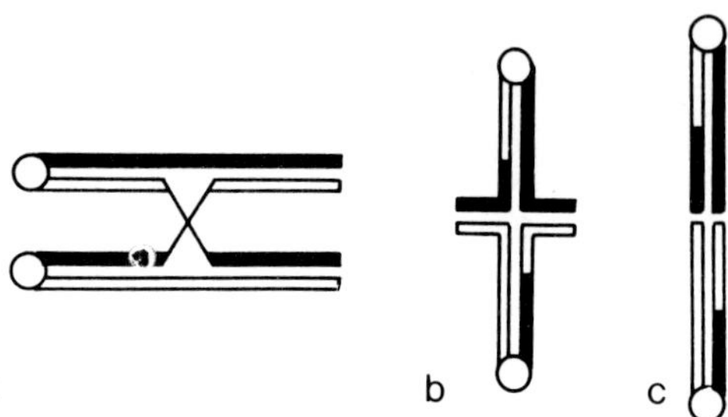

FIGURE 5. The expected consequences of chiasma terminalisation in a differentially stained meiotic bivalent. Distal movement of the chiasma from the point of exchange (a) should produce regions of iso-stained associations of chromatids between the displaced chiasmata and the points of exchange (b and c).

anaphase I and metaphase II chromosomes (Tease & Jones, 1979). Estimates of SCE frequencies obtained by these two methods showed reasonable agreement and also agreed quite well with estimates of meiotic SCE frequencies obtained by autoradiographic methods from other Orthopteran species. Observations on a small number of binucleate spermatocytes containing two X chromosomes which differed as regards SCEs provide evidence that at least some SCEs are meiotic events and not simply relics of spermatogonial exchanges. However, a number of observations suggest that the SCEs of meiotic chromosomes do not reflect the special exchange characteristics of meiotic cells. The mean meiotic SCE frequencies of *Locusta* are very similar to those observed in somatic chromosomes of ovariole wall cells. Moreover, the frequencies of meiotic SCEs in *Locusta* show a positive relationship to chromosome length and a Poissonian distribution among similar sized M group and X chromosomes, in broad agreement with observations on somatic SCEs. The question of whether meiotic SCEs, or a proportion of them, occur spontaneously or are induced by the incorporated BrdU has not been specifically investigated, but in view of the similarities of meiotic and somatic SCEs the current opinion which suggests a low spontaneous incidence of somatic SCEs probably applies equally to meiotic SCEs.

The frequencies of meiotic SCEs in mouse spermatocytes (Kanda & Kato, 1980) and mouse oocytes (Polani *et al.* in press) after BrdU hamsters, but 2 older animals showed an excess of hidden exchanges. Kanda & Kato (1980) similarly report an excess of hidden exchanges in autosomal bivalents of the male mouse. An inherent scoring bias favouring hidden exchanges cannot be ruled out at present and so these results must be viewed with caution. Nevertheless they raise the possibility that under certain conditions, non-sister exchanges may preferentially involve chromatids of the same labelling status.

An important feature of the visible crossover exchanges observed in *Locusta migratoria* bivalents is that they coincide exactly with chiasmata. This not only furnishes proof of the chiasmatype theory, but also demonstrates that in this species there is no movement or terminalisation of chiasmata, since this would be readily detected as dislocations of points of exchange from chiasmata (FIGURE 5). No such dislocations were observed by us among many hundreds of chiasmata in BrdU labelled *Locusta* spermatocytes. Kanda & Kato similarly report that exchange points invariably coincide with chiasmata in mouse spermatocytes and they also conclude that terminalisation of chiasmata does not occur in male meiosis of the mouse. However, neither Polani *et al*. (in press) nor Allen (1979) exclude the possibility of some terminalisation of chiasmata in the bivalents of mouse oocytes and hamster spermatocytes. In the absence of clear supporting evidence showing real dislocations of exchange points from chiasmata, and *close* associations of similarly stained chromatids proximal to the chiasmata the inference of chiasma terminalisation remains very questionable. Stretching distortions introduced by air drying could account for the exceptional bivalents figured by Allen (1979), none of which conform to the ideal 'terminalised chiasma' configurations of FIGURE 5.

The differential staining of meiotic sister chromatids also allows the detection of sister chromatid exchanges (SCEs) in meiotic chromosomes, with the important qualification that all SCE events will be revealed as visible exchanges. SCEs can be directly observed and counted in monochiasmate bivalents at diplotene-diakinesis or, alternatively, SCE frequencies can be calculated by subtracting the expected numbers of visible exchanges produced by chiasmata from the total numbers of visible exchanges observed in treatment show good agreement, but are much lower than that observed in Locusta. However, such interspecific comparisons are notoriously difficult to interpret in view of the known dependence of SCE frequencies on genome size and the lack of control over numerous environmental factors known to influence SCE frequencies, particularly BrdU concentration. Kanda & Kato (1980) report that meiotic SCE frequency in mouse spermatocytes approximates to the spontaneous level of SCE shown by pre-meiotic spermatogonia, and they comment that SCEs might therefore be much less frequent during meiosis.

TABLE 2. A comparison of the incidence of anomalous exchanges and the mean frequency of SCEs in autosomal monochiasmate bivalents of 5 different locusts.

Anomalous exchanges	No. of bivalents	% anomalous exchanges	Mean SCE frequency
31	236	9.5	0.291
25	255	9.8	0.231
38	264	14.4	0.216
24	269	8.9	0.171
32	259	12.5	0.210

As previously stated, approximately half the monochiasmate bivalents observed in Locusta carried a visible exchange of dark and light chromatids at the chiasma. The majority of these, classed as visible exchanges, showed the expected arrangement of dark and light chromatid material, but a significant proportion (approximately 10%) showed an anomalous arrangement, such that 'parental' and 'recombinant' chromatids were adjacent rather than alternately placed in the bivalent (Tease & Jones, 1978). Similar anomalous exchange configurations have been seen in the hamster and the mouse (Allen, 1979; Kanda & Kato, 1980). These anomalous exchanges cannot be readily explained by conventional non-sister chromatid crossing-over, and various alternative explanations have been proposed. One suggestion is that these exchanges could result from the coincidence of crossovers and SCEs, or alternatively from two closely spaced crossovers of the 3 strand-double type (FIGURE 13, Tease & Jones, 1978). However, the frequency of anomalous exchanges in Locusta appears too high to result directly from the chance coincidence of independently occurring crossovers and SCEs and, furthermore, the frequencies of anomalous exchanges in five different locusts were not related in any obvious way to their mean meiotic SCE frequencies (TABLE 2). Non-independence of crossovers and SCEs would imply that an initial exchange event, say a crossover, could trigger an SCE or another non-sister crossover in its immediate vicinity. Alternatively, these 'double exchanges' could be regarded as single complex exchange events simultaneously involving three chromatids.

The final aspect of meiotic exchanges which has been analysed concerns the relationships of chromatids involved in adjacent chiasmata (Jones & Tease, 1979). Mather (1933) proposed the term 'chromatid interference' for the non-random involvement of chromatids in adjacent pairs of chiasmata, and evidence for this phenomenon has been sought in both genetical and cytological investigations over many years, with rather conflicting results (Whitehouse, 1965). The differential chromatid staining method offers an unusually direct approach to this question. Given that hidden and visible crossover exchanges have an equal probability of occurring. and assuming no chromatid interference, expectations for double crossovers can be formulated in terms of various combinations of hidden and visible exchanges (TABLE 3). The differentially stained Locusta bivalents yielded 67 pairs of chiasmata which were

TABLE 3. The derivation of the expected proportions of the different pairwise combinations of hidden and visible crossovers, assuming no chromatid interference, and the expected and observed numbers of the different combinations for a sample of 67 analysable chiasma pairs.

Probability of hidden crossover, H = 0.5

Probability of visible crossover, V = 0.5

Then:-			Exp.	Obs.	χ^2_3	P
HH = 0.5 x 0.5		= 0.25	16.750	17		
HV = 2(0.5 x 0.5)		= 0.5	33.500	33	2.94	0.3
VV = 0.5 x 0.5 = 0.25	2-STD	= 0.125	8.375	12		
	4-STD	= 0.125	8.375	5		

sufficiently clear for unambiguous classification. The observed numbers of chiasma pairs in the different classes agreed closely with the numbers expected on the assumption of no chromatid interference (TABLE 3). Consequently there is no evidence for the operation of chromatid interference in *Locusta migratoria* spermatocytes. It has been suggested that inter-chiasma distance may influence the strand relationships of pairs of chiasmata and it would therefore be of interest to investigate this possibility using this technique applied to larger samples of chiasma pairs.

ACKNOWLEDGEMENT. We are grateful to Professor P.E.Polani for allowing us to study and quote from his unpublished manuscript.

REFERENCES

Allen, J.W. 1979. BrdU-dye characterization of late replication and meiotic recombination in Armenian hamster germ cells. *Chromosoma* (*Berl*.) 74, 189 - 207.

Allen, J.W. and S.A. Latt. 1976. In vivo BrdU-33258 Hoechst analysis of DNA replication kinetics and sister chromatid exchange formation in mouse somatic and meiotic cells. *Chromosoma* (*Berl*.) 58, 325 - 340.

Brown, S.W. and D. Zohary. 1955. The relationship of chiasmata and crossing-over in *Lilium formosanum*. Genetics 40, 850 - 873.

Church, K. and D. E. Wimber. 1969. Meiotic timing and segregation of H^3-thymidine labelled chromosomes. *Canad. J. Genet. Cytol*. 11, 573 - 581.

Craig-Cameron, T. and G. H. Jones. 1970. The analysis of exchanges in tritium-labelled meiotic chromosomes I. *Schistocerca gregaria*. *Heredity 25*, 223 - 232.

Jones, G.H. 1971. The analysis of exchanges in tritium-labelled meiotic chromosomes. II. *Stethophyma grossum*. *Chromosoma* (*Berl*.) 34, 367 - 382.

Jones, G.H. and C. Tease. 1979. Analysis of exchanges in differentially stained meiotic chromosomes of *Locusta migratoria* BrdU-substitution and FPG staining III. A test for chromatid interference. *Chromosoma* (*Berl*.) 73, 85 - 91.

Kanda, N. and H. Kato. 1980. Analysis of crossing over in mouse meiotic cells by BrdU labelling technique. *Chromosoma* (*Berl*.) 78, 113 - 122.

Kato, H. 1974. Spontaneous sister chromatid exchanges detected by a BrdU-labelling method. *Nature* (*Lond*.) 251, 70 - 72.

Latt, S.A. 1973. Microfluorometric detection of DNA replication in human metaphase chromosomes. *Proc. Natl. Acad. Sci.* (*Wash*.) 70, 3395 - 3399.

Mather, K. 1933. The relation between chiasmata and crossing-over in diploid and triploid *Drosophila melanogaster*. *J. Genet*. 27, 243 - 259.

Peacock, W.J. 1968. Chiasmata and crossing-over. In Replication and Recombination of Genetic Material, W.J. Peacock and R.D. Brock eds., 242-252. Canberra : Australian Academy of Science.

Peacock, W.J. 1970. Replication, recombination and chiasmata in Goniaea autralasiae (Orthoptera : Acrididae) Genetics 65, 593-617.

Perry, P. and S. Wolff. 1974. New Giemsa method for the differential staining of sister chromatids. Nature (Lond.) 251. 156-158.

Polani, P.E., J.A. Crolla, M.J. Seller and F. Moir, 1979. Meiotic crossing over exchange in the female mouse visualised by BudR substitution. Nature (Lond.) 278, 348-349.

Polani, P.E., J.A. Crolla and M.J. Seller. In press. An experimental approach to female mammalian meiosis. Differential chromosome labelling and an analysis of chiasmata in the female mouse. Bioregulators of reproduction, P. and S. Biological Sciences Symposium, Vogel and Jagiello eds. New York: Academic Press.

Taylor, J.H. 1965. Distribution of tritium-labelled DNA among chromosomes during meiosis I. Spermatogenesis in the grasshopper. J. Cell Biol. 25, 57-67.

Tease, C. 1978. Cytological detection of crossing-over in BudR substituted meiotic chromosomes using the fluorescent plus Giemsa technique. Nature (Lond.) 272, 823-824.

Tease, C. and G.H. Jones. 1978. Analysis of exchanges in differentially stained meiotic chromosomes of Locusta migratoria after BrdU-substitution and FPG staining I. Crossover exchanges in monochiasmate bivalents. Chromosoma (Berl.) 69, 163-178.

Tease, C. and G.H. Jones. 1979. Analysis of exchanges in differentially stained meiotic chromosomes of Locusta migratoria after BrdU-substitution and FPG staining. II. Sister chromatid exchanges. Chromosoma (Berl.) 73, 75-84.

Whitehouse, H.L.K. 1965. Towards an understanding of the mechanism of heredity. London : Edward Arnold.

Wilson, E.B. 1925. The cell in heredity and development. New York : Macmillan.

POPULATION CYTOGENETICS

Heterochromatin variation in natural populations

Bernard John

Australian National University, Canberra, Australia

1. INTRODUCTION

The advent of C-banding has made it possible to differentially stain constitutively heterochromatic regions at condensed stages of the division cycle and, hence, at a time when such regions are normally indistinguishable from euchromatin. Apart from confirming overt cases this technique has also revealed the presence of hitherto unsuspected and sometimes quite subtle systems of heterochromatin variation. Indeed since its introduction it has become clear that probably the most common category of chromosome variation involves the occurrence of quantitative differences in both the number and the size of heterochromatic segments between otherwise homologous chromosomes. Variation of this sort may take one of three principal forms:

(1) It may be interspecific, serving to distinguish related species, or

(2) It may be intraspecific, in which case it may either

(a) distinguish different populations of the same species, creating a polytypism, or else

(b) it may distinguish different individuals of the same population, creating a polymorphism.

Although such variation has long been recognised by conventional cytological techniques its occurrence has assumed added importance in recent years following the finding that constitutive heterochromatic regions commonly harbour highly repetitive DNA sequences. Surprisingly, however, those in search of a function for highly repetitive DNA have chosen largely to ignore the variation in heterochromatin content found within and between natural populations of many species and have instead given their attention predominantly to differences between related, or in some cases even unrelated, species. Comparisons of this sort suffer from the inherent disadvantage that different species, even related ones, may differ in a number of genetic properties. Consequently it is not always easy to confidently assign particular properties of different species directly to differences in their heterochromatin content.

An alternative approach is to examine naturally occurring polytypic or polymorphic systems. Here other genetic differences are less likely to assume significance. Let me now illustrate the potential power of this approach by reference to two examples which my colleague Max King and I have been analysing over the past three years. But before I turn to the actual details there are two very general statements that need to be made:

(1) Whatever else these polytypic or polymorphic systems may tell us they make it clear that the heterochromatin variation in question cannot be essential for either basic cell function or for fundamental aspects of organismic development. That is, whatever the heterochromatin difference is doing it cannot have any indispensable function and, at best, can only serve to modify the performance of an activity or activities that go on perfectly adequately in its absence.

(2) In seeking a possible role for these heterochromatin differences we need to pay particular attention to their effects on the meiotic process. There are three reasons for this:

(a) Chromosome mutations, in general, have their most pronounced, indeed in many cases their only known, effects on meiosis where they influence either the pattern of chromosome pairing or else the pattern of recombination.

(b) In at least some organisms heterochromatin is known either to be specifically removed from, or else under-represented in, the somatic tissues. By contrast it is never lost from, or reduced in content in, the germ line. Its universal retention within the germ line suggests it may have a special role there (John and Miklos 1979).

(c) In keeping with this latter point, the only substantive evidence so far produced for the transcription of highly repetitive DNA comes from meiotic chromosomes. Varley, Macgregor and Erba (1980), using a cloned 330 bp monomer satellite sequence isolated from the total DNA of *Triturus cristatus carnifex*, have found good evidence for the transcription of this sequence in the oocyte lampbrush loops of that region of the long arm of chromosome-1 which is known to be C-band positive at mitosis in both sexes as well as at male meiosis.

Bearing these points in mind, let us now turn to consider the two specific examples in question.

2. POLYTYPISM IN CRYPTOBOTHRUS

The endemic grasshopper *Cryptobothrus chrysophorus* is distributed in the south east region of Australia. We have sampled 42 different populations covering the greater part of this distribution and have found it to include two distinct chromosome races. One of these, the northern race, is confined to a region in the north of New South Wales and southern Queensland. The second, or southern, race is much more extensive and occupies the remainder of the distribution (John and King 1977a).

Both races have an identical chromosome number (2n = 23,XO ♂; 24,XX ♀). They also have superficially very similar mitotic karyotypes. Thus, if the chromosomes are numbered in order of decreasing size both include three long pairs (L1-3), six medium pairs (M4-9) and two small pairs (S10-11) of autosomes together with a large X-chromosome. There is, however, an indication that the M-chromosomes of the northern race are relatively longer than their southern counterparts. This impression is confirmed by an examination of the pachytene and diplotene chromosomes at male meiosis where one finds that, in the northern race, chromosomes 4, 5, 6, 8 and 9 are characterised by the presence of fixed distal blocks of heterochromatin. Those on 4, 6, 8 and 9 appear as C-band positive structures but the blocks on 5 do not C-band. The two races are also consistently distinguished by the C-banding character, and sometimes the size too, of the M7 chromosome which in this species represents the nucleolar organising and megameric element. Thus the M7 is multiply C-banded in the northern race but not in

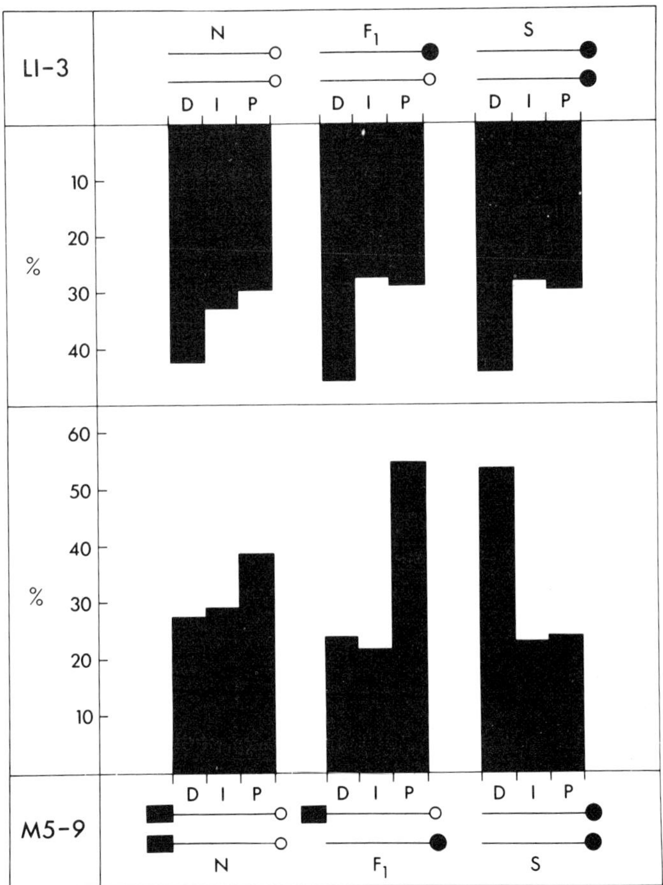

Fig. 1 The influence of terminal heterochromatic blocks on chiasma distribution in male diplotene meiocytes of the southern (S) and northern (N) races of Cryptobothrus chrysophorus and in first generation laboratory-synthesised hybrids between them (F_1). In the case of both S and N, ten cells from each of twenty individuals have been scored giving a total of 200 cells for each distribution histogram and hence 600 bivalents for the three pairs of long chromosomes (L1-3) and 1200 bivalents for the six pairs of medium chromosomes (M4-9). Sixteen F_1 hybrids were scored giving a total of 160 cells and hence 480 long bivalents (L1-3) and 960 medium bivalents (M4-9). For the purpose of scoring chiasma location the euchromatic portion of each bivalent has been divided into three segments of equal length - proximal (P), interstitial (I) and distal (D) - and the numbers of chiasmata falling into these categories have been pooled over all chiasma classes (normally 1 or 2 chiasmata per bivalent, rarely 3).

the southern. Additionally it occurs in two size classes in the northern race. The smaller of these is equivalent in size to that found in the southern race, whereas the other is considerably longer (John and King 1977b). The two races can be successfully hybridised in the laboratory and a comparison of the mitotic chromosomes of interracial F_1 hybrids indicates that, on average, the medium members of the complement are collectively some 16% longer in the northern race than in the southern (John and King 1980). This difference, as expected, is paralleled by an equivalent difference in DNA content (Rees, Shaw and Wilkinson 1978).

A detailed comparison of male meiosis in the two races is possible because the meiotic bivalents are readily distinguishable in terms of size classes, both in normal and in C-banded preparations. Consequently one can consistently identify the three different classes of bivalents - long, medium and short - as well as being able to distinguish clearly between their centric and noncentric ends. Two facts are clear from the meiotic studies. First, the presence of heterochromatic blocks in the M-chromosomes, whether homozygous as in northern individuals or heterozygous as in synthetic F_1 hybrids, has no effect on chromosome pairing. Second, there is a marked effect of such blocks on recombination. Thus by dividing each chromosome arm into three intervals of equal size one can partition the chiasmata in each bivalent into one of three categories - proximal, interstitial and distal. When the chiasma distribution pattern of the 3 long pairs, which lack terminal heterochromatic blocks, is compared for all chiasma classes in the two races and in their F_1 hybrids, they agree. This is not the case, however, in the medium pairs. Here chiasmata are predominantly distal and interstitial in the southern race but predominantly interstitial and proximal in the northern race. Thus the presence of the heterochromatic blocks is associated with a pronounced modification in chiasma distribution (Fig. 1). Notice that the effect is maintained in the F_1 hybrids which means that a single heterochromatic block is as efficient in producing the effect as is a homozygous block combination.

3. POLYMORPHISM IN ATRACTOMORPHA

The pyrgomorph grasshopper *Atractomorpha similis* is distributed in a broad arc across the northern and eastern regions of Australia. We have examined 50 population samples covering the entire distribution range. As the demonstration poster we have presented at this conference shows, this species is extraordinarily polymorphic for both the presence and the size of C-bands. All 10 members of the haploid set (2n = 19♂XO, 20♀XX) are affected with numerous variants in each chromosome and in every population. Some of these involve proximal, some interstitial and some terminal blocks of heterochromatin, while still others involve the development of either partially or totally heterochromatic short arms. Different combinations of chromosome morphs are found in different populations though, as in *Cryptobothrus*, the total amount of euchromatin appears to remain essentially constant.

Demonstrable effects of these differences in heterochromatin content can again be found at male meiosis. Let me exemplify the situation by referring to the three most readily appreciated cases, namely those relating to chromosomes 4, 5 and 6. All three include variants which either have or else lack C-band positive and terminal heterochromatic blocks. Added to this the blocks themselves may vary in size. Thus any given individual may be homozygous for the absence of blocks (--), heterozygous for the presence in one homologue and the absence in the other (-+) or else homozygous (++) for blocks of the same or different size.

By analysing chiasma distribution in C-banded diplotene cells from individuals with different block combinations one can again examine the relationship between the occurrence of heterochromatic blocks and the observed patterns of pairing and chiasma distribution. To maximise the number of individuals I have pooled individuals from different populations with equivalent karyomorph characteristics in respect of bivalents 4, 5 and 6, recognising the three classes of karyomorph referred to above, namely --, -+ and ++. The pooling of individuals with equivalent karyomorphs from different populations is permissible because the mean cell chiasma frequency is similar in all individuals from all populations and is in fact near minimal, ranging from 9.5 to 10.4 per cell. This means, of course, that bivalents with a single chiasma constitute by far the most common class, occurring in some 90% of all male meiocytes. For this reason I have concentrated on the single chiasma class of bivalents.

The data points unmistakably to the fact that when either one or two heterochromatic blocks are present terminally the chiasma pattern is radically readjusted within a bivalent and in precisely the same manner as in *Cryptobothrus* (Fig. 2). Moreover, and again as in *Cryptobothrus*, meiotic pairing is again in no sense disturbed by the presence of either homozygous or heterozygous block combinations. These results validate and extend the work which my colleagues George Miklos and Neil Nankivell (1976) carried out on this same species. In their case they compared only two karyomorphs of one chromosome (-- and -+) and their comparison involved only a single population.

In *Drosophila* it is possible to construct a fly which mimics the situation in *Atractomorpha*. Thus by experimentally translocating a block of Y heterochromatin to the distal euchromatic section of the long arm of the X one obtains an X^Y chromosome with a novel terminal heterochromatic block. George Miklos has compared the extent of recombination for a series of X-linked markers in XX and XX^Y females. He finds that the presence of the distal Y block reduces crossing-over in the adjacent section of X-euchromatin (see Fig. 6 in Miklos and John 1979). This experiment is instructive in another context too since it demonstrates that there is an increase in recombination values in the euchromatic regions near the centromeres of both of the major autosomes, II and III. Inter as opposed to intra-chromosomal effects of supernumerary heterochromatic blocks have been recorded elsewhere and heterochromatic supernumerary chromosomes too sometimes have equivalent effects (John and Miklos 1979).

4. GENERALITY AND EXCEPTION

On the basis of the evidence presented above I believe there are grounds for arguing that one of the functions of the heterochromatin variation to be found in natural populations is the regulation of recombination and, through this, the regulation of the variation present within and between populations. This view can be challenged on two grounds:

(1) First, that the presence of heterochromatic blocks within a genome does not invariably influence recombination. This is true.

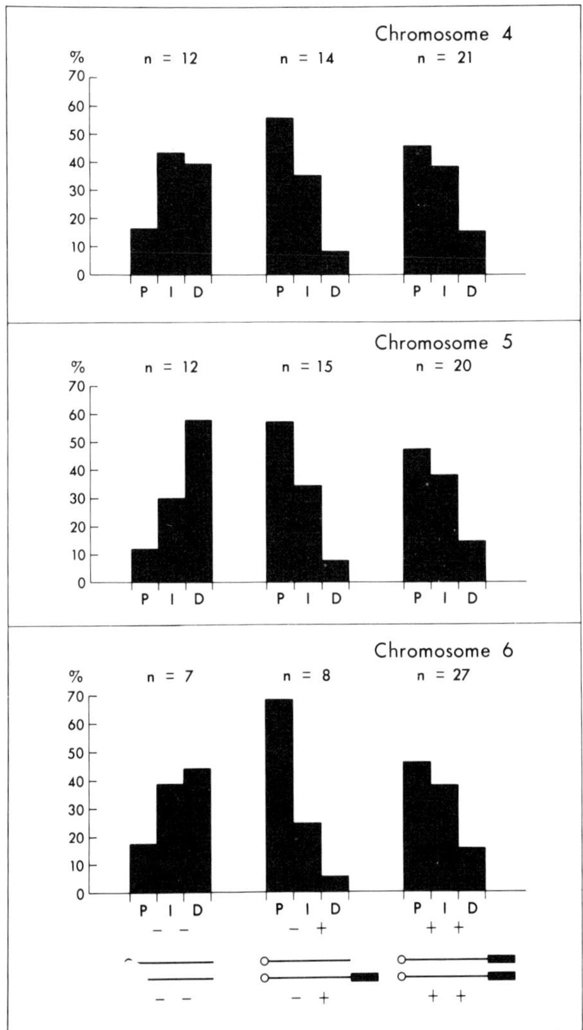

Fig. 2 Chiasma distribution patterns in bivalents 4, 5 and 6 of *Atractomorpha similis* when these lack (--) or else are heterozygous (-+) or homozygous (++) for terminal heterochromatic blocks. For the purpose of scoring chiasmata the euchromatic portion of each bivalent has been divided into three segments of equal length - proximal (P), interstitial (I) and distal (D) - and the numbers of chiasmata in each of these segments pooled for all bivalents carrying a single chiasma. The symbol (n) refers to the total number of individuals scored in each of the three classes of bivalent and ten male diplotene cells were scored per individual.

For example in rye both chiasmata and C-bands are located distally. This might lead the unwary to conclude that chiasmata may form preferentially at or near heterochromatic-euchromatic junctions. Fortunately in rye it is possible through hybridisation to produce recombinant genotypes with an abnormal pattern of chiasma distribution (Jones 1965) in which many of the exchanges occur in interstitial or even proximal positions. Since the C-band patterns are similar in all rye species, with distal heterochromatic segments (Bennett *et al*. 1977), and since the recombinant F_2 hybrid segregants used by Jones to obtain the abnormal chiasma pattern carried no structural changes we can safely conclude that the relationship normally shown between chiasmata and C-bands in rye depends not on the heterochromatin as such but rather on the genotype.

A similar situation obtains in the genus *Allium*. Here too all the species that have been studied have C-bands in distal to terminal positions (Vosa 1976, 1977). In different species, however, chiasmata may be proximal, as in *fistulosum*, distal as in *flavum*, or random, as in *cepa* and *paniculatum* (Levan 1933, 1935). Here too then genotype determines chiasma distribution without regard to the distribution of the heterochromatic segments normally present in the genome. Whether this situation would continue to hold were novel heterochromatic blocks to be introduced into the genome is not known. But let me remind you that in maize naturally occurring polymorphic heterochromatic knob systems are known which influence both chiasma formation and genetic recombination (Rhoades 1978).

It is also worth drawing attention to the fact that in *Drosophila* the centromere has long been known to exert an inhibitory effect on recombination. Consequently when heterochromatin is located next to the centromere its effect may be confounded by that of the centromere itself. It is not without interest to note therefore that the heterochromatic blocks which have known intra-chromosomal effects on chiasma distribution are all terminal.

(2) A second objection that can be raised is that such effects as have been demonstrated are no more than correlations so that the evidence is, at best, circumstantial. This too is true. In

biological science, however, corroborating evidence has much more significance than contrary evidence and the fact that comparable correlations are known in a range of animals and plants (John 1973, Jones 1975) adds up to a convincing argument that heterochromatin variation plays an important, though certainly not invariable, role in the regulation of recombination. Thus as Thoreau once observed "some circumstantial evidence is very strong, as when you find a trout in the milk."

5. REFERENCES

Bennett, M.D., Gustafson, J.P. and Smith, J.B. 1977. Variation in nuclear DNA in the genus Secale. Chromosoma 61, 149-176.

John, B. 1973. The cytogenetic systems of grasshoppers and locusts II. The origin and evolution of supernumerary segments. Chromosoma 44, 123-146.

John, B. and King, M. 1977a. Heterochromatin variation in Cryptobothrus chrysophorus I. Chromosome differentiation in natural populations. Chromosoma 64, 219-239. 1977b. II. Patterns of C-banding. Chromosoma 65, 59-79. 1980. III. Synthetic hybrids. Chromosoma 78, 165-186.

John, B. and Miklos, G.L.G. 1979. Functional aspects of heterochromatin and satellite DNA. Int. Rev. Cytol. 58, 1-114.

Jones, R.N. 1975. B-chromosome systems in flowering plants and animal species. Int. Rev. Cytol. 40, 1-100.

Levan, A. 1933. Cytological studies in Allium IV. Allium fistulosum. Svensk Bot. Tid. 27, 211-232. 1935. Cytological studies in Allium VI. The chromosome morphology of some diploid species of Allium. Hereditas 20, 289-330.

Miklos, G.L.G. and Nankivell, R.N. 1976. Telomeric satellite DNA functions in regulating recombination. Chromosoma 56, 143-167.

Miklos, G.L.G. and John, B. 1979. Heterochromatin and satellite DNA in man: properties and prospects. Amer. J. Hum. Genet. 31, 264-280.

Rees, H., Shaw, D.D. and Wilkinson, P. 1978. Nuclear DNA variation among acridoid grasshoppers. Proc. Roy. Soc. Lond. B. 202, 517-525.

Rhoades, M.M. 1978. Genetic effects of heterochromatin in maize. Pp. 641-671 in "Maize breeding and genetics" (Ed. D.B. Walder). Wiley (Interscience), N.Y.

Varley, J.M., Macgregor, H.C. and Erba, H.P. 1980. Satellite DNA is transcribed in lampbruch chromosomes. Nature 283, 686-688.

Vosa, C.G. 1976. Heterochromatic patterns in Allium I. The relationship between the species of the cepa group. Heredity 36, 383-392. 1977. Heterochromatic patterns and species relationships. The Nucleus 20, 33-41.

Chromosome manipulations for insect pest control

C. F. Curtis

London School of Hygiene, Keppel St, London WC1E 7HT

Biological control methods for insect pests have undergone a revival in popularity in recent years because of the problem of the evolution of insecticide resistance and the harmful effects, in certain cases, of insecticides to non-target organisms. One of the forms of biological control which has been studied is genetic control (Davidson 1974), whose fundamental principle is the harnessing of the very efficient mate-seeking behaviour of male insects to introduce genetic abnormalities into the eggs of the pest species as a result of mating with wild females. These abnormalities are induced in, or inherited by, males which are artificially reared and released. It is essential that the rearing and release processes and any necessary mutagenic treatment is carried out in such a way that the males can compete efficiently with wild males for mating with wild females. Single genes and cytoplasmically inherited factors have been used in genetic control systems, but in this paper I will concentrate on factors which involve cytogenetically observable abnormalities. The intended function of these factors may be one or a combination of the following: (i) sterilisation, i.e., the prevention of egg hatching, (ii) systems for eliminating females from batches of males being prepared for release, (iii) systems for causing the replacement of a pest population by a less harmful genotype or one more easily controlled in other ways.

Chromosomes today, volume 7   George Allen & Unwin 1981

Dominant lethals

The only forms of genetic control which have been used in practice so far involve the use of dominant lethal mutations, i.e., the so called 'sterile male technique'. The largest application of this technique is to the Screw Worm Fly (*Cochliomyia hominovorax*) in the southern United States and Mexico, which has saved and is saving the cattle industry tens of millions of dollars of damage per year. Other large projects include attempts to prevent the Mediterranean Fruit Fly (*Ceratitis capitata*) invading Mexico from Guatemala and the Melon Fly (*Dacus cucurbitae*) invading the main islands of Japan from the Ryukyu Islands. Extensive field trials have also been carried out with this technique against, for example, tsetse flies in Upper Volta and Tanzania, malaria mosquitoes in Central America, and Codling Moth in apple orchards in western Canada.

The dominant lethals on which all these programmes depend are induced by treatment of males with gamma rays or alkylating agents before release. These mutagens have their dominant lethal effect mainly by breaking chromosomes, which interferes with mitosis. In most insects mitosis and cell division are virtually completed by the late pupal or adult stages so that chromosome breakages do not usually have disastrous somatic effects but are stored up in the gametes and, after fertilisation, they disrupt the embryonic cleavage divisions. Thus in most insects, unlike mammals, it is possible to induce 100% dominant lethality in the gametes without killing the treated individual. In general, the treatments required for 100% dominant lethality do not interfere with the ability of sperms to take part in fertilisation. This has the important consequence that if a female mates to a sterilised and a fertile male a proportion of the eggs will be sterilised so that it makes little difference to the outcome of a release of a given number of sterile males whether the species is one in which the female accepts several inseminations or whether it only accepts one.

The simplest route by which a chromosome breakage could yield a dominant lethal effect is by detachment of a chromosome segment from its centromere so that it is left behind at anaphase.

Chromosome fragments have frequently been seen at the first cleavage division in embryos fathered by radiation or chemically sterilised males. However, bridges as well as fragments are also seen at later cleavage divisions in such eggs (LaChance 1967) and this suggests that there are frequently more complex consequences of initial breakage such as sister strand fusion causing bridge-breakage-fusion cycles (Fig. 1) and translocations between two centromeric fragments. In Diptera and Hymenoptera the deaths caused by dominant lethals occur very early in development - much earlier than those due to the loss of whole chromosome arms - and it is thought that the bridges disrupt the timing of the mitotic process and thus kill the embryo.

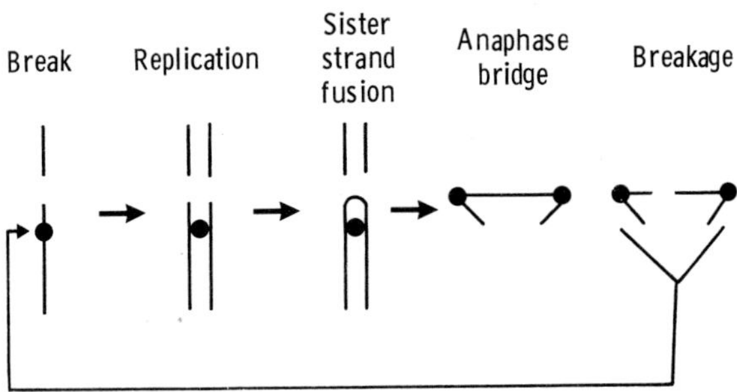

FIGURE 1. Chromosome breakage leading to a fusion-bridge-breakage cycle.

Inherited partial sterility due to chromosome translocations

Translocations and peri-centric inversions produce inherited partial sterility because of their well known effects on meiosis. They were first suggested as a means of pest control by Serebrovskii (1940) and more recently they have been induced in many species of pest insect (Robinson 1976). The easiest type of translocation to propagate for a release programme is a male linked heterozygote. In species with a differentiated Y chromosome, such as most flies and Anopheline mosquitoes, any translocation involving this chromosome can be propagated indefinitely without culling. In Culicine mosquitoes, however, there is a sex locus or chromosome segment on a chromosome which is otherwise homologous and (as in all mosquitoes) there is crossing over in the male. Thus in all these cases only stringently selected translocations can be relied upon to remain male linked under conditions of mass rearing.

It seems to me unlikely that semi-sterility associated with a single translocation or peri-centric inversion will be sufficient to control a pest population effectively. Multiple aberrations can be made with higher levels of sterility but if these are propagated as heterozygotes the captive colonies will suffer from as much sterility as can be introduced into the wild population. To compensate for this, larger adult colonies would have to be kept and this would involve some extra cost compared with the rearing of a fully fertile stock. A possible solution is to rear and cross homozygous stocks. It has proved unexpectedly difficult to produce viable and fertile translocation homozygotes but this has been done in a few species such as the yellow fever mosquito, _Aedes aegypti_. To further increase the effectiveness of double heterozygotes a meiotic drive factor which distorts the sex ratio in favour of males was linked to one of the translocations (Suguna _et al_. 1976). Only female mosquitoes bite and the reproductive potential of the population almost certainly depends on the numbers of the egg laying sex and not on the sperm producing sex. Thus distortion of the sex ratio in favour of males is doubly beneficial and matings by the distorter-double heterozygotes show overall 95% reduction in daughter production (Fig. 2) with considerable inheritance of the partial sterility and distortion into later generations. Despite their load of genetic abnormalities the distorter-double heterozygotes were found to compete well for mates after release into a natural _Ae. aegypti_ habitat (Grover _et al._ 1976).

It is important to emphasize that with virtually all of these systems, although there is some degree of inheritance after matings by released males, natural selection will tend to eliminate partial sterility from wild populations and, in the case of meiotic drive, it will favour the increase of resistance factors which suppress the sex ratio distortion.

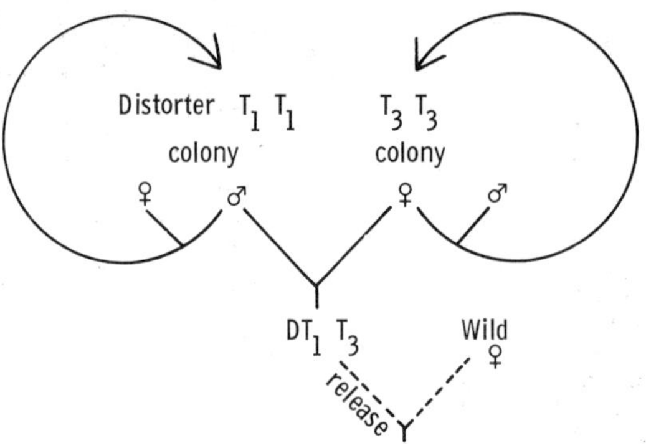

FIGURE 2. The production of sex ratio distorter-double translocation heterozygotes in *Aedes aegypti* (Suguna *et al.*, 1976).

Translocations and inversions in the construction of sex separation systems

As already mentioned, there is generally excess male mating capacity in wild insect populations. Thus releasing sterile females with sterile males is generally neutral to the working of the genetic control mechanism and in the large release programmes so far carried out both sexes have been released and care is taken that the mutagenic treatment induces female sterility as well as male sterility. However, the mass release of females is objectionable in some species, especially mosquitoes, where sterile females still bite and can transmit disease. Another reason for wishing to eliminate females is that if this can be done early in larval life there is a large saving in rearing facilities which are the main cost of genetic control programmes.

Genetic systems for sex separation have been constructed with inversions and/or translocations. In the mosquito *Culex tritaeniorhynchus* either recessive or dominant temperature sensitive genes have been utilized which kill larvae at 32° but not at 26°. The recessive mutant is linked to the *m* (female determining) gene and kept from crossing over on to *M* (male determining) chromosome by an inversion. The system is self replicating at 26° but females can be eliminated from batches being prepared for release by increasing the temperature to 32°.

The existing dominant temperature sensitive mutant (DTS in Fig. 3) is homozygous lethal and therefore setting the system up for use involves selecting and sexing the parents. However, Baker et al. (1979) consider it advantageous that the system allows the use of wild type females as the parents of the males for release so as to minimise the chances that the released males have a genome which adapts them to the laboratory and not to the field. The system uses the fact that there is no crossing over in female C. tritaeniorhynchus to keep the marker bw in repulsion to DTS (Fig. 3). It also includes a peri-centric inversion-translocation complex which causes 85% sterility in the released males and also prevents crossing over between DTS and M^3, a male determining gene situated on chromosome 3. Although the system may look rather unwieldy it has been used for experimental releases of male mosquitoes in Pakistan (Baker et al. 1979).

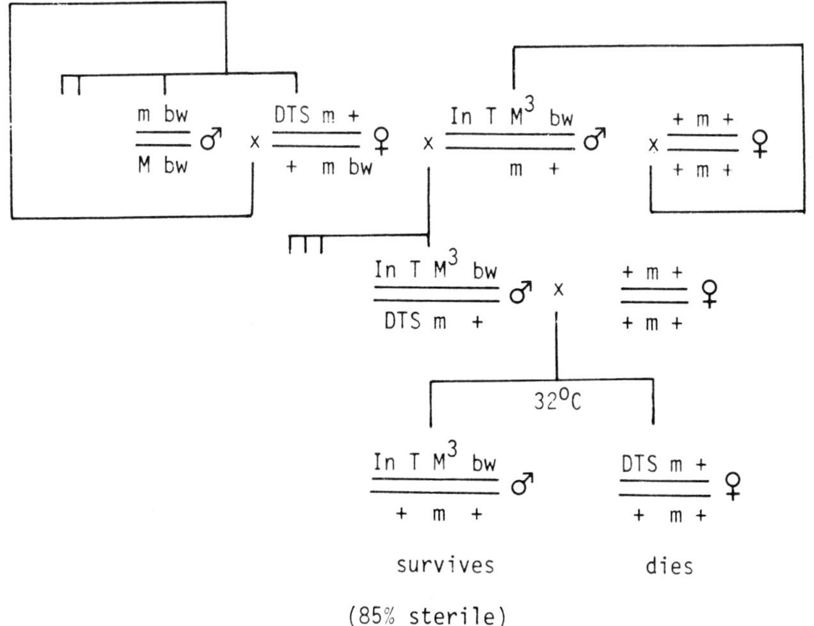

FIGURE 3. Combination of a dominant temperature sensitive (DTS) mutant with a peri-centric inversion and translocation in *Culex tritaeniorhynchus* to produce males with an 85% sterility for release (Baker *et al.*, 1979).

In the Australian Sheep Blowfly (*Lucilia cuprina*) and in Anopheline mosquitoes there is a conventional Y chromosome without gene homology with the X. A different principle has therefore been adopted for sex separation, namely the translocation of a resistance gene on to the Y chromosome (Fig. 4). The genes used have been those causing resistance to the insecticides dieldrin in the Sheep Blowfly (Whitten and Foster 1975) and in the *An. gambiae* complex (Curtis 1979) or propoxur in *An. albimanus* (Seawright *et al.* 1977). In the latter case selective killing of the female susceptible homozygotes was carried out by treatment at the egg stage. Crossing over between the resistance gene and the translocation break point was suppressed by an inversion. This system was successful in the production of males for a release programme at a rate of about 1 million per day.

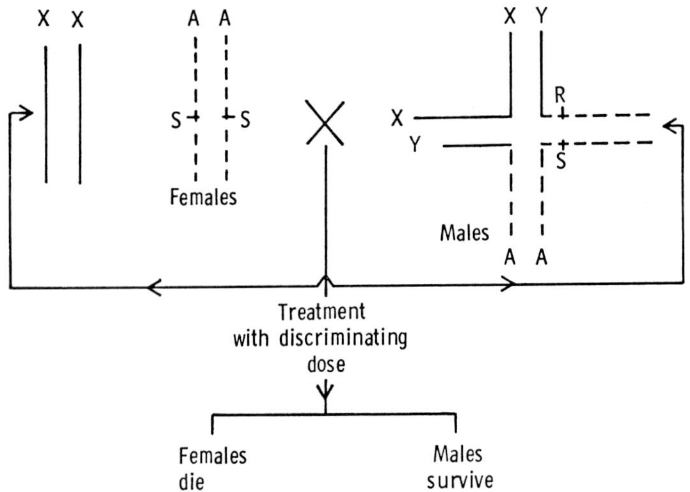

FIGURE 4. Translocation of an insecticide resistance on to the Y chromosome to allow elimination of females from batches of males being prepared for release.

Population replacement by negatively heterotic systems

If matings between two genotypes yield fewer or less fertile progeny than matings within each genotype, selection will tend to favour the initial majority type with a point of unstable equilibrium at an intermediate frequency. The equilibrium point will be affected if one of the genotypes is less fit than the other but, as illustrated in Fig. 5, selection in favour of a less fit type is possible provided that it is given a sufficient initial numerical advantage. Chromosome abnormalities which might behave in this way include autosomal translocations (Serebrovskii 1940; Curtis 1968) and compound chromosomes in which the two left arms and the two right arms of a chromosome have become joined (Foster *et al*. 1972).

Matings	Frequency of matings	Assumed fertility of matings	Progeny		
			Type	Relative no.	Frequency
A x A	0.01	1	A	0.01	0.04
A x B	0.09	0	-	-	-
B x A	0.09	0	-	-	-
B x B	0.81	0.25	B	0.202	0.96
			Total =	0.212	

FIGURE 5. The effect of one generation of mating where there is full sterility in crosses between A and B, 25% fertility in B and an initial frequency of 90% B, 10% A.

Population replacement might be made useful for pest control as follows:-

1. The low fertility of the replacing population might ultimately eradicate it or hold it below a density at which it constitutes a pest.
2. A conditional lethal gene might be combined with the chromosomal abnormality. This gene might be a temperature sensitive or cause insecticide susceptibility. It could be arranged that the gene was no handicap during the replacement process but ensured destruction of the population under changed conditions.
3. The replacing strain might carry a gene for harmlessness to man. There are about a dozen examples of mosquito strains selected for inability to transmit malarial, filarial or

viral pathogens which the species normally transmits (Curtis 1979). So far, however, these almost all refer to 'laboratory-model' pathogen-vector systems and extension of them to human pathogens and their natural vectors is proving to be difficult.

Population replacement has been demonstrated with autosomal translocations in Spider Mites (Tetranychus urticae) by Feldmann and Sabelis (1980) and with compound chromosomes in a Drosophila population in a winery by Mackenzie (1976). A trial is in progress in an isolated valley with compound chromosomes which have been produced in the Australian Sheep Blowfly.

In the case of autosomal translocations, only genes closely linked to the break points could be fixed in a population as a result of the replacement process. With compounds, however, where there is full sterility in crosses to wild type, all genes initially associated with the compound would remain so throughout the replacement process. This is advantageous with regard to a gene which it is desired to fix in a population but also means that lack of adaptation to field conditions in the reared stock could not be remedied by a process of recombination and selection after release.

Ideally population replacement by means of negative heterosis could be achieved despite a continual influx of a minority of immigrants. However, the resilience of the system to a combination of reduced fitness of the released strain and immigration of wild types is strictly limited (Dietz 1976). Where the aim is to introduce conditional lethals, these genes must, in the long run, be seriously harmful to the insect if they are to be of any use in a control programme. It seems unlikely in practice that the system could be so finely adjusted as to give stable population replacement together with effective population control. However, genes for harmlessness to man may have little or no adverse effect on fitness of the insect and in this case it may be possible by a release programme of short duration to produce population replacement which has long term stability and could continuously 'absorb' and sterilise a limited number of immigrants of the original wild type. This would seem to be an ideal form of control for insect vectors of disease if only the numerous practical difficulties can be overcome.

REFERENCES

Baker, R. H., Reisen, W. K., Sakai, R. K., Hayes, G. G., Aslamkhan, M., Saifuddin, U. T., Mahmood, F., Perveen, A. and Javed, S. 1979. Field assessment of mating competitiveness of male *Culex tritaeniorhynchus* carrying a complex chromosomal aberration. *Ann. Ent. Soc. Am.* 72, 751-758.

Curtis, C. F. 1968. Possible use of translocations to fix desirable genes in insect populations. *Nature* 218, 368-369.

Curtis, C. F. 1979. Translocations, hybrid sterility and the introduction into pest populations of genes favourable to man. In *Genetics in relation to insect management*, 19-30. Rockefeller Foundation Symposium, Bellagio, 1978.

Davidson, G. 1974. *Genetic control of insect pests*. London & New York: Academic Press.

Dietz, K. 1976. The effect of immigration on genetic control. *Theoret. Pop. Biol.* 9, 58-67.

Feldmann, A. M. and Sabelis, M.W. 1980. Karyotype displacement in a laboratory population of the two spotted spider mite *Tetranchus urticae*. *Genetica*, in press.

Foster, G. C., Whitten, M. J., Prout, T. and Gill, R. 1972. Chromosome rearrangements for the control of insect pests. *Science* 176, 825-878.

Grover, K. K., Suguna, S. G., Uppal, D. K., Singh, K.R.P., Ansari, M. A., Curtis, C. F., Singh, D., Sharma, V. P. and Panicker, K. N. 1976. Field experiments on the competitiveness of males carrying genetic control systems for *Aedes aegypti*. *Ent. Exp. & Appl.* 20, 8-18.

LaChance, L. E. 1967. The induction of dominant lethal mutations in insects as related to the sterile-male technique of insect control. In *Genetics of insect vectors of disease*, J. W. Wright and R. Pal, eds, 617-649. Amsterdam: Elsevier.

McKenzie, J. A. 1976. The release of a compound chromosome stock in a vineyard cellar population of *Drosophila melanogaster*. *Genetics* 82, 685-695.

Robinson, A. S. 1976. Progress in use of chromosomal translocations for control of insect pests. *Biol. Rev.* 51, 1-24.

Seawright, J. A., Kaiser, P.E., Dame, D.A. and Lofgren, C. 1977. Genetic sexing of *Anopheles albimanus*. *Science* 200, 1303-1304.

Serebrovskii, A. S. 1940. On the possibility of a new method for the control of insect pests. *Zool. Zh.* 19, 618-630.

Suguna, S. G., Curtis, C. F., Kazmi, S. J., Singh, K.R.P., Razdan, A. K. and Sharma, V. P. 1977. Distorter double translocation systems in *Aedes aegypti*. *Genetica* 47, 117-123.

Whitten, M. J. and Foster, G. G. 1975. Genetical methods of pest control. *Ann. Rev. Entomol.* 20, 461-477.

CHROMOSOMES AND SPECIATION

Homosequential species of Hawaiian *Drosophila*

H. L. Carson

Department of Genetics, University of Hawaii, Honolulu

Comparative chromosomal cytology of groups of closely related species at the diploid level has seen a great rebirth of interest in recent years. Whereas earlier techniques permitted only a rather simple estimation of the length of chromosome arms in a karyotype (e.g. Babcock 1947), the new banding methods, especially when coupled with various heterochromatin and molecular characterizations, now provide sensitive data for systematic and evolutionary karyology (e.g. Yunis et al., 1980). Indeed, interspecific comparisons, when viewed in conjunction with data on certain kinds of intraspecific polymorphism, have been used to construct dynamical theories bearing on the origin of species (White 1978; Bush et al., 1977).

In most plants and animals, the determination of the linear differentiation of the chromosome is limited to a rather gross type of banding, even with the best of modern methods. Yet genetic evidence is overwhelming that even a moderate-sized chromosome harbors a sequence of genes which number in the hundreds if not thousands. The giant chromosomes of the nuclei of salivary gland cells of certain Diptera reflect the sequence of genes on a chromosome in extraordinary detail. Here is displayed, under simple light-microscope procedures, a wealth of banding detail and which, under favorable circumstances, lends itself to detailed and sensitive comparisons between species.

I review here certain cytological data which have accumulated over the past fifteen years with respect to more than a hundred

Chromosomes today, volume 7   George Allen & Unwin 1981

closely related Drosophila species, all of which are endemic to the Hawaiian Archipelago. The most outstanding feature of these data is the precision and detail with which the banding sequence of each chromosomal element of each species may be mapped. Although interspecific sequence comparisons have been possible in a number of other species groups of Drosophila and indeed other Diptera, it has only rarely been possible to characterize completely all the banding sequences of all chromosomes in two or more related species. The extraordinary favorability of the polytene chromosomes of certain Hawaiian Drosophila (Figure 1),

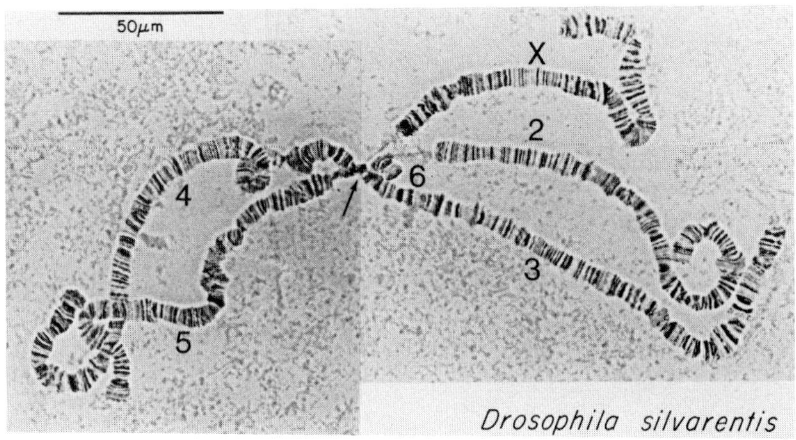

FIGURE 1. Photomicrograph of the polytene chromosomes of Drosophila silvarentis. This is one of a cluster of six homosequential species (see Table 2). Relative to the Standard of D. grimshawi there is one fairly large fixed inversion in each of the chromosomes X, 2, 3 and 4; their positions are mapped in Carson and Stalker (1968). The characteristically small chromocenter is shown at the arrow. Prepared and photographed by Jong Sik Yoon.

coupled with a degree of evolutionary conservatism, has indeed made it possible to ascertain the relative position of each cytologically resolvable band of the genome in a more than a hundred species. This wealth of detailed comparative data has been coupled with a growing body of information on intraspecific polymorphism and metaphase conditions. Thus, there is provided an especially clear view of chromosomal evolution in a geographically and phylogenetically well-defined group of species. Some inferences concerning the role of gross chromosomal variability in the speciation process will be attempted.

MATERIALS AND METHODS

Among the more than 400 described species of *Drosophila* (subgenus *Drosophila*) endemic to Hawaii is a group of about 120 spectacular species called the "picture-winged" flies because most of them have dark maculations on the wings. With some exceptions, these species are very large and live in rainforests above 1000 m elevation. Except for two or three species, they breed only on endemic plants. Like many of their plant hosts, the flies exist in small isolated populations. A great majority of these species are confined to single islands and, indeed, sometimes to a single volcano of an island.

Wild-caught females have been brought to the laboratory and placed individually into culture tubes and cytological examinations were carried out on F_1 larvae. F_1 progeny were raised as vouchers or for the establishment of stocks. Chromosomes were sequenced by direct comparison with an arbitrarily chosen standard, the polytene sequences found in *Drosophila grimshawi* Oldenberg from Auwahi, Maui (see Carson and Stalker, 1968). The standard stock is monomorphic in all six polytene elements. The polytene sequences of each species may be described in terms of this single set of standards. Aiding in this procedure is a drawing-tube viewing system which permits a sort of artificial synapsis of homologous chromosome regions (Carson 1970). Thus, the image of the chromosome under the microscope may be juxtaposed to a photographic cutout of the standard on a black table surface. Since the chromosomes are so favorable, it is possible to recognize even quite small inverted sections in the homozygous state. The sequential genome of 103 species of "picture-winged" flies has been read against this standard. All species show 2n = 12; there are no Robertsonian alterations. Like most species, the metaphase of *Drosophila grimshawi* shows five acrocentrics and one microchromosome with only minimal heterochromatin near the centromeres. This condition is characterized by the formula 5R, 1D (five rods, one dot) in the Tables which follow.

Intraspecific inversion polymorphisms, of course, may be recognized in the usual manner by synaptic configurations. Throughout this work, which has been reported in a series of papers cited by Carson and Kaneshiro (1976), and Carson and Yoon (1981), an attempt has been made, by continued collecting and analysis of wild-caught specimens, to examine as many isofemale lines of each species as possible. For some species this number is in the hundreds; at the other extreme, a few species are known only from a single larva. Such a single larva, however, has a high content of sequential information, although it is of little use in determining intraspecific polymorphism.

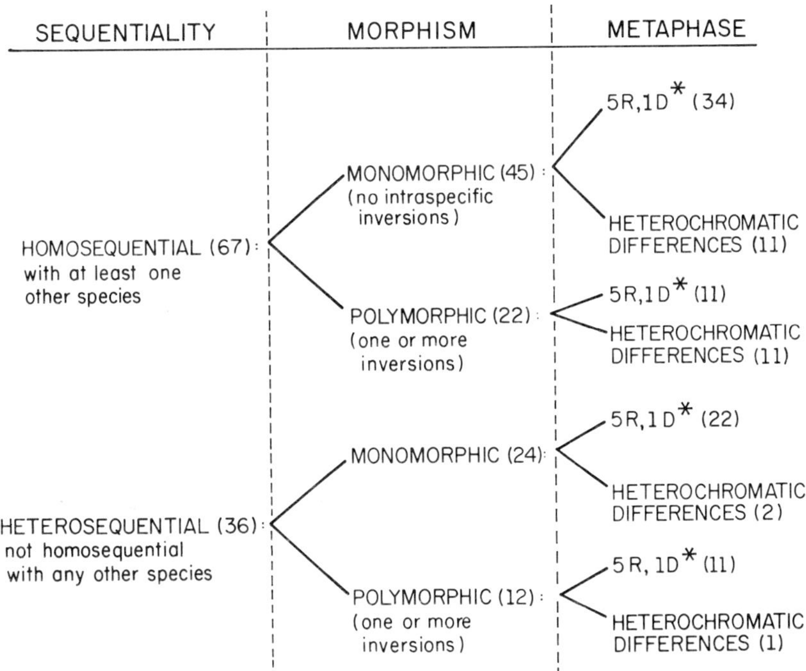

FIGURE 2. Chromosomal sequentiality, morphism and metaphase condition in 103 species of "picture-winged" Hawaiian Drosophila (number of species in each category in parentheses). All are 2n = 12. Those with asterisk (*) show no discernable difference from five rods (acrocentrics) and one dot (microchromosome).

RESULTS

Figure 2 and Tables 1-4 are self explanatory. Data have been

TABLE 1. Eighteen clusters of homosequential species among 67 species of picture-winged Hawaiian Drosophila.

No. of species in homosequential cluster	Number of such clusters	Total number of species
two	4	8
three	7	21
four	3	12
five	2	10
six	1	6
ten	1	10
Total	18	67

taken from the summaries of Carson and Kaneshiro (1976) and Carson and Yoon (1981). The total number of species examined is 103. It should be emphasized that no species is included unless the entire genome has been completely sequenced in terms of the standard of *Drosophila grimshawi*. On the whole, these species are cytologically very conservative; the total number of inversions observed is 213; that is, about two inversions per species. These inversions, however, are unevenly distributed among the species. This is best seen by considering the number of species which are homosequential (see Carson et al., 1967 for origin of this term) with one or more other species. Two or more species are homosequential if they lack any fixed inversion differences. Almost two-thirds of the species (67) may be so described (Fig. 2 and Table 1). There are eighteen clusters of homosequential species, including from two to ten species in each cluster. Further details on these clusters are given in Tables 2 and 3. The most extensive cluster consists of those species which happen to include the standard, *Drosophila grimshawi*.

Tables 2 and 3 include the formulae for the polytene gene arrangement for each species given in terms of the standard. For example, in the *ochracea* cluster (Table 2) all gene orders are identical to standard except for chromosome 5 which is homozygous for an inversion called 5a. This and all other inversions men-

Table 2. Six clusters of homosequential species within the Standard 4 and 4u phylads of picture-winged Drosophila from Hawaii. 2n = 12 in all 28 species. Lower case letters refer to inversions relative to the grimshawi Standard. H = Hawaii, K = Kauai, L = Lanai, Ma = Maui, Mo = Molokai and O = Oahu.

Species	Island	Polytene Chromosome Gene Arrangements						Metaphase
pullipes	H	X	2	3	4	5	6	5R, 1D
sodomae	Mo	X	2	3	4	5	6	5R, 1D
obatai	O	X	2	3	4	5	6	5R, 1D
villosipedis	K	X	2	3	4	5	6	5R, 1D
atrimentum	O	X	2	3	4	5	6	5R, 1D
grimshawi	K,O,Ma,Mo,L	X	2	3	4*	5	6	5R, 1D
orphnopeza	Ma	X	2	3*	4	5	6	5R, 1D≠
bostrycha	Mo	X	2	3	4*	5	6	5R, 1D≠†
affinidisjuncta	Ma	X	2	3	4*	5	6	3V, 2J, 1D≠†
disjuncta	Ma	X	2*	3	4*	5	6	5R, 1D≠
ochracea	H	X	2	3	4	5a	6	5R, 1D
sejuncta	K	X	2	3	4	5a	6	5R, 1D
limitata	Ma,Mo	X	2	3	4	5a	6	5R, 1D; 6R≠
balioptera	Ma,Mo,L	Xg	2	3	4	5	6	5R, 1D
sobrina	O	Xg	2	3	4	5	6	5R, 1D
orthofascia	Ma,L,H	Xg	2	3*	4	5	6	5R, 1D
murphyi	H	Xg	2	3*	4	5	6	5R, 1D
reynoldsiae	O	Xg	2	3o	4	5	6	5R, 1D
ciliaticrus	H	Xg	2	3o	4*	5	6	5R, 1D
villitibia	Mo	X	2b	3	4	5	6	5R, 1D
lasiopoda	Ma	X	2b	3	4	5	6	6R≠
flexipes	O	X	2b	3	4*	5	6	5R, 1D
musaphilia	K	Xa^2	2b	3g	4u	5	6	5R, 1D
gymnobasis	Ma	Xa^2	2b	3g	4u	5	6	5R, 1D≠
heedi	H	Xa^2	2b	3g	4u	5	6	6R≠
recticilia	Ma	Xa^2	2b	3g	4u	5*	6	5R, 1D≠
hawaiiensis	H	Xa^2	2b	3g*	4u*	5	6	5R, 1D
silvarentis	H	Xa^2	2b	3g	4u	5*	6	5R, 1D≠

TABLE 3. Twelve clusters of homosequential species within the 4b phylad of picture-winged *Drosophila* from Hawaii. 2n = 12 in all 39 species. H = Hawaii, K = Kauai, L = Lanai, Ma = Maui, Mo = Molokai and O = Oahu.

Species	Island	Fixed Polytene Chromosome Gene Arrangements						Metaphase
pilimana	O	X	2	3	4b	5	6	5R, 1D
glabriapex	K	X	2	3	4b	5	6	5R, 1D
vesciseta	Ma	X	2	3	4b	5	6	5R, 1D
aglaia	O	X	2	3	4b*	5	6	5R, 1D
assita	H	Xk^3l^3	2	3	4b*	5	6	5R, 1D
montgomeryi	O	Xk^3l^3	2	3	4b	5	6	6R≠
tarphytrichia	O	X	2	3i	4b	5d	6	5R, 1D
spaniothrix	O	X	2	3i	4b	5d	6	5R, 1D
odontophallus	Ma	X	2	3i	4b	5d	6	5R, 1D
macrothrix	H	X	2	3i	4b	5d	6	5R, 1D
psilophallus	O	X	2	3i	4b	5d	6	6R≠
distinguenda	O	Xc^3d^3	2r	3	4b	5	6	5R, 1D
divaricata	O	Xc^3d^3	2r	3	4b	5	6	5R, 1D
inedita	O	Xc^3d^3	2r	3	4b	5	6	5R, 1D
virgulata	Ma	X	2	3	4b	5d	6	5R, 1D
digressa	H	X	2	3	4b	5d	6	5R, 1D≠
liophallus	Ma	Xh	2	3i	4b	5d	6	5R, 1D
gymnophallus	O	Xh	2	3i	4b	5d	6	5R, 1D
punalua	O	Xef	2	3z	4befg	5	6	5R, 1D
ocellata	K	Xef	2	3z	4befg	5	6	5R, 1D
paucicilia	O	Xef	2	3z	4befg	5	6	5R, 1D
paucipuncta	H	Xef	2	3z	4befg	5	6	5R, 1D
uniseriata	O	Xef	2	3z	4befg	5	6	6R≠
planitibia subgroup: Standard X (X^P) = Xijkopqs								
neopicta	Mo,Ma	X^P*	2*	3d	4b*	5	6	5R, 1D
obscuripes	Ma	X^P*	2	3d	4b	5	6	5R, 1D
substenoptera	O	X^P	2	3d	4b	5	6	5R, 1D
oahuensis	O	X^Pt*	2	3d	4b	5	6	5R, 1D

neoperkinsi	Mo	$X^P t$	2*	3d	4b*	5	6	5R, 1D
hanaulae	Ma	$X^P t$	2	3d	4b	5	6	5R, 1D
planitibia	Ma	$X^P rt$	2	3d	4b	5	6	5R, 1D
differens	Mo	$X^P rt$	2	3d	4b	5	6	5R, 1D
heteroneura	H	$X^P rt$	2	3d*	4b	5	6	5R, 1D
silvestris	H	$X^P rt$*	2*	3d*	4b*	5	6	5R, 1D
		adiastola subgroup: Standard X (X^A) = Xikouvwyz						
adiastola	Ma,L	X^A	2cd	3fjk	4bopq	5f	6	5R, 1D
peniculipedis	Ma	X^A	2cd	3fjk	4bopq	5f	6	5R, 1D
cilifera	Mo	X^A	2cd	3fjk	4bopq	5f	6	5R, 1D
varipennis	Mo	$X^A y^2$	2cd	3fk	4bopq	5f	6	5R, 1D
paenehamifera	Ma	$X^A y^2$	2cd	3fk	4bopq	5f	6	5R, 1D
hamifera	Ma	$X^A y^2$	2cd	3fk	4bopq	5f	6	5R, 1D

* polytene chromosome element shows at least one intraspecific inversion polymorphism.

≠ metaphase with distinctive pattern of heterochromatin distribution.

† according to the interpretation of Baimai and Ahearn (1978) some chromosome pairs are metacentric or submetacentric.

TABLE 4. Fixed inversion differences+ among 36 heterosequential picture-winged species of Drosophila from Hawaii.

No. of inversion differences from that species which is closest sequentially	No. of species in category
1	20
2	5+
3	2
4	3
5	1
8	2
11	3

\+ includes D. formella in which chromosome 4 has acquired two long inversions in tandem "trans" position. Neither of these is fixed. Crossing over in heterozygotes is not observed. Thus, the species does not retain Standard 4. If it did, it would be considered a homosequential species in the villitibia cluster (Table 2).

tioned here are designated by lower-case letters (sometimes with superscripts) and have been described and break-points located in earlier papers (see Carson and Yoon 1981).

Each homologue marked with an asterisk (*) in Tables 2 and 3 shows at least one intraspecific inversion polymorphism. Thus, within each cluster of homosequential species it is possible to recognize those species which are both polymorphic and homosequential (Fig. 2 and Tables 2 and 3). There are forty-five species in this category (Fig. 2) although some of these may eventually be shown to be polymorphic as further studies are carried out. Monomorphism is nonetheless a real category. For 12 species of the *adiastola* subgroup, 1916 wild chromosomes have been examined without discovery of any intraspecific inversions (Carson 1971).

Information on metaphase condition is also included in Figure 2 and Tables 2 and 3. Fig. 2 gives, for each category of sequentiality and morphism, two categories of metaphase. These latter are: 5R, 1D (five acrocentrics and one microchromosome without easily discernable heterochromatic differences) and metaphases of species which show some alteration due to accumulation of heterochromatin. The Y chromosome is not included in these characterizations. A word of caution may be advanced here. Undoubtedly there are some species included here which are marked 5R, 1D which, on closer scrutiny, will be shown to have some heterochromatin alteration. Baimai and Ahearn (1978), for example, have shown that *bostrycha*, *affinidisjuncta* and *disjuncta* may be so differentiated. From Figure 2, it may be seen that 5R, 1D is by all odds the most frequent metaphase; it has been observed in 78 of 103 species, including 34 which are also homosequential and monomorphic.

Even among heterosequential species, the amount of fixed inversion difference is rather small (Table 4). Thus, 25 of the 36 species differ from their closest relative by no more than two inversions. Certain individual chromosomes are very conservative. Thus, the *grimshawi* chromosome 2 gene arrangement is found in 61 other species and shows intraspecific polymorphism in only four of these species.

DISCUSSION AND CONCLUSIONS

Virtually all the picture-winged species may be easily recognized morphologically. In fact, among the 103 species, only two might be described as morphologically cryptic or "sibling" species. These are D. primaeva and D. attigua, which are found sympatrically on the island of Kauai (Carson and Stalker 1969). These two species, however, are strongly heterosequential, differing from one another by eleven inversions.

The grimshawi cluster of ten homosequential species (Table 2) includes species with widely variant color and wing-maculation patterns. Males exhibit strikingly different secondary sexual characters from one species to the next. The species in this

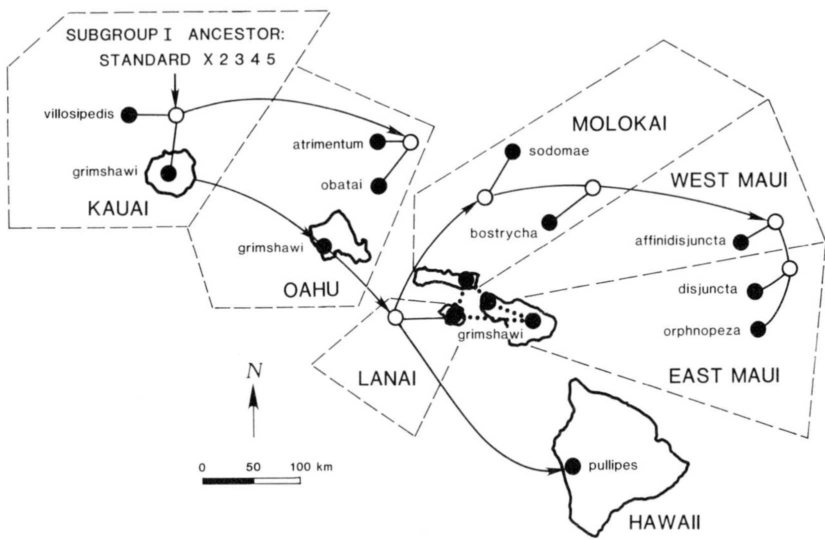

FIGURE 3. Geographical distribution of ten homosequential species in the D. grimshawi cluster in the Hawaiian Archipelago. Closed circles, present-day species; open circles, putative ancestral populations. Lines joining the circles hypothesize a parsimonious evolutionary scheme based on various non-cytological lines of evidence (for details, see Carson and Yoon 1981).

cluster are found on all major islands. Fig. 3 shows their island distributions; the arrows indicate the probable pattern of colonization, based on various non-cytological lines of evidence.

Ecologically, they range from ovipositional generalists (e.g. *villosipedis* of Kauai) to specialists such as *bostrycha* of Molokai (breeds on *Freycinetia* stems) and *obatai* of Oahu (breeds on *Dracaena* stems). Even more striking is the fact that Oahu and Kauai populations of *grimshawi* itself are specialists, that is, they are confined to breeding on *Wikstroemia* bark. A related, very close species, *D. pullipes* of Hawaii, is also confined to this host plant. On the Maui complex of islands (Maui-Molokai-Lanai) *D. grimshawi* demonstrates generalism; thus, the species has been reared from 12 different plant families on those islands. (Montgomery 1975; Carson and Ohta 1980).

Among the species groups of the genus *Drosophila*, perhaps the most cogent comparisons may be made between the Hawaiian picture-winged species and the *repleta* group, found in the xeric American tropics. Thus, Wasserman (1981) has sequenced 62 species of the latter, using polytene chromosomes. Of these, less than one-third (18) are homosequential. Twenty-six (42%) are monomorphic. The homosequential species fall into six clusters. Thus, although there are many more homosequential species among the picture-winged Drosophila of Hawaii, this condition is by no means confined to them.

Accordingly, chromosomal sequentiality in Hawaiian *Drosophila* shows no correlation with either morphological or ecological differentiation. Thus, the incorporation of cytologically detected aberrations, or indeed, heterochromatin alterations as well, do not seem to have been important in the dynamics of the speciation process. Wasserman (1981) has drawn a similar conclusion.

This conclusion does not agree with the suggestion of Bush et al. (1977) that a chromosomal mutation might act " . . . at a molecular level as a regulatory mutation, producing an altered pattern of gene expression that results in an organism with a new and fitter phenotype". In addition, the absence of interspecific translocation differences in the entire picture-winged group precludes a role for stasipatric mechanisms such as have been proposed by White (1978) for other groups of organisms. A regulatory role for translocations, furthermore, seems unlikely.

That chromosomal mutations do not appear to be involved in regulatory processes does not mean that interspecific differences in regulation of structural loci at the genic level do not exist and serve as an important factor in the genetic adaptation of these species. Indeed several highly specific cases of such regulatory differences have been described for several species of Hawaiian *Drosophila* (Dickinson and Carson 1979; Dickinson 1980). Inversions play no role in these cases.

Extensive genetic work has recently been completed on the natural populations of a sympatric pair of closely related but distinctive species of Hawaiian *Drosophila* (*D. silvestris* and *D. heteroneura*, Table 3). Thus Sene and Carson (1976) and Craddock and Johnson (1979) have shown that not only are these two species homosequential but that they are also virtually indistinguishable in their structural genes; indeed, there are no fixed allelic differences between them. Further, these species also do not display regulatory differences affecting structural genes of the kind described by Dickinson and Carson (1979).

All evidence indicates that these two species are recently evolved. Accordingly, what stand out as the most important differences arising during the speciation process are the easily observed morphological and behavioral differences. In the case of *silvestris* and *heteroneura*, these differences have been shown to be polygenic in nature (Val, 1977; Bryant and Carson, 1979). These differences cannot now be related to any of the chromosomal, molecular or regulatory differences discussed above.

I conclude that the speciation process in these groups of flies is facilitated neither by visible chromosomal mutations nor by structural gene changes or, indeed, by genes responsible for the regulation of the latter. A pronounced allopatric speciation abetted by the founder effect is considered to be the main mechanism of species proliferation (Carson, 1971). The initial changes which occur as species are formed are reflected genetically in polygenic differences controlling mating behavior and correlated morphological traits. I have suggested (Carson, 1975) that the founder event creates optimal conditions for abrupt shifts in the balance of such genes, in a manner emphasized for many years by Wright (1931, 1978).

SUMMARY

There are approximately 120 species in the group known as "picture-winged" Drosophila endemic to the Hawaiian Islands. The species are mostly large, easily distinguishable morphologically and show diverse behavioral and other ecological adaptations. Polytene chromosomes from larval salivary gland cells are extraordinarily favorable. The six elements have been completely sequenced in 103 species; the relative banding order of each has been described in terms of a single set of standard sequences. The qualitative appearance of the bands has not been significantly altered during evolution and there have been no Robertsonian fusions among these species (2n = 12). With the exception of one deletion, all interspecific differences in banding order are due to paracentric inversions (N = 213; 2.07 inversions per species). Sixty percent of these inversions occur in the fixed state. Two or more species are judged homosequential if they lack fixed inversion difference. Two-thirds (67) of the species are involved in 18 homosequential grouping with from one to ten other species. Forty-five species are both homosequential and monomorphic, that is, intraspecific polymorphisms are unknown in their populations. A number of species in both of the above categories show some interspecific variation due to differential distribution of fixed heterochromatic segments. Of the 45 which are both homosequential and monomorphic, a total of 34 show metaphases which have had no easily discernable addition or alteration of heterochromatin; all demonstrate the commonly observed condition of five acrocentrics with minimal centromeric heterochromatin and one microchromosome. Although these chromosomal characters provide very valuable phylogenetic and populational information, there is no evidence that this chromosomal variability plays an active role in the dynamics of the speciation process. Neither electrophoretic loci nor genes which regulate them can be implicated as pivotal in speciation. A simple allopatric model of species formation is favored for this group. The founder principle appears to play an important role by creating optimal conditions for abrupt shifts in the balance of genes controlling mating behavior and correlated morphological traits. Conventional adaptation by mutation and selection may follow, rather than accompany, the process of speciation.

REFERENCES

Babcock, E. B. 1947. The Genus Crepis. University of California Publications in Botany 21:1-195.

Baimai, V. and J. N. Ahearn 1978. Cytogenetic relationships of *Drosophila affinidisjuncta* Hardy. Amer. Midl. Nat. 99:352-360.

Bryant, P. J. and H. L. Carson 1979. Genetics of an interspecific difference in a secondary sexual character in *Drosophila*. Genetics 91:s15.

Bush, G. L., S. M. Case, A. C. Wilson and J. L. Patton 1977. Rapid speciation and chromosomal evolution in mammals. Proc. Nat. Acad. Sci. USA 74:3942-3946.

Carson, H. L. 1970. Chromosome tracers of the origin of species. Science 168:1414-1418.

Carson, H. L. 1971. Speciation and the founder principle. Stadler Genetics Symp. 3:51-70.

Carson, H. L. 1975. The genetics of speciation at the diploid level. Am. Nat. 109:83-92.

Carson, H. L., F. E. Clayton and H. D. Stalker 1967. Karyotypic stability and speciation in Hawaiian Drosophila. Proc. Nat. Acad. Sci. USA 57:1280-1285.

Carson, H. L. and K. Y. Kaneshiro 1976. Drosophila of Hawaii: Systematics and Ecological Genetics. Ann. Rev. Ecol. Syst. 7:311-345.

Carson, H. L. and A. T. Ohta 1980. Origin of the genetic basis of colonizing ability. Proc. IInd Intern. Congr. System. Evol. Biol. (in press).

Carson, H. L. and H. D. Stalker 1968. Polytene chromosome relationships in Hawaiian species of *Drosophila* I. The *D. grimshawi* subgroup. Univ. Texas Publ. 6818:335-354.

Carson, H. L. and H. D. Stalker 1969. Polytene chromosome relationships in Hawaiian species of *Drosophila* IV. The *D. primaeva* subgroup. Univ. Texas Publ. 6918:85-94.

Carson, H. L. and J. S. Yoon 1981. Genetics and evolution of Hawaiian Drosophila. *in* The Genetics and Biology of Drosophila. Ed. M. Ashburner, H. L. Carson and J. N. Thompson. Vol. 3 Academic Press, London (in press).

Craddock, E. M. and W. E. Johnson 1979. Genetic variation in Hawaiian *Drosophila* V. Chromosomal and allozymic diversity in *Drosophila silvestris* and its homosequential species. Evolution 33:137-155.

Dickinson, W. J. 1980. Tissue Specificity of Enzyme Expression Regulated by Diffusible Factors: Evidence in Drosophila Hybrids. Science 207:995-997.

Dickinson, W. J. and H. L. Carson 1979. Regulation of the tissue specificity of an enzyme by a cis-acting genetic element: evidence from interspecific Drosophila hybrids. Proc. Nat. Acad. Sci. USA 76:4559-4562.

Montgomery, S. L. 1975. Comparative breeding site ecology and the adaptive radiation of picture-winged Drosophila. Proc. Hawaii

Entomol. Soc. 22:65-102.

Sene, F. M. and H. L. Carson 1977. Genetic variation in Hawaiian Drosophila IV. Close allozymic similarity between D. silvestris and D. heteroneura from the Island of Hawaii. Genetics 86:187-198.

Val, F. C. 1977. Genetic analysis of the morphological differences between two interfertile species of Hawaiian Drosophila. Evolution 31:611-629.

Wasserman, M. 1981. Evolution of the repleta group. in The Genetics and Biology of Drosophila. Ed. M. Ashburner, H. L. Carson and J. N. Thompson Vol. 3 Academic Press, London (in press).

White, M. J. D. 1978. Modes of Speciation. San Francisco: W. H. Freeman Co., pp. 455.

Wright, S. 1931. Evolution in Mendelian populations. Genetics 16:97-159.

Wright, S. 1978. Evolution and the Genetics of Populations. Chicago: The University of Chicago Press, Vol. IV, pp. 580.

Yunis, J. J., J. R. Sawyer and K. Dunham 1980. The Striking Resemblance of High-Resolution G-Banded Chromosomes of Man and Chimpanzee. Science 208:1145-1148.

ACKNOWLEDGEMENT

This work has been supported by grants from the National Science Foundation (BMS 74-22532). I thank Professor Jong Sik Yoon for allowing the use of his photograph reproduced as Figure 1.

Chromosome architecture of the parthenogenetic grasshopper *Warramaba virgo* and its bisexual ancestors

M. J. D. White and N. Contreras

Research School of Biological Sciences, Australian National University

The chromosome architecture of the Australian parthenogenetic grasshopper *Warramaba virgo* is now better known than that of any other all-female species of organism. Discovered in 1961 (White *et al.*, 1963), in west-central New South Wales, its karyotype was at first misinterpreted, because its hybrid origin was not appreciated. The bisexual ancestral species were, in fact, not yet known and their karyotypes were not described until much later (White and Webb 1968; White *et al.* 1973). The "hybrid interpretation" of *W. virgo* then became inevitable (Hewitt, 1975) and was clinched when the hybridization was repeated in the laboratory and "synthetic *virgo*" were obtained (White *et al.* 1977; White and Contreras 1978). Until 1973 the only natural populations of *virgo* known were in eastern Australia, whereas the ancestral species (designated as 'P169' and 'P196', pending a taxonomic treatment of the genus *Warramaba* by Dr K.H.L. Key) are confined to small areas of Western Australia. However, in 1973 populations of *W. virgo* were found in Western Australia, south of the areas occupied by P169 and P196.

THE DUAL ORIGIN OF *W. VIRGO*

The statement that *W. virgo* arose by hybridisation between populations ancestral to the present day species P169 and P196 needs clarification. Was there a single hybridization, several or many? When and where did hybridization occur? One extreme model would be that all clones of *virgo* are descended from a single hybrid individual that resulted from a unique mating between the ancestral bisexual species. Another extreme model would postulate numerous hybridizations, widely distributed in space and time, giving rise to the existing clones of *virgo* and doubtless to others that have become extinct. Intermediate models can easily be imagined.

Definite answers to these questions cannot for the most part be given. But the range of possibilities can be narrowed. Two important conclusions have already been stated. White and Contreras (1979) showed that in the Coolgardie-Kalgoorlie region of Western Australia the ranges of *virgo* and P196 were parapatric, but that no mixed colonies could be found, even though the food-plants of the two species are the same in this area. In 1980 we found several individuals of *virgo* 100 m from a colony of P196, but still no geographic mixing occurred. Since the two species mate readily in the laboratory and produce triploid hybrids that are essentially sterile (White *et al.* 1977), mixed colonies should be unstable and tend to become extinct or once more monospecific. Mating between P169 and *virgo* takes place equally easily in the laboratory, with essentially the same result.

From these facts there follows conclusion (1), namely that successful hybridization to produce *virgo* could only have occurred in Western Australia where the periphery of the range of one sexual species intersected that of the other, with *virgo* then invading territory not occupied by either of them. The second deduction arrived at recently is that *virgo* must then have migrated to central New South Wales, 2300 km away, through its own locomotory activity, since no accidental transportation over long distances is conceivable. Because the insect is wingless and extremely sedentary, this forces us to conclusion (2), namely that the hybridization or hybridizations that produced the first *virgo* individuals took place a very long time ago, *i.e.* at least 500,000 years B.P. (White 1980).

Conclusion (3), evidence for which will be presented below, is that there were two hybridizations, or groups of hybridizations, one of which gave rise to the majority of the *virgo* clones while the other gave rise to the Boulder and Zanthus clones. Since these two clones are confined to a relatively small area of Western

Australia and never reached eastern Australia, they may have originated much more recently.

Altogether, 25 cytological clones of *virgo* are now known. The karyotypes of 15 were described and given geographical designations by Webb *et al.* (1978) and one additional one (Spargoville) has been described since (White 1980). The remainder will be described in a forthcoming paper. Some clones have a 'standard' karyotype and only differ in C-band patterns (presence or absence of certain bands or differences in their length). Others differ in respect of major chromosomal rearrangements such as translocations, centric fusions or inversions. The standard karyotype of *virgo* consists essentially of a haploid set (8 chromosomes) from P169 and another (7 chromosomes) from P196.

In general, only one clone is present at each locality, but a number of instances exist where two coexist at a locality and at Spargoville, in Western Australia, three clones (Spargoville, Boulder and Coolgardie) live together on the same foodplant, an undescribed *Acacia* species. It is quite possible that some cytological clones, especially the more widespread ones, will prove to be genetically composite, when their allozymes have been more thoroughly studied.

Webb *et al.* (1978) realised that the closely related Western Australia clones Boulder and Zanthus differed greatly in karyotype and banding pattern from all the others. They are unique in lacking C-segments 4 and 17 (in the X+A chromosome), 32 (in the AB chromosome), 44 (in the B+5 chromosome), 49 (in the X_1 chromosome) and 60.5 (in the CD_{169} chromosome). There are six additional C-segments, 23 (in the AB), 36 (in the B+5), 64.5 (in the CD_{169}), 74 (in the 1_{169}), 93 (in the 5_{196}) and 97 (in the X_2). However, segment 64.5 may be the missing segment 60.5, shifted by a paracentric inversion. The X+A chromosome is shorter than in other clones and the X_1 is unequal-armed instead of equal-armed, as it is in other clones. There are altogether 15 cytological differences between Boulder-Zanthus and the other clones, of which 8 are in chromosomes derived from P169, 7 in ones derived from P196. There are also quite significant phenotypic and physiological differences between the Boulder-Zanthus clones and the rest. The morphometric studies of Atchley (1978) confirm the distinctness of the Boulder and Zanthus clones (the latter represented in his material by the "Newman Rock population") from other Western Australian clones. In addition, the eggs of Boulder and Zanthus individuals are more slender and, under laboratory conditions, have a very poor hatchability.

The studies on the C-banding patterns and DNA replication profiles of P169 and P196 confirmed the hybrid origin of *virgo*, the differences between the chromosomes of the parental species and the corresponding chromosomes of *virgo* clones (other than Boulder and Zanthus) being relatively minor. Those studies were, in both instances, carried out on material from relatively northern localities. However, it had become apparent in the meanwhile that there were very considerable biological differences between northern and southern populations of P196 (White and Contreras 1979). The northern individuals, such as those used in the cytological investigations referred to above, were much larger than southern ones from the vicinity of Kalgoorlie and Coolgardie; moreover they laid, under laboratory conditions, 2 to 3 times as many eggs per lifetime. The data could be interpreted as a north-south cline but, because of paucity of information for the middle part of the range, they are equally compatible with the existence of two distinct races, a northern one of large, high-fecundity individuals and a southern one of much smaller grasshoppers having a very low fecundity.

It has been found recently that there are quite considerable karyotypic differences between the northern and southern races of P196 (Fig. 1). The chromosome number and the general structure of the karyotype is the same, but there are four distinct differences, as follows:

	Northern Race	Southern Race
C-segment	23 absent	present
"	32 present	absent
"	49 "	"
X_1	chromosome nearly equal-armed	unequal-armed

The interesting thing is that all the diagnostic cytogenetic features of the southern race of P196 (as seen in individuals from 3 km NW of Spargoville, 9 km NE of Coolgardie and 1 km N of

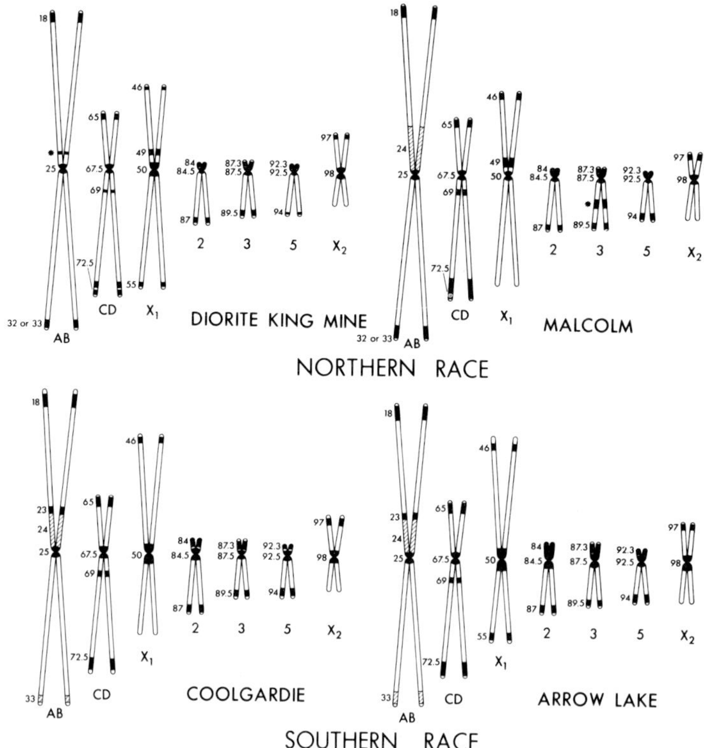

FIGURE 1 Diagrams of the C-banding patterns of the northern and southern races of *Warramaba* P196.

Arrow Lake) are present in the Boulder and Zanthus clones of *virgo* , but not in other clones.

From these observations, it is clear that the Boulder-Zanthus clones are derived from a hybridization involving the southern race of P196, whereas the other clones are descended from one or more hybridizations involving the northern race. This situation is shown diagrammatically in Fig. 2, although it is not implied that the arrows representing hybridizations A and B accurately show the precise points of origin or the migration routes of the two parthenogenetic stocks. Furthermore, it is possible that each of these arrows should really be a bundle of arrows, if the two events were mass hybridizations of local populations rather than single pair matings.

Since there are a number of significant features in which the Boulder-Zanthus clones differ from both 'normal' clones of *virgo*

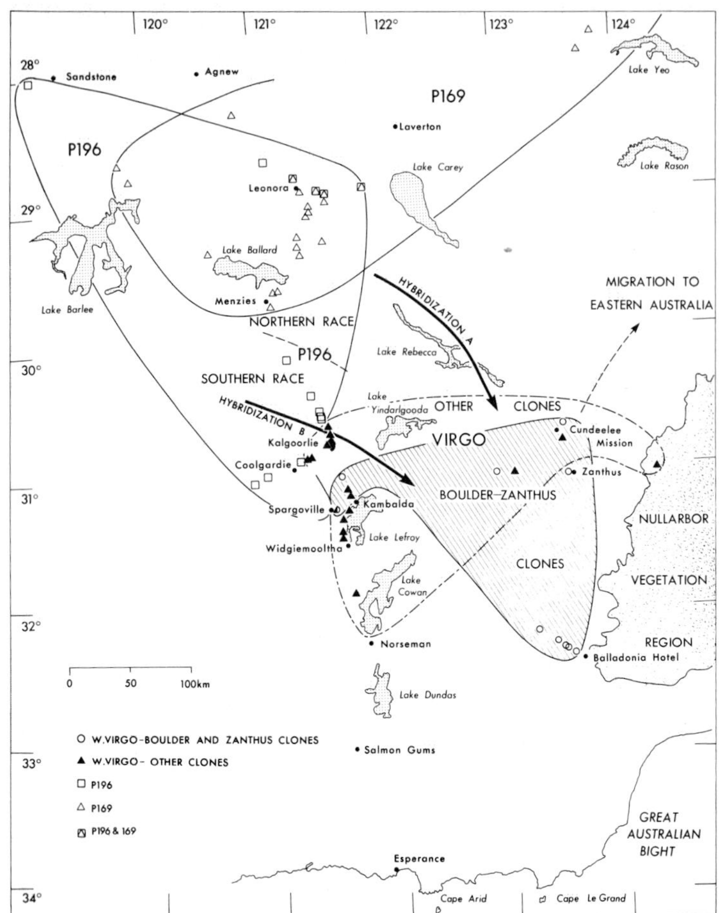

FIGURE 2 Map showing the present day distributions, as far as known, of *Warramaba* spp. P169 and P196 and of the clones of *W. virgo* in Western Australia. The arrows indicate the two hybridizations that gave rise to the 'other clones' and 'Boulder-Zanthus clones' of *virgo*. The distribution of Nullarbor type vegetation, blocking the eastward spread of *virgo*, is based on Beard (1970); the Kitchener population of *virgo*, apparently located on Nullarbor vegetation, is on a small ecotonal area of mulga (*Acacia aneura*). Mixed populations of P196 and P169 existing at the present time, without hybridization, indicated by a special symbol. The northern and eastern limits of the distribution of P169 are unknown, and it is possible that it occurs further south than indicated, near Lake Carey and Lake Rebecca.

and from P169 (as analyzed cytologically by Webb *et al.* 1978) it is plausible that there exists a southern race of P169, differing in a number of karyotypic features from the more northerly material. Such a population might be expected to have a rather shorter X+A, lacking C-band 4, and might show band 36 but not band 44 in the B+5 chromosome. However, this southern race of P169 may be extinct, or may be more eastern than southern. Conceivably, it never existed, the various changes in the P169-derived chromosomes having taken place in the Boulder-Zanthus stock after hybridization B had occurred.

The laboratory hybrids between P169 and P196 that we were able to obtain (White *et al.* 1977; White and Contreras 1978) all involved the southern race of P196; we have never been able to hybridize P169 with the northern race of P196 successfully. Thus all the "synthetic *virgo*" individuals referred to in those papers were really "synthetic Boulder-Zanthus" individuals.

We have no real means of estimating how long ago hybridization B took place. Obviously, the Boulder-Zanthus clones have had time to fan out from their point of origin (Fig. 3) over a considerable area of territory (roughly, 230 km from east to west and 180 km from north to south), which suggests that event B occurred at least some thousands of years ago. Two facts - that the descendents of event B never reached eastern Australia and that the southern race of P196 is still capable of producing laboratory

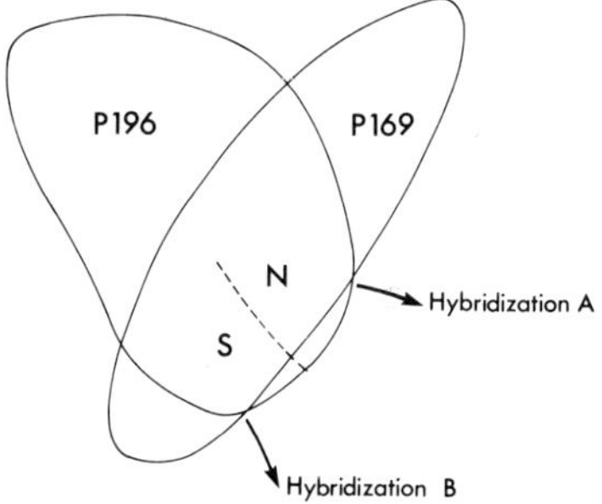

FIGURE 3 Diagram showing the postulated dual origin of *W. virgo*, with the hybrid populations spreading out from two points where the periphery of the range of P169 intersected that of P196 into territory not inhabited by either of the parent species.

hybrids with P169 whereas the northern race is not - suggest that hybridization B took place more recently than hybridization A. Also the Boulder-Zanthus stock did not give rise to clones with major structural chromosome rearrangements (the stock derived from hybridization A has produced at least 9 such clones). Thus the evidence suggests that in contrast to the undoubtedly ancient hybridization A, hybridization B may be much more recent.

P169 is not known to be sympatric with the southern race of P196, although it has an extensive area of overlap with the northern one (Fig. 2). Lack of sympatry with the southern race may be due to ecological factors, *e.g.* the foodplant of P169, *Acacia aneura*, does not extend as dense or continuous stands into the area inhabited by the southern race of P196. But it is also possible that the absence of genetical isolation between P169 and the southern race of P196 is an additional reason for lack of sympatry between them. However, fieldwork has not been sufficiently extensive to completely exclude the possibility of an area of sympatry with the southern race at the present time - only if it exists it must be narrow. In the area of sympatry with the northern race the two species occur together on *Acacia aneura* at four different localities with no indication that mating ever takes place between them in nature at the present time.

REPLICATION PATTERNS IN THE KARYOTYPES OF *VIRGO* AND ITS ANCESTORS

Using tritiated thymidine autoradiography, we have studied the distribution of late-replicating segments along the length of the chromosomes of five clones of *virgo*, P169 and the northern race of P196 (White *et al.* 1980). It was found that the replication patterns of the *virgo* clones are generally similar, but that the Boulder ones are significantly different from those of the other four. Some, but not all, of the strongly late replicating segments correspond to C-bands. Some differences between the replication profiles of the different clones are clearly due to variation in the length of particular C-segments that must be due to amplification or diminution of special DNA sequences. Thus segment 4 appears strongly late-replicating in the Broken Hill clone in which band 4 is amplified, but not late replicating in the Hayes Hill clone in which the band is reduced to a mere hairline across the chromosome. The telomeric segment 33-33.3, which contains a 'gray' C-band that does not stain as darkly as standard C-segments, is strongly late-replicating in all clones, including the Boulder one.

The replication patterns of P169 and P196 proved to be generally similar to those of *W. virgo*, as far as the larger chromosomes, at any rate, are concerned. That is to say, the X+A, B+5 and CD chromosomes of P169 and the AB, X, and CD chromosomes of P196 have 'replication profiles' that are remarkably similar to those of the corresponding chromosomes in the hybrid karyotype of *virgo*. Clearly, replication patterns have been remarkably stable. Since the replication pattern of the southern race of P196 has not been studied, we do not know whether it shows resemblances to that of the Boulder clone which are not seen in the case of the northern race. A few anomalous features are not easily explained. Thus the end of the long arm of the CD is late replicating in P196 (northern race) and in the Boulder clone, but not in the other *virgo* clones.

DISCUSSION

Two strongly contrasted viewpoints have dominated past thinking on the subject of thelytokous genetic systems. According to one of these such systems are evolutionary 'dead ends' incapable of progressive change and adaptation. The other viewpoint states that such organisms are destined to undergo mutational changes in a more or less uncontrolled manner (that is, controlled only by natural selection against those mutants that have seriously impaired viability or fecundity) and consequently soon become diversified into complexes of numerous divergent clones that are almost impossible to classify by conventional methods. Both viewpoints have suffered severely from lack of quantification. What do we mean by a 'dead end' - one that will become extinct in a thousand, a million, ten million or a hundred million years? Since most lineages of sexual organisms eventually become extinct, what difference exists between thelytokous and sexual lineages in this respect? What sort of mutations establish themselves in thelytokous lineages and at what rates? How much do thelytokous organisms diversify in relation to niche-diversity? To what extent are thelytokous species of monophyletic or polyphyletic origin? How does the genetic diversity of thelytokous 'species' compare with that of related sexual ones?

Since there are a number of quite diverse cytogenetic types of thelytoky that have arisen in organisms with very different genetic systems and life styles it is unlikely that most of the above questions can be answered in any simple universally valid manner.

Clearly the amount of cytogenetic diversification that has occurred in *W. virgo*, which may be related to and in part explain its adaptability to different foodplants, climates and soils across the Australian continent, is not as great as we formerly assumed, on the assumption of a unique origin by hybridization. Thus, most, but probably not all, the differences between the Boulder-Zanthus clones and the others were already present in the parent species and have not arisen under conditions of thelytokous reproduction. But considerable cytogenetic diversification can be proved quite rigorously to have arisen under parthenogenetic conditions. This is particularly the case with translocations and fusions that involve one chromosome derived from P169 and one from P196. Such rearrangements are known in the Monia Gap, Yatpool, Spargoville, Hayes Hill, Kambalda and Woolibar karyotypes (the last two still undescribed). Thus it is quite unreasonable to argue from the cytogenetic diversity of the *virgo* clones in favor of a highly multiple origin, with each clone derived from a separate hybridization event.

Since the Spargoville clone of *W. virgo* is widely divergent, karyotypically, from the other clones, it is obvious that the possibility of a third independent origin of *virgo* does have to be considered. But the most outstanding peculiarities of the Spargoville clone are two major rearrangements (a translocation between the AB and 3_{169} and a fusion between 1_{169} and 5_{196}) which must have arisen since the hybrid origin (because they involve in each case chromosomes derived from each of the parent species). Thus the Spargoville clone *may* have had an independent origin, but these peculiarities are not an argument in favor of this interpretation since they could not have been inherited from special local races of the parental species (in the way that the more outstanding peculiarities of the Boulder-Zanthus clones have been derived from a 'special' race of P196).

Acknowledgements

We are grateful to W.R. Atchley, J.B. Gibson and I.M. White for assistance with the field collecting. The work has been supported by grant 1 RO1-GM22710 from the Division of General Medical Sciences, U.S. National Institutes of Health.

REFERENCES

Atchley, W.R. 1978. Biological variability in the parthenogenetic grasshopper *Warramaba virgo* (Key) and its sexual relatives. II. The Western Australian taxa. *Evolution* 32, 375-388.

Beard, J.S. 1970. Vegetation Survey of Western Australia. 1:1,000,000 Map Series. Nullarbor sheet. Univ. Western Australia Press and Australian Biological Resources Study.

Hewitt, G.M. (1975. A new hypothesis for the origin of the parthenogenetic grasshopper *Moraba virgo*. *Heredity* 34, 117-136.

Webb, G.C., White, M.J.D., Contreras, N. and Cheney, J. 1978. Cytogenetics of the parthenogenetic grasshopper *Warramaba* (formerly *Moraba*) *virgo* and its bisexual relatives. IV. Chromosome banding studies. *Chromosoma* 68, 309-339.

White, M.J.D. 1980. The genetic system of the parthenogenetic grasshopper *Warramaba virgo*. In: *Insect Cytogenetics*, Xth Symposium of the Royal Entomological Society of London (ed. R.L. Blackman, M. Ashburner and G.M. Hewitt). Oxford: Blackwell.

White, M.J.D., Cheney, J. and Key, K.H.L. 1963. A parthenogenetic species of grasshopper with complex structural heterozygosity (Orthoptera:Acridoidea). *Austral. J. Zool.* 11, 1-19.

White, M.J.D. and Contreras, N. 1978. Cytogenetics of the parthenogenetic grasshopper *Warramaba* (formerly *Moraba*) *virgo* and its bisexual relatives. III. Meiosis of male "synthetic *virgo*" individuals. *Chromosoma* 67, 55-61.

White, M.J.D. and Contreras, N. 1979. Cytogenetics of the parthenogenetic grasshopper *Warramaba* (formerly *Moraba*) *virgo* and its bisexual relatives. V. Interaction of *W. virgo* and a bisexual species in geographic contact. *Evolution* 33, 85-94.

White, M.J.D., Contreras, N., Cheney, J. and Webb, G.C. 1977. Cytogenetics of the parthenogenetic grasshopper *Warramaba* (formerly *Moraba*) *virgo* and its bisexual relatives. II. Hybridization studies. *Chromosoma* 61, 127-148.

White, M.J.D. and Webb, G.C. 1968. Origin and evolution of parthenogenetic reproduction in the grasshopper *Moraba virgo* (Eumastacidae: Morabinae). *Austral. J. Zool.* 16, 647-671.

White, M.J.D., Webb, G.C. and Cheney, J. 1973. Cytogenetics of the parthenogenetic grasshopper *Moraba virgo* and its bisexual relatives. I. A new species of the *virgo* group with a unique sex chromosome mechanism. *Chromosoma* 40, 199-212.

White, M.J.D., Webb, G.C. and Contreras, N. 1980. Cytogenetics of the parthenogenetic grasshopper *Warramaba* (formerly *Moraba*) *virgo* and its bisexual relatives. VI. DNA replication patterns of the chromosomes. *Chromosoma* (in press).

Chromosomal evolution in primates

B. Dutrillaux, J. Couturier, Evani Viegas-Pequignot

Institut de Progenese, 75270 Paris, Cedex 06, France

Progress in comparative karyology of primates has followed the progress in human cytogenetics. In the early sixties, Chiarelli (1961), Hamerton et al (1961), Chu and Bender (1962) and others found similarities between the karyotypes of man and those of the great apes. This was followed by the analysis of most living species, and a considerable amount of information was assembled in a large catalogue (Hsu and Bernirschke 1967-1977). However, the low resolution of then conventional techniques hindered the making of comparisons of value, except for a few closely related species.

With the seventies came the development of chromosome banding and gene mapping. These new possibilities for comparative cytogenetics were exploited by Turleau et al (1972), Bobrow and Madan (1973), Dutrillaux et al (1973), Lejeune et al (1973), Pearson (1973), Warburton et al (1973), and others. However, these comparisons remained limited to a few species, namely the great apes (Chimpanzee, Gorilla and Orang-utan) and man, until Garver et al (1977) and Grouchy et al (1977) proposed a comparative study of chromosome banding and gene mapping for some chromosomes in the Pongidea and in two species of Cercopithecoidea. The banding comparisons were completed for all chromosomes (Dutrillaux et al 1978a,b) in several Cercopithecoidea, and, more recently, in many other primates (Dutrillaux 1979b).

At present, the karyotypes of approximately half the living species of primates have been compared, and some general conclusions concerning the chromosomal evolution of primates can be proposed.

KARYOTYPIC COMPARISONS

Identity of euchromatic bands

Starting from the human karyotype, which was the best known, a systematic comparison has been carried out with those of more and more distantly related species. Between man and the great apes (Chimpanzees, Gorilla, and Orang-utan), an almost complete analogy was found (Dutrillaux 1975). The same conclusions were also reached from comparisons between man and several Cercopithecoids, such as baboons, macaques, and various *Cercopithecus* (Dutrillaux et al 1978a,b). A clear analogy of chromosome banding was also found between man and some New World monkeys, such as Capuchin and woolly monkeys (*Cebus capucinus* and *Lagothrix lagotricha*) (Dutrillaux, 1979a, Dutrillaux et al 1980a). The study was extended to prosimians, such as *Microcebus murinus*, and once more, a considerable analogy of chromosome banding was found (Dutrillaux 1979b). Finally, these analogies do not seem to be restricted to primates; in many respects, human chromosomes look quite similar to those of the rabbit (Dutrillaux et al 1980b) or to those of several species of Carnivora (unpublished).

If we try to quantify these analogies, about 99% are found to exist between man and the great apes, about 90% between man and Cercopithoids, about 80% between man and New World monkeys, and about 70% between man and prosimians, man and rabbit, and man and Carnivora. A complete analogy could not be demonstrated for technical reasons in all instances, such as the occurrence of complex rearrangements or the presence of very small chromosomes which could not be analysed accurately. However, in each of the species compared, the unmatched chromosomes representing the same number of bands, it is likely that the euchromatic material is the same for all the species studied.

Comparative gene mapping

Comparative gene mapping has been carried out for a few species and the conclusions can be summarised as follows:

- among the great apes and man, identical genes have been localised in nearly all the chromosomes which were presumed homologous after banding comparisons had been made. (Garver et al 1977, Grouchy et al 1977).

- among Cercopithecoids, several chromosomes of *Macaca mulatta*, *Papio papio*, and *Cercopithecus aethiops*, were found to carry the genes expected from banding comparisons with man and the great apes (Garver et al 1977, Grouchy et al 1977).
- in one species of New World monkey (*Cebus capucinus*), 5 genes have been mapped on 2 chromosomes (Creau-Goldberg et al 1980), which again were the presumed carriers from banding comparisons.

Although these studies are still very limited as regards the number of genes and the number of species, there is a remarkable agreement between comparative chromosome banding and comparative gene mapping, and this agreement strengthens the validity of the two approaches to the question. The few remaining discrepancies, mostly in the comparison of Cercopithecoids and man, probably reflect only technical difficulties in the methods used. Thus, it can be concluded that, in general, chromosomes having the same banding pattern also possess the same genic content, in the species studied so far.

Unfortunately, there are no comparative studies of gene mapping on rabbit and man, nor on Carnivora and man. The extensive data on gene mapping of mouse is, for the moment, difficult to relate to chromosome banding comparisons. From our unpublished results on Rodentia, it is clear that mouse possesses a highly differentiated karyotype, many translocations and fissions having probably occurred during its evolution. However, in the few chromosomes for which banding analogies could be found, such as: MMU (*Mus musculus*) 4 = HSA (*Homo sapiens*)1 p, MMU 11(distal) = HSA 17, MMU 12 (distal) = HSA 14, and MMU 16 (distal) = HSA 21, gene mapping is in good agreement.

Thus, it may be expected that in the very near future, and after acquiring a general view of the chromosome evolution of rodents, a direct comparison between man and mouse will be possible.

High Resolution Chromosome Banding

Synchronisation procedures, making it possible to study long chromosomes with about 1000 bands per haploid set, have been used for the comparison of a few species. The results obtained in

Pongidae (Yunis 1980, unpublished), in Cercopithecoids (unpublished) in New World monkeys (Dutrillaux et al 1980a) and in non-primate mammals (Dutrillaux et al 1980b), generally confirm those obtained after more classical chromosome banding techniques were used, but also substantially extend the potentialities of the method. Figure 1 shows a comparison of human chromosomes with those of *Allenopithecus nigroviridis*, a Cercopithecoid with a relatively primitive karyotype.

The DNA-Replication Pattern

The DNA-replication pattern, which is highly specific for each chromosome, has been studied in detail for certain species (Viegas-Pequignot et al 1978, Couturier and Dutrillaux in preparation). This specific pattern was found in all the species analysed, and it was demonstrated that the sequence of replication time of the bands is the same in chromosomes presumed analogous after banding comparison. This replication pattern was not found to be altered by the occurrence of structural rearrangements.

Finally, all these comparative studies can be summarized as follows: The euchromatic components of the chromosomes (i.e. R- and G- bands) are mostly, and perhaps entirely, the same in all primate species, and probably also in other non-primate mammals (Lagomorpha, Rodentia, Carnivora). This conservatism is valid for staining properties to the highest level of analysis, for DNA-replication time, and in the few species analysed, for the genic content of the chromosomes.

Variability of Heterochromatin

In contrast with the stability of euchromatin, heterochromatin is extremely variable. Besides the juxta-centromeric heterochromatin additional heterochromatin is present in some species. This is generally, but not always, C-band positive, and is either near to the telomeres, or near to the centromeres, or intercalated between euchromatic segments. Its amount varies in considerable proportions, from less than 1% in baboons and macaques, to more than 10% in *Cebus*, and even more than 15% of the whole karyotype in *Lemur coronatus*.

The staining properties are also quite variable, and may be C-band, R-band and Q-band positive or negative, with various com-

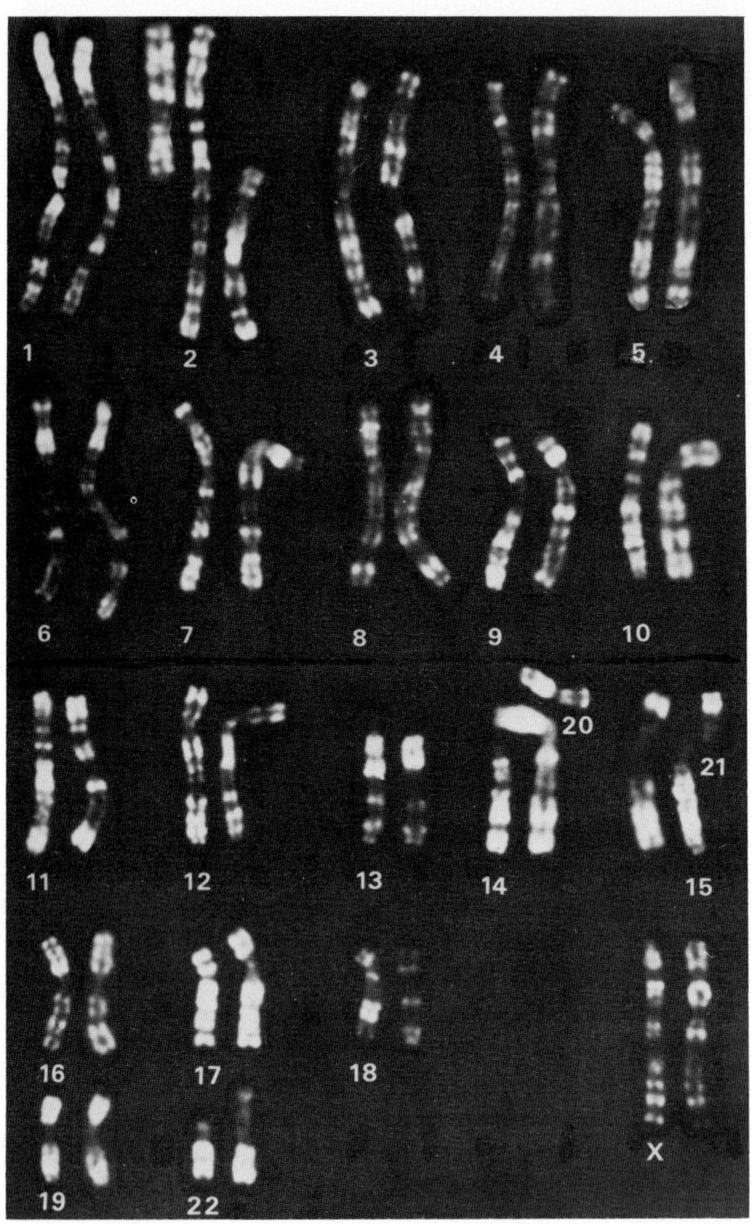

Figure 1: Comparison of human chromosomes (left) to those of Allenopithecus nigroviridis (right). Human chromosome variation was used. Although the two karyotypes differ by about 30 re-arrangements, the analogies remain obvious for many chromosomes.

binations. In the few cases where DNA composition was analysed, good correlation was found between a positive R-banding and the presence of a G-C rich satellite DNA (unpublished). A positive Q-banding was correlated with an A-T rich satellite DNA (Jalal et al 1974), but not all A-T rich satellites are Q-band positive. It was not possible to relate any particular phenotypic character to the presence or absence of heterochromatin, but the fact that its total amount seems fairly stable in a given species,when random chromosome segregation would lead to large individual variations, supports the existence of a regulatory system, and thus of a possible, though unknown, role of heterochromatin (Dutrillaux 1979).

Moreover, the fact that heterochromatin is not distributed at random among the chromosomes, but is always located at similar sites (telomeric, juxta-centromeric, or intercalary) in a given species or genus, supports the existence of special chromosomal structures with the potential ability to develop heterochromatin: for instance, it could be dependent on specific base sequences in DNA susceptible to undergo amplification. Particularly interesting is the fact that heterochromatin can be located exactly in the same place on the same chromosomes of two distantly-related species, whereas it does not exist in species closely related to each of these.

CHROMOSOMAL PHYLOGENY

Two sets of information can be obtained from chromosome comparisons with regard to phylogenic problems.

First, the finding that two or more species possess the same unchanged chromosome is a good argument for considering that this chromosome was already present in the karyotype of their common ancestors. Progressively, by comparison of an increasing number of species, more and more chromosomes of a more and more ancestral karyotype can be found. Then, ancestral karyotypes of different groups can be compared, and similarities between them strengthen the validity of the working hypothesis. At present, the ancestral karyotype for primates, Lagomorpha, Rodentia and Carnivora can be reconstructed, even though a few uncertainties remain, as, for example, the exact configuration of the X chromosome. Figure 2 gives an idea of its general constitution.

The second type of information is obtained from the study of the chromosomal rearrangements. It has been possible to reconstruct more than 200 changes, leading to the progressive modification of the ancestral karyotype into the differentiated karyotypes observed in living species.

The sequence of the rearrangements affecting each chromosome

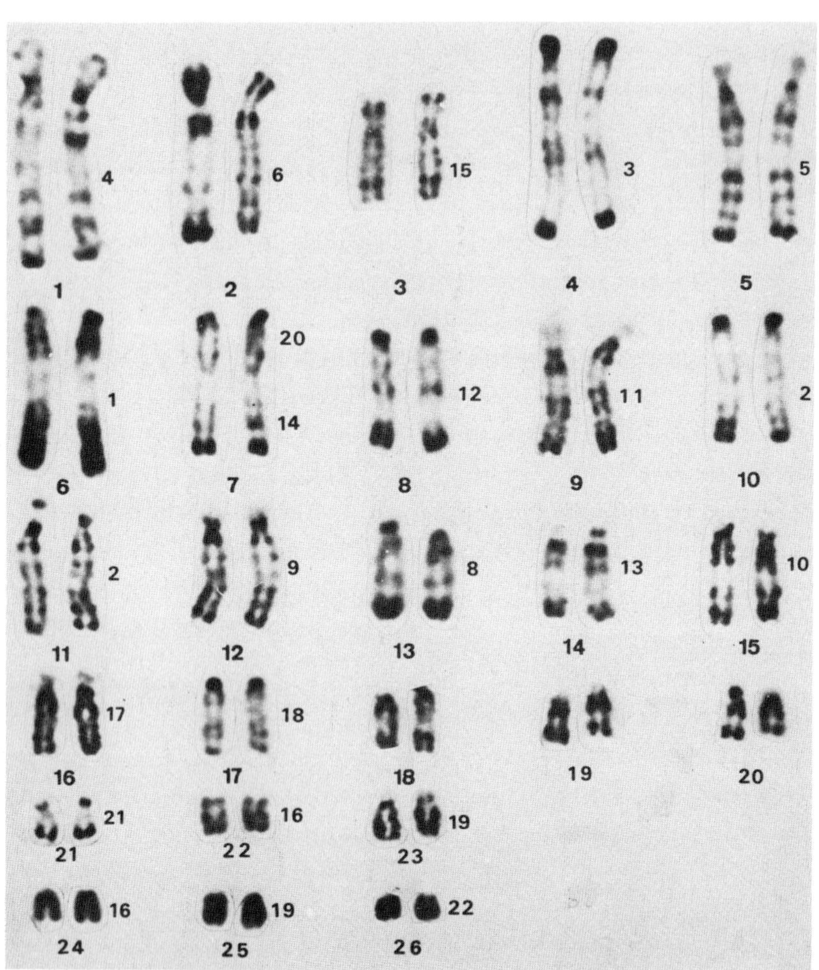

Figure 2: Reconstitution of the presumed karyotype of the common ancestor of Primate, Lagomorpha, Carnivora and Rodentia. Numbers on the right side indicate analogies with human chromosomes. It was not possible to choose between several possibilities for sex chromosomes. Chromosomes 3, and the small acrocentrics are uncertain.

indicates the order in which the branches leading to the various sub-orders, families, genera and species have separated, and Figure 3 shows the phylogeny of the Catarrhini, with the exception of Colobidae and Hylobatidae.

As shown in Figure 3, a strict dichotomic evolution cannot be established, probably because a single chromosomal change was insufficient to induce a reproductive barrier. In several instances a "populational" evolution of chromosomes has occurred. Thus, the role of chromosome rearrangements is not as clear-cut as might be thought, and this enlarges the question of the relationship between speciation and chromosomes.

According to our study, less than 3/4 of species possess a unique karyotype. Among Papioninae, 17 species belonging to Papio, Macaca and Cercocebus share between them only 3 karyotypes, and 10 species have the same one. On the other hand, among the Cercopithecinae, the most closely related sub-family, nearly all of the 14 species studied possess their own karyotypes, and differences can

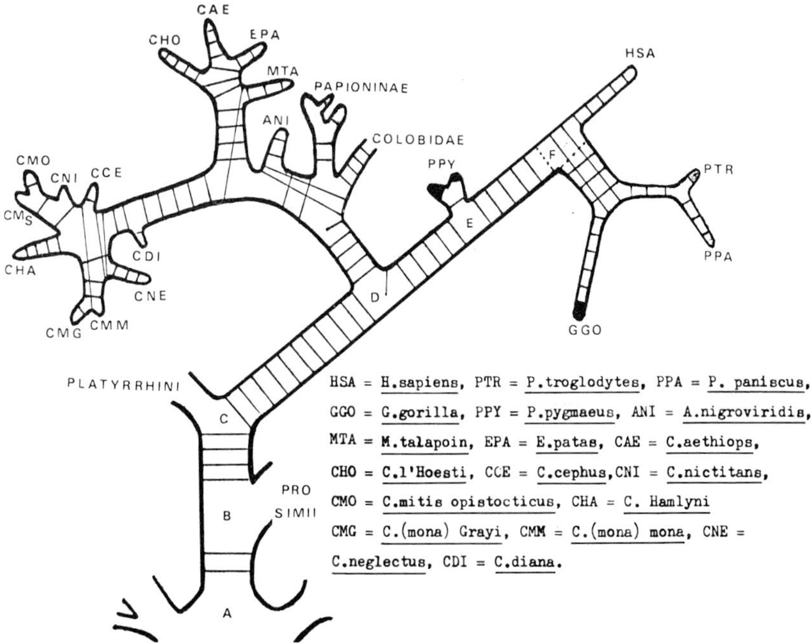

Figure 3: Chromosomal phylogeny of Catarrhini. Each line indicates a structural rearrangement.

be observed at the level of their sub-species. This clearly indicates that, over the same period of time, the speciation process has given two equal-sized groups of species independently of the number of the chromosomal changes accumulated by each group.

However, it cannot be concluded that chromosomal mechanisms are not involved in speciation, the situation of the Cercopithecoidae not being representative of that of the whole order of primates. In our opinion, each case must be considered apart, but also in the general context of evolution.

Figure 4 shows another representation of the phylogeny of the primates, which has been simplified in some respects, where the types of rearrangements have been indicated, and where, in relation to Figure 3, lemurs have been added. The analysis of Figure 4

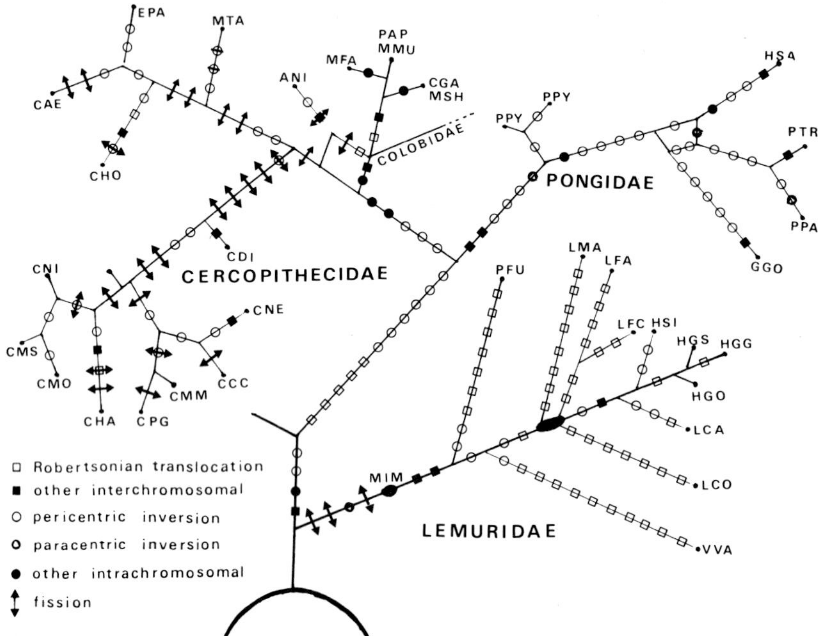

Figure 4: Simplified scheme indicating chromosomal changes. PFU = Phanerfurcifer, LMA = Lemur macaco, LFF = L. fulvus fulvus, LFC = L.f. collaris, LFA = L.f. albocollaris, LCO = L. coronatus, LCA = L. catta, VVA = Varecia variegata, HSI = Hapalemur simus, HGG = H. griseus griseus, HGO = H. g. occidentalis, HGS = H.g. spec., MFA = Macaca fascicularis, MMU = M. mulatta, PAP = Papio papio, CGA = Cercocebus galeritus, MSH = Mandrillus sphinx. Other three-letter codes are given in Fig. 3.

clearly indicates that rearrangements do not occur at random. Many Robertsonian translocations have occurred in the Lemurs. many fissions in the Cercopithecoidae, and many inversions in the Pongidae and in man's ancestors. This fact must be explained by a differential selection, by a differential mutagenesis, or by both of these.

As the reconstructed rearrangements have occurred in ancestral species for which reproductive behaviour, population dynamics, and sensitivity to mutagens cannot be tested, the only possibility is to consider living species, although this is not entirely satisfactory. Furthermore, the only species for which population cytogenics is informative at present is man, and caution must be used for any generalisation. Nevertheless, human data shows that Robertsonian and reciprocal translocations are the rearrangements most frequently observed in populations (1 per 1000 for each, in new-borns) while pericentric inversions are more rare (1 per 10,000 new-borns) (Hamerton et al 1975). Thus, most of the translocations seem to have been eliminated from the speciation process, leading to an almost exclusive accumulation of the pericentric inversions.

If we focus on this class of rearrangements, it is interesting to compare those which occurred during evolution, and those detected in human population. It appears that many abnormal chromosomes in man reproduce monkey chromosomes. It is too early to give the frequency of this phenomenon of resemblance, but the simple fact that several identical elements have been observed in two small samples is highly suggestive, particularly when we consider that the number of possibilities for making inversions at random is theoretically very large. Usually the rearrangements observed at the heterozygote status in man reproduce elements that were considered as ancestral. They can be regarded as reverse mutations. But convergent mutations, making the mutant human chromosomes look like more differentiated chromosomes of another species, are also observed. Figure 5 shows examples of such mutations.

Finally, it can be concluded that the breakpoints leading to inversions tend to be similar, both in evolution and in human pathology even if the relative frequencies are not the same. This is rather surprising, since the two sets of data are theoretically biased, due to the effect of a strong selection acting in somewhat

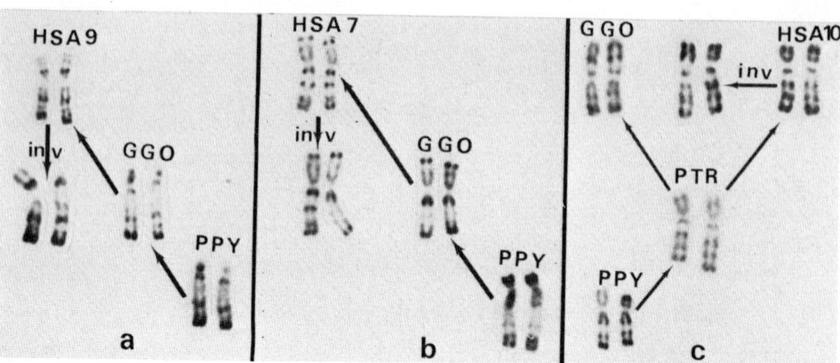

Figure 5: a and b. Reverse mutations. The human heterozygote carriers (HSA) possess a derivative chromosome, after pericentric or paracentric inversion, similar to the ancestral element still observed in other species (GGO = gorilla, PTR = chimpanzee, PPY = orang-utan). c. Convergent mutation. The normal human chromosome 10 identical to that of chimpanzee, is ancestral, as regards to its equivalent in gorilla, which has undergone a pericentric inversion. The same inversion is observed in a heterozygote carrier.

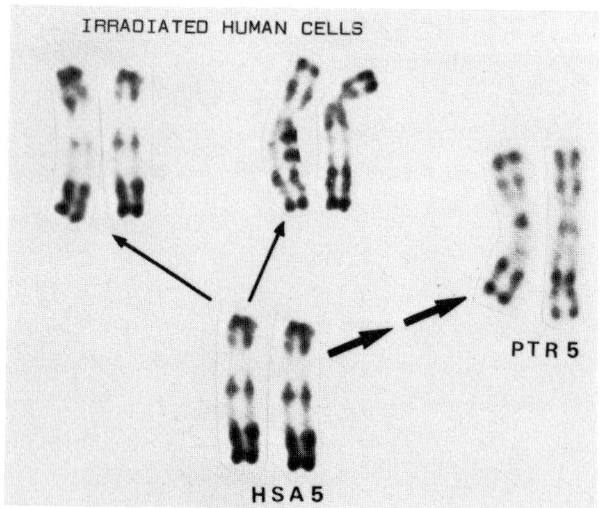

Figure 6: Radio-induced pericentric inversions of human chromosome 5 reproducing the equivalent chromosome in chimpanzee (PTR 5).

opposite directions: evolution should have maintained non-deleterious changes, while most of the inversions observed in humans were ascertained through abnormal probands and should confer a selective disadvantage.

Thus, the following hypothesis can be proposed: the chromosomal rearrangements result from a limited number of possibilities, which explains why the same mutant chromosomes tend to be observed in various samples even after selection. For instance, it can be postulated that in a given chromosome a dozen points only are able to exchange. If this is the case, many intrachromosomal changes like inversions should be similar.

This hypothesis is being tested by an experiment on cell irradiation of human lymphocytes and an analysis of the induced pericentric inversions. For the moment, only 50 pericentric inversions have been collected, which does not permit valuable statistical analysis, but the results are highly suggestive. For instance, two inversions affect chromosome 5; they result from the same break-points, although they are observed in independent experiments (Fig.6); and furthermore, the derivative chromosomes look identical to the chimpanzee equivalent of human chromosome 5. This is a typical case of radio-induced convergent mutation. The same observation was made with chromosome 10, with an inversion reproducing the equivalent chromosome 10 in Gorilla, and also an inversion previously observed in pathology (Fig.5).

In these experiments, the mitoses were collected between the first and the fourth or fifth cell cycle after irradiation. A cellular selection cannot be excluded, but even if this exists, it must be very limited in comparison with the selection at the level of living individuals, or at the level of evolution, and it is logical to consider that the anomalies detected here reflect the chromosomal mutagenesis rather well. Thus our hypothesis of limited possibilities of chromosome mutations seems credible, and experiments are being pursued to demonstrate it significantly.

Coming back to Figure 4, another argument for the non-random nature of the rearrangements is afforded by their distribution, and a complementary hypothesis can be formulated. The non-random distribution of the types of rearrangements (inversions, fusions, fissions) may also result from the fact that the types of mutation are determined, or predetermined, by the genetic constitution transmitted by the ancestral species.

Another assay of irradiation was started on a Cercopithecus (C. cephus), because many fissions have occurred during the evolution of this genus. On the other hand, fissions are never observed in irradiated human cells, and have been reported only exceptionally elsewhere. Our preliminary results indicate that fissions can be radio-induced in C. cephus fibroblasts, and can lead to the formation of two derivative chromosomes with apparently active centromeres. Figure 7 shows two independent cases of fission of chromosomes equivalent to human chromosome 4 (HSA 4). C. cephus possesses this chromosome in its entirety, differing from HSA 4 by one or two pericentric inversions. This chromosome is the largest of its karyotype, being one of the few large elements which have not undergone fission. At least 3 different fissions of this chromosome were observed after irradiation. One of them (upper row

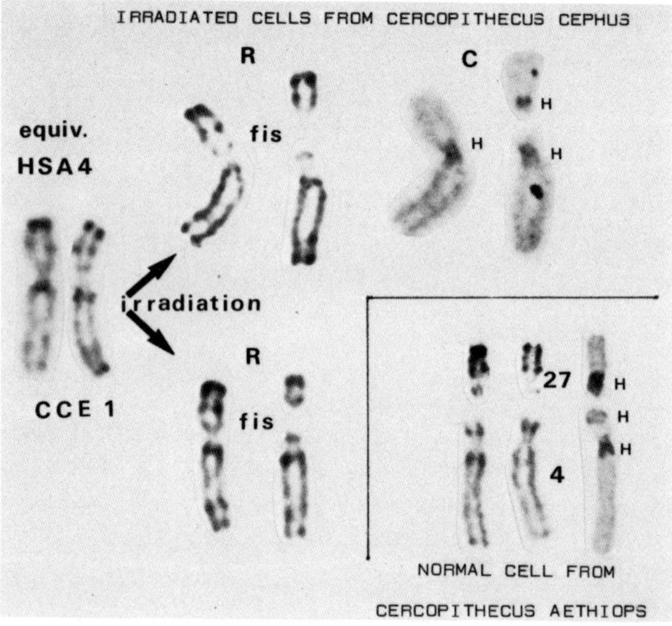

Figure 7: Radioinduced fissions (fis) of chromosome equivalent to HSA in Cercopithecus cephus (CCE 1), in R- and C- banding. The fission of the upper row makes derivative chromosomes very similar to the equivalent elements (4 and 27) in C. aethiops. H = C-band positive heterochromatin.

in Fig.7) reproduces exactly the chromosomes of C. aethiops, another Cercopithecus which has undergone a fission of the equivalent of HSA 4 during evolution (Dutrillaux 1979b). C-banding is positive in the two new chromosomes. Experiments are in progress to confirm these findings. This could give valuable information for the understanding of heterochromatin modifications, on the existence of potential intercalary centromeres, and other chromosomal mechanisms.

Our preliminary results are thus in favour of the genetic constitution having a role in the induction of rearrangements, and this leads us to reconsider the possible role of chromosomes in the speciation process: their modification appears to be partially a consequence of genic mutations. When such a mutation is acquired by a given ancestor, chromosomal evolution will then follow a certain specialisation and the karyotypes will become characteristic in descendant species, making the gametic barrier highly efficient between one group and another.

Finally, in spite of the role of selection, which should conceal mutagenesis, it may not be so unrealistic to compare rearrangements which occurred during evolution with those occurring now, finding many similarities. We hope that this work on comparative cytogenetics will shed some light on the understanding of the fundamental question in cytogenetics: what is a chromosomal change?

REFERENCES

Bobrow, M. and Madan, K. 1973. A comparison of chimpanzee and human chromosomes, using the Giemsa-11 and other chromosome banding techniques. Cytogenet. Cell Genet. 12, 107-116.

Chiarelli, B. 1961. Chromosomes of the orang-utan (Pongo pygmaeus). Nature, 192, 285.

Chu, E.H.Y. and Bender, M.A. 1962. Cytogenetics and evolution of primates. Ann. N.Y. Acad. Sci. 102, 253-266.

Creau-Goldberg, N., Cochet, C., Turleau, C., Finaz, C., Grouchy, J de 1980. Comparative gene mapping of man and Cebus capucinus for PGD, Eno, PGM 1, PGM 2, and SOD 1. Cytogenet. Cell Genet. In press.

Dutrillaux, B. 1975. Sur la Nature et l'Origine des Chromosomes humains. Expansion, Paris.

Dutrillaux, B. 1979a. Very large analogy of chromosome banding between Cebus capucinus (Platyrrhini) and man. Cytogenet. Cell Genet. 24, 84-98.

Dutrillaux, B. 1979b. Chromosomal evolution in primates; tentative phylogeny, from Microcebus murinus (Prosimian) to man. Hum. Genet. 48, 251-314.

Dutrillaux, B., Rethore, M.O., Prieur, M. and Lejeune, J. 1973. Analyse de la structure fine des chromosomes du Gorille (Gorilla gorilla). Comparaison avec Homo sapiens et Pan troglodytes. Humangenetik 20, 347-354.

Dutrillaux, B., Viegas-Pequignot, E., Couturier, J. and Chauvier, G. 1978a. Identity of euchromatic bands from man to Cercopithecidae (Cercopithecus aethiops, Cercopithecus sabaeus, Erythrocebus patas, Miopithecus talapoin). Hum. Genet. 45, 283-296.

Dutrillaux, B., Viegas-Pequignot, E., Dubos, C. and Masse, R. 1978b Complete or almost complete analogy of chromosome banding between the baboon (Papio papio)and man. Hum. Genet. 43, 37-46.

Dutrillaux, B., Couturier, J., Fosse, A-M. 1980a. The use of high resolution banding in comparative cytogenetics: comparison between man and Lagothrix lagotricha (Cebidae). Cytogenet. Cell Genet. 27, 45-51.

Dutrillaux, B., Viegas-Pequignot, E. and Couturier, J. 1980b. Tres grande analogie de marquage chromosomique entre le lapin (Oryctolagus cuniculus) et les primates dont l'homme. Ann. Genet. 23, 22-25.

Garver, J.J., Estop, A., Pearson, P.L., Dijkman, T.M., Wijnen, L.M.M. Meera Khan, P. L977. Comparative gene mapping in the Pongidea and Cercopithecoidea. Chromosomes Today, Vol.6, Chapelle, A. de la,Sorsa, M. (eds), pp.191-199. Amsterdam: Elsevier/North Holland Biomedical Press.

Grouchy, J. de, Finaz, C., Nguyen van Cong. 1977. Comparative banding and gene mapping in primates evolution. Evolution of chromosome 1 during fifty million years. Chromosomes Today, Vol.6, Chapelle, A de la, Sorsa, M. (eds), pp.183-190. Amsterdam, Elsevier/North Holland Biomedical Press.

Hamerton, J.L., Fraccaro, L., de Carli, L., Nuzzo, F., Klinger, H.P., Hullinger, L., Taylor, A. and Lang, E.M. 1961. Somatic chromosomes of the gorilla. Nature 192, 225-228.

Hamerton, J.L., Canning, N., Ray, M., Smith, S. 1975. A cytogenetic survey of 14,069 new-born infants. I. Incidence of chromosome abnormalities. Clin. Genet. 8, 223-243.

Hsu, T.C., Bernirschke, K. 1967-1977. Mammalian chromosome atlas. New York, Springer.

Jalal, S.M., Clark, R.W., Hsu, T.C. and Pathak, S. 1974. Cytological differentiation of constitutive heterochromatin. Chromosoma, 48, 391-403.

Lejeune, J., Dutrillaux, B., Rethore, M.O.and Prieur, M. 1973. Comparaison de la structure fine de chromatides d'Homo sapiens et de Pan troglodytes. Chromosoma 43, 423-444.

Pearson, P.L. 1973. The uniqueness of the human karyotype. Chromosome Identification Techniques and Application in Biology and Medicine, pp.145-151. Eds. T. Carpersson and L. Zech. Academic Press, New York.

Turleau,C., de Grouchy, J., and Klein, M. 1972. Phylogenie chromosomique de l'homme et des primates hominiens (Pan troglodytes, Gorilla gorilla and Pongo pygmaeus) essai de reconstitution du caryotype de l'ancetre commun. Ann. Genet. 15, 225-240.

Viegas-Pequignot, E., Couturier, J., Dutrillaux, B. 1978. Comparison of DNA-replication chronology in chromosomes of chimpanzee and man. Primates 19, 209-213.

Warburton, D., Firschein, I.L., Miller, D.A. and Warburton, F.E. 1973. Karyotype of the chimpanzee, Pan troglodytes based on measurements and banding patterns: comparison to the human karyotype. Cytogenet. Cell Genet. 12, 453-461.

Yunis, J.J., Sawyer, J.R., Dunham, K. 1980. The striking resemblance of high-resolution G-banded chromosomes of man and chimpanzee. Science, 208, 1145-1148.

CHROMOSOMES AND PLANT BREEDING

Chromosome manipulation in wheat

C. N. Law

Plant Breeding Institute, Trumpington, Cambridge

The allohexaploid bread wheat of agriculture, Triticum aestivum (2n=6x=42), is composed of three sets of 14 chromosomes. Each set or genome is descended from a diploid species, the three diploid donor species in their turn being related to a common ancestral diploid. Thus, although each wheat genome is distinct in the sense that strict homologous chromosome pairing takes place at meiosis in wheat, the chromosomes of each genome are genetically related and there is ample evidence that identical loci occur in each of the genomes. This triplication of genetic information permits the loss of or increased dosage of whole chromosomes or chromosome arms without drastically reducing the viability of the wheat plant. These aneuploid types have been assembled over the years for each of the 21 chromosomes of wheat.

Aneuploids have been used to classify the genomic origins of each chromosome as well as to define the genetical relationships between the chromosomes of each genome. This has led to a further classification of wheat chromosomes (Sears, 1954, 1966) into seven genetically similar or homoeologous groups, each having three chromosomes and each having one representative from each of the genomes (see Table 1).

By far the greatest usage of these aneuploids has been in the development and exploitation of a now extensive methodology which permits the manipulation of chromosomes either between different wheat varieties or between wheat and related species. These methods provide a means of performing genetical analyses and of transferring whole or parts of chromosomes which carry genes of importance in plant breeding.

TABLE 1. The chromosome classification of hexaploid wheat, *Triticum aestivum*.

		Genomes		
		A	B	D
	1	1A	1B	1D
	2	2A	2B	2D
Homoeol-	3	3A	3B	3D
ogous	4	4A	4B	4D
groups.	5	5A	5B	5D
	6	6A	6B	6D
	7	7A	7B	7D

The relatively recent applications of chromosome banding techniques in wheat cytogenetics, as well as the use of DNA probes by *in situ* hybridisation have yet to be used directly in the chromosome manipulation of wheat. Their success in identifying wheat chromosomes and chromosomes from related species (Singh and Röbbelen, 1975; May and Appels, 1980; Miller, Gerlach and Flavell, 1980) suggest that they will have an important role in chromosome manipulation in the future.

Chromosome addition and substitution lines.

Although aneuploid methods are used to study the genetics of wheat by transferring chromosomes from one wheat variety into another (Sears, 1953; Law and Worland, 1973), perhaps the greatest impact of these methods has been in the transfer of useful genes from related species into wheat. Alien chromosome addition lines in which single pairs of homologous chromosomes from a related species are added to wheat were first produced by O'Mara (1940) who succeeded in adding rye (*Secale cereale*) chromosomes to wheat by backcrossing a wheat-rye hybrid (*Triticale*) to wheat. Since that time chromosome addition lines have been obtained from a range of alien species and include other examples of *Secale cereale* (Riley and Chapman, 1958; Jenkins, 1966), *Secale montanum* (Riley, Chapman and Miller, 1973), *Aegilops umbellulata* (Sears, 1956; Kimber, 1967), *Aegilops comosa* (Riley, Chapman and Johnson, 1968), *Agropyron elongatum* (Dvorak and Knott, 1974) and

Agropyron intermedium (Wienhues, 1963; Cauderon, 1977), and more recently cultivated barley, *Hordeum vulgare* (Islam, Shepherd and Sparrow, 1978) and *Hordeum chilense* (Chapman and Miller, 1978).

In most instances, the development of these addition series was prompted by the possibility of introducing desirable genes from the alien species into wheat, or by the desire to unravel the chromosomal genetics of the alien species itself. In terms of their direct value to plant breeding, chromosome addition lines have been a failure since without exception they have proved to be chromosomally unstable and the addition line rapidly reverts to the recipient variety. They are important however in providing information about the genetic potential of the added chromosome as well as providing a starting point for chromosome substitution and translocation.

The development of alien chromosome substitution lines depends upon the availability of wheat aneuploids, particularly monosomics. Early on in the development of substitution lines it was found that most alien chromosomes could only be substituted for the three wheat chromosomes of a homoeologous group (Riley and Kimber, 1966). In such substitution lines, the alien chromosome compensated for the genetical activities of the wheat chromosome to produce vigorous plants. Attempts to substitute outside this group failed. A classification of homoeology between wheat and alien chromosomes has therefore been assembled, so that it is now possible to state the genetical relationship between wheat chromosomes and most rye chromosomes, most chromosomes of *Ae. umbellulata*, several *Agropyron* and barley chromosomes. The chromosome classification of wheat is therefore being extended gradually to many members of the tribe *Triticeae*.

In terms of their contribution to wheat breeding, alien chromosome substitution lines are a much better prospect than addition lines if only because of their increased chromosome stability. However, no directed alien chromosome substitution line has achieved the status of a commercial variety. This is because in all examples studied, the alien chromosomes carry genes whose adverse effects on the plant phenotype outweigh the advantages of the useful genes being transferred. This has led to the development of techniques which transfer only parts of an alien chromosome.

However, before moving on to describe these, it should be noted that the triplication of genes in wheat does permit the selection of backgrounds having genes which compensate for or mask the effects of deleterious genes carried by an alien chromosome. This approach has not been tried, although it is known now that several spontaneous rye chromosome substitutions have been unwittingly selected by breeders in the past, presumably following natural outcrossing to the wheat-rye hybrid, *Triticale*. Some of these alien introductions have been released as varieties commercially (Zeller, 1973).

Induced translocations.

The transfer of a small segment of an alien chromosome carrying a desirable gene was first accomplished by Sears (1956) who selected a translocated chromosome carrying a gene for resistance to leaf-rust following irradiation of a wheat plant possessing an iso-chromosome of *Ae. umbellulata* (2n=14). Several other workers have introduced single genes for disease resistance using this method (Table 2). As might have been expected, all the successful induced translocations have involved homoeologous chromosomes only.

A more precise and conceptually more satisfying solution to the transfer of alien genes into wheat evolved from the discovery that the strict homologous chromosome pairing that occurs in hexaploid wheat arose from the activities of a gene, *Ph*, on chromosome 5B which suppresses meiotic chromosome pairing between homoeologues (Riley and Chapman, 1958; Sears and Okamoto, 1958). Removal of 5B using aneuploids or suppressing the activities of the gene by hybridising with an appropriate alien species results in pairing and recombination between homoeologues but more importantly between wheat chromosomes and their homoeologues from an alien species. In this way desirable genes from these species can be introduced directly into wheat.

The first example of this type of transfer was carried out by Riley *et al.* (1968) using an addition line of chromosome 2M of *Ae. comosa* carrying a gene *Yr8* for yellow-rust resistance. They succeeded in obtaining a translocated chromosome composed of a

TABLE 2. Genes for disease resistance introduced into wheat from related species using chromosome engineering techniques.

Disease	Gene	Chromosome location	Source	Method	Workers
Leaf-rust	Lr9 (Transfer)	6B	*Aegilops umbellulata* (2n = 14)	Irradiation	Sears (1956)
Stem-rust	Sr26	6A	*Agropyron elongatum* (2n = 70)	Irradiation	Knott (1964)
Leaf-rust and stem-rust	Lr19, Sr25 (Agatha)	7D	*Agropyron elongatum* (2n = 70)	Irradiation	Sharma & Knott (1966)
Leaf-rust, stem-rust and yellow-rust		7A	*Agropyron intermedium* (2n = 14)	Irradiation	Wienhues (1973)
Leaf-rust and mildew	Lr25, Pm7 (Transec)	4A	*Secale cereale* (2n = 14)	Irradiation	Driscoll and Jensen (1965)
Yellow-rust	Yr8 (Compair)	2D	*Aegilops comosa* (2n = 14)	Homoeologous pairing	Riley, Chapman and Johnson (1968)
Leaf-rust and stem-rust	Lr19, Sr25	7D	*Agropyron elongatum* (2n = 70)	Homoeologous pairing	Sears (1973)
Leaf-rust and stem-rust	Lr24, Sr24	3D	*Agropyron elongatum* (2n = 70)	Homoeologous pairing	Sears (1973)
Leaf-rust	Lr24 (Agent)		*Agropyron elongatum* (2n = 70)	Spontaneous translocation	Smith, Schlehuber, Young and Edwards (1978)
Eye-spot		7D	*Aegilops ventricosa* (2n = 28)		Dosba and Doussinault (1977)

part of 2M with *Yr8* and part of 2D. More recent uses of this technique to transfer genes by inducing homoeologous recombination are described in Table 2.

Some of these transferred alien genes have been exploited in wheat breeding. The gene *Sr26* for stem-rust resistance from *Ag. elongatum* (Knott, 1964) has been used in Australia and occurs in a number of commercial varieties. *Lr9* for leaf-rust resistance from *Ae. umbellulata* has been exploited in the United States in the development of the variety Riley 67. In the case of *Yr8* for yellow-rust resistance obtained from *Ae. comosa* (Riley *et al.*, 1968), its incorporation into wheat coincided with yellow-rust epidemics in the U.K. arising from rapid genetical changes in the pathogen population in response to the release of varieties carrying specific genes for resistance. The use of such genes as *Yr8* was therefore discouraged at that time and *Yr8* has yet to be used effectively in any wheat breeding programme.

Despite the ability to induce recombination between alien and wheat chromosomes, the problem of close linkage between desirable and undesirable genes still occurs. An example of this is the association between leaf- and stem-rust resistance and an undesirable yellow flour colour in an *Ag. elongatum* translocation with chromosome 7D of wheat (Sharma and Knott, 1966; Dvorak, 1975). Attempts to break this linkage have failed either because the genes are physically close together or crossing-over between the *Agropyron* chromosome and its wheat homoeologue is localised. However, recent attempts to mutate the gene using EMS have proved successful (Knott, personal communication).

Limitations to the use of the 5B technique also occur in attempts to transfer genes from the more distant relatives of wheat such as rye. The frequency of homoeologous pairing between rye and wheat chromosomes is very low and for some chromosomes is probably zero. It is possible that this barrier may be overcome by the exploitation of genes other than *Ph* which affect homoeologous pairing (Mellor-Sampayo, 1971), or by increasing the dosage of genes affecting pairing (Miller and Riley, 1972), or from the use of environmental agencies. For the time being, however, transfer from these species will probably depend upon the use of irradiation techniques, and the selection of spontaneous translocations of whole chromosome arms resulting from rare centric fusions that can occur in plants simultaneously hemizygous for a wheat and an alien chromosome (Sears, 1972).

The problem of choosing genes for transfer.

The majority of transfers described in Table 2 refer to genes having qualitative effects on disease resistance. This is not surprising since these genes, besides being important in breeding, are readily recognisable so that it is possible to follow their passage through a complex hybridisation programme.

The choice of other genes is more difficult and underlines one of the major problems of the plant chromosome engineer and that is the need to recognise easily those genes which have sufficiently large and useful effects on a plant phenotype as to make their transfer worthwhile. Indeed, this is almost certainly going to be an equal if not greater problem when the molecular genetic engineer arrives at the position where transfers can be made.

In wheat, apart from the genes for disease resistance, only one other potentially useful set of easily identifiable genes is open to consideration at the moment. These are the genes controlling the endosperm proteins which influence the baking and nutritional properties of bread. In UK wheats and possibly other wheats there is a positive correlation between bread-making quality and the presence of high molecular weight (HMW) glutenin proteins (Payne, Corfield and Blackman, 1979). A survey of these proteins amongst hexaploid wheats showed that the largest glutenins were those having MW between 100,000 to 140,000. In no instance, were proteins larger than this found. However, in another survey carried out in the genus *Aegilops* (Harris, Payne and Law, 1981) glutenins having larger MW were identified. In the case of one of these species, *Ae. umbellulata*, the chromosome carrying the genes for some of these HMW glutenins has been substituted for homoeologous group 1 chromosomes of wheat, the group known to carry the structural genes for glutenin (Payne, Law and Mudd, 1980). It should therefore be possible to transfer the genes responsible for these HMW glutenins into wheat using the techniques of induced homoeologous recombination and then to study the consequences of such changes on bread-making.

Apart from these two classes of genes it is not immediately obvious what other readily identifiable genes having desirable attributes are available for transfer. Undoubtedly, many of the relatives of wheat possess properties which could be useful in breeding improved wheats. Examples of such features might include increased photosynthetic activity, resistance to freezing and drought, tolerance of salt and various minerals, insect resistance and so on. The genetics of these characters are not understood and the means of assessing them are often quantitative and time consuming. In some instances, it is likely that the characters are polygenically controlled so that their transfer will be a formidable if not an impossible task.

One approach to the transfer of the genes affecting such characters is to select amongst the backcross derivatives of an intergeneric hybrid deficient for chromosome 5B. This was carried out by Riley (1966) who was successful in producing lines having high yields from a cross between the low yielding wheat variety Holdfast and *Aegilops bicornis*. Further attempts to use this method have however proved disappointing, since the initial recombinant derivatives are often so feeble that only a few plants survive and provide too narrow a genetic base for subsequent selection. Interest has therefore turned to a more systematic approach where the initial material is a promising chromosome addition or substitution line. A good example of this approach is the introduction of higher grain protein levels into wheat.

The study of grain protein variation caused by alien chromosomes related to homoeologous group 2 of wheat

Alien chromosome substitution lines in the variety Chinese Spring (CS) in which each of the chromosomes of homoeologous group 2 had been replaced by either chromosome 2M from *Ae. comosa*, or chromosome $2C^u$ from *Ae. umbellulata*, or chromosome $2R^m$ from *S. montanum*, were assessed for grain protein amount (Table 3). Analysis of the results indicated that chromosome 2A produced a greater amount of protein than 2B, followed by 2M, $2C^u$, 2D and $2R^m$ (Law *et al.*, 1977). Thus, only the substitution of 2M for 2D in CS gave increased levels of grain protein compared with CS. This result illustrates the rather obvious point that the consequences of substituting an alien chromosome are not only dependent upon the alien chromosome being substituted but also the relative magnitudes of the effects of the chromosomes being replaced. For homoeologous transfers three sites and, as the results from the group 2 alien chromosome substitutions indicate, three different

TABLE 3. Total grain protein (gms) produced per plant amongst alien chromosome substitution lines of homoeologous group 2 in the varieties Chinese Spring, Maris Widgeon and Rothwell Perdix (Law, Worland, Chapman and Miller, 1977).

Chinese Spring (CS)	1.22
CS 2A (2M)	1.11
CS 2B (2M)	1.17
CS 2D (2M)	1.45*
CS 2A ($2C^u$)	0.67*
CS 2B ($2C^u$)	1.19
CS 2D ($2C^u$)	1.22
CS 2A ($2R^m$)	0.39*
CS 2D ($2R^m$)	0.47*
† Maris Widgeon	50.2
Maris Widgeon translocation 2D/2M	53.8*
† Rothwell Perdix	49.9
Rothwell Perdix 2D (2M)	53.1*

Substitution for CS 2A by 2M is denoted as CS 2A (2M) and so on for the other substitution lines.

* Significantly different from recipient variety

† Data based on plots rather than single plants.

phenotypes are possible. To know something about the variation between the homoeologues of a wheat variety could therefore be crucial to achieving the successful transfer of alien genes.

Although it would seem unlikely that the group 2 homoeologous variation of CS should be found in other varieties, 2M substitutions for 2D and a translocation between 2M and 2D have been produced in the UK varieties Maris Widgeon and Rothwell Perdix and have also been found to produce higher grain protein amounts (Table 3). It is possible therefore that the variation between these chromosomes may have been genetically conserved and the substitution of 2M for 2D would produce similar results irrespective of the recipient variety. The extent of the variation within hexaploid wheats would suggest however that such a result is more likely to be the exception rather than the rule.

Conclusions

The methods of chromosome manipulation in wheat have achieved a high level of sophistication. Given the ability to produce fertile hybrids then there is no major barrier to the transfer of useful chromosomes to wheat. In the case of rye and probably barley and even more distant relatives of wheat, barriers to homoeologous chromosome pairing and recombination exist and there is a need for a greater understanding of the processes controlling chromosome behaviour between these species. However, a wealth of 'useful' genetic variation undoubtedly exists in the more closely related species where restrictions to homoeologous chromosome pairing and recombination do not occur. Here, it is the lack of understanding of the genetics of the characters of interest in plant breeding which is the major hindrance. How many genes are involved and how to identify those which are important, are the questions that need to be answered if the methods of chromosome manipulation are to be used widely in wheat breeding. But these questions are after all those basic to plant breeding itself and their answer can only come about from the joint endeavours of both geneticists and physiologists as well as those in related disciplines in studying wheat and other crop plants.

REFERENCES

Cauderon, Y. 1977. Alloploidy. In Interspecific Hybridisation in Plant Breeding, Proc. 8th Eucarpia Congress, Madrid, Spain, 131-143.

Chapman, V. and Miller, T.E. 1978. Alien chromosome addition and substitution lines. Plant Breeding Institute, Cambridge, Annual Report: 124-125.

Dosba, F. and Doussinault, G. 1977. Introduction into wheat of the resistance to eyespot in *Aegilops ventricosa*. In Interspecific Hybridisation in Plant Breeding, Proc. 8th Eucarpia Congress, Madrid, Spain, 99-107.

Driscoll, C.J. and Jensen, N.F. 1965. Release of a wheat-rye translocation stock involving leaf-rust and powdery mildew resistances. Crop Sci. 5, 279-280.

Dvorak, J. 1975. Meiotic pairing between single chromosomes of diploid *Agropyron elongatum* and decaploid *A. elongatum* in *Triticum aestivum*. Can. J. Genet. Cytol. 17, 329-336.

Dvorak, J. and Knott, D.R. 1974. Disomic and ditelosomic additions of diploid *Agropyron elongatum* chromosomes to *Triticum aestivum*. Can. J. Genet. Cytol. 16, 399-417.

Harris, P.A., Payne, P. I. and Law, C. N. 1981. Variation for High Molecular Weight grain protein sub-units among species of *Triticum* and *Aegilops* (In preparation).

Islam, A. K. M. R., Shepherd, R. W. and Sparrow, D. H. B. 1978. Production and characterisation of wheat-barley addition lines. Proc. 5th Int. Wheat Genet. Symp. New Delhi, India, 365-371.

Jenkins, B. C. 1966. *Secale* additions and substitutions to common wheat. Proc. 2nd Int. Wheat Genet. Symp., Lund, Sweden. 301-310.

Kimber, G. 1967. The addition of the chromosomes of *Aegilops umbellulata* to *Triticum aestivum* (var. Chinese Spring). Genet. Res. 9, 111-114.

Knott, D. R. 1964. The effect on wheat of an *Agropyron* chromosome carrying rust resistance. Can. J. Genet. Cytol. 6, 500-7.

Law, C. N. and Worland, A. J. 1973. Aneuploidy in wheat and its uses in genetic analysis. Plant Breeding Institute, Cambridge, Annual Report 1972, 25-65.

Law, C. N., Worland, A. J., Chapman, V. and Miller, T. E. 1977. Homoeologous chromosome transfers into hexaploid wheat and their influence on grain protein amounts. In *Interspecific Hybridisation in Plant Breeding*, Proc. 8th Eucarpia Congress, Madrid, Spain, 73-80.

O'Mara, J. G. 1940. Cytogenetic studies on *Triticale*. I. A method of determining the effect of individual *Secale* chromosomes on *Triticum*. Genetics, 25, 401-408.

May, C. E. and Appels, R. 1980. Rye chromosome translocations in hexaploid wheat: a re-evaluation of the loss of heterochromatin from rye chromosomes. Theor. Appl. Genet. 56, 17-23.

Mello-Sampayo, T. 1971. Genetic regulation of meiotic chromosome pairing by chromosome 3D of *Triticum aestivum*. Nature New Biology, 230, 23-24.

Miller, T. E. and Riley, R. 1972. Meiotic chromosome pairing in wheat-rye combinations. Genét. Ibér. 24, 1-10.

Miller, T.E., Gerlach, W. L. and Flavell, R. B. 1980. Nucleolus organiser variation in wheat and rye revealed by *in situ* hybridisation, Heredity, 45.

Payne, P. I., Law, C. N. and Mudd, E. E. 1980. Control by Homoeologous group 1 chromosomes of the High-Molecular-Weight Subunits of Glutenin, a major protein of wheat endosperm. Theor. Appl. Genet. 58, 113-120.

Riley, R. 1966. Cytogenetics and wheat breeding. Proc. 5th Yugoslav. Symp. on research in wheat, Novi Sad, 107-116.

Riley, R. and Kimber, G. 1966. The transfer of alien genetic variation to wheat. Plant Breeding Institute, Cambridge, Annual Report, 1964-65, 6-36.

Riley, R. and Chapman, V. 1958. Genetic control of the cytologically diploid behaviour of hexaploid wheat. Nature, 182, 713-715.

Riley, R., Chapman, V. and Johnson, R. 1968. Introduction of yellow-rust resistance of Aegilops comosa into wheat by genetically induced homoeologous recombination. Nature, 217, 383-384.

Riley, R., Chapman, V. and Miller, T. E. 1973. Alien chromosome additions and substitutions. Plant Breeding Institute, Cambridge, Annual Report, 143-144.

Sears, E. R. 1953. Nullisomic analysis in common wheat. Amer. Nat. 87, 245-252.

Sears. E.R. 1954. The aneuploids of common wheat. Missouri Agr. Exp. Sta. Res. Bull. 572, 59.

Sears, E. R. 1956. The transfer of leaf-rust resistance from Aegilops umbellulata to wheat. Brookhaven Symp. Biol. 9, 1-22.

Sears, E. R. 1966. Nullisomic-tetrasomic combinations in hexaploid wheat. In Chromosome Manipulations and Plant Genetics, ed. R. Riley and K. R. Lewis, suppl. Heredity 20, 29-45. Oliver and Boyd, Edinburgh.

Sears, E. R. 1972. Chromosome engineering in wheat. Stadler Symp. 4, 23-38, Columbia, Missouri.

Sears, E. R. 1973. Agropyron-wheat transfers induced by homoeologous pairing. Proc. 4th Int. Wheat Genet. Symp. Columbia, Missouri, 191-199.

Sears, E. R. and Okamoto, M. 1958. Intergenomic chromosome relationships in hexaploid wheat. Proc. 10th Int. Cong. Genet. Montreal, 258-259.

Sharma, D. and Knott, D. R. 1966. The transfer of leaf-rust resistance from Agropyron to Triticum by irradiation. Can. J. Genet. Cytol. 8, 137-143.

Singh, R. J. and Röbbelen, G. 1975. Comparison of Somatic Giemsa banding pattern in several species of rye. Z. Pflanzenzüchtg. 74, 270-285.

Smith, E. L., Schlehuber, A. M. and Edwards, L. H. 1978. Registration of Agent wheat. Crop Sci. 8, 511-512.

Weinhues, A. 1963. Transfer of rust resistance of Agropyron to wheat by addition, substitution and translocation. Proc. 2nd Int. Wheat Genet. Symp. Lund, Sweden, 328-340.

Wienhues, A. 1973. Translocations between wheat chromosomes and an Agropyron chromosome conditioning rust resistance. Proc. 4th Int. Wheat Genet. Symp, Columbia, Missouri, 20 -2

Zeller, F. 1973. 1B/1R wheat-rye chromosome substitutions and translocations. Proc. 4th Int. Wheat Genet. Symp., Columbia, Missouri, 209-221.

Plant cell hybrids and somatic hybrid plants

E. C. Cocking

Plant Genetic Manipulation Group, Department of Botany, University of Nottingham, Nottingham NG7 2RD

Only recently has another process become available for higher plants that can lead to genetic recombination. By manipulating somatic cells in such a way that their cell walls are removed and fusing their protoplasts, an alternative method of hybridisation to sexual hybridisation has been found to be possible. This process of somatic hybridisation is one of the several processes described by Haldane (1955) as "Alternatives to Sex". There is a basic difference between sexual hybridisation and somatic hybridisation in that in sexual hybridisation there is usually unilateral exclusion of the cytoplasm. No such exclusion normally exists in the case of somatic hybridisation, since both somatic cell protoplasts initially contribute more or less equally to the cytoplasmic status of the resultant somatic hybrid. Protoplast fusion therefore makes possible the fusion of two different cytoplasms, allowing genetic analysis of cytoplasmic factors.

Much interest centres on the analysis of nuclear and cytoplasmic behaviour in somatic hybrid cells, and in any plants regenerated from such cells and a comparison with the behaviour in any sexual hybrid counterpart. There is now a very extensive review literature on this general subject, the most recent being that of Vasil *et al*. 1979.

PLANT CELL HYBRIDS

Practical details of the various procedures involved in protoplast isolation and fusion to produce heterokaryons have been fully described previously (Cocking and Peberdy 1974). Although there is still considerable on-going work aimed at increasing the percentage of heterokaryons that can be obtained when protoplasts of different species are fused, it is clear that fusion itself is not a major incompatibility consideration. Usually approximately 1% heterokaryon formation can be obtained, and provided the cultural conditions are satisfactory, and provided an adequate selection pressure can be put on the system, hybrid callus (or hybrid embryoids) can be selected. Sometimes it is possible to select heterokaryons visually.

Kao (1977) studied chromosome behaviour in somatic hybrid callus cells resulting from the fusion of soybean and *Nicotiana glauca* protoplasts. Chromosomes of *N. glauca* which had a tendency to stick together and break into pieces, were randomly lost from the hybrid cells. Some of the *N. glauca* chromosomes were still present in the hybrid tissue after 6-7 months of culturing. Our own earlier studies on the consequence of fusion of *Parthenocissus* protoplasts with *Petunia* protoplasts indicated that a significant feature of the callus obtained, as a result of the selective culture of fused protoplasts, was that the callus was shown to possess the chromosomes of *Parthenocissus* only, yet showed iso-peroxidases of both *Parthenocissus* and *Petunia*. In discussing these results we noted that Schwartz *et al*. (1971) had obtained some evidence, after fusion of chick erythrocytes with cultured mouse cells, that a structural gene for check inosinic acid pyro-phosphorylase was incorporated into the mouse nucleus in some cells during post-mitotic reconstitution. We suggested that a similar happening could be occurring with plant protoplasts, as a result of which genes for Petunia isoperoxidases had become incorporated into the *Parthenocissus* nucleus. More recent studies on intergeneric cell hybrids have also resulted in the production of a significant reduction in the size of one parental genome introduced into the hybrids; and it has been suggested that fusion between dividing and mitotically inactive protoplasts accentuates the elimination process, and that irradiation of protoplasts of one of the parents may direct and accelerate genome elimination (Dudits *et al*. 1980). As recently discussed (Cocking 1980), there are often disadvantages in attempting to combine the total genetic structures of two species, and advantages in attempting to incorporate in the recipient species some limited, perhaps single, genetic attribute of a donor species. We are currently investigating whether such protoplast fusions could be used to transfer nitrate reductase genes between different species. We are utilising nitrate reductase minus mutants of tobacco, and fusing these with irradiated cereal, and legume protoplasts, and then selecting for nitrate reductase proficiency among the tobacco cells.

These studies on somatic hybrid cells are providing good evidence that selective chromosome transfer is possible. However, it is clear that we require a better knowledge of the control of plant chromosomal behaviour at the somatic hybrid cell level.

SOMATIC HYBRID PLANTS

Results obtained so far on the consequences of fusion of protoplasts have provided good evidence that, in many instances, fusions between those from sexually compatible species will result in the formation of heterokaryons in which both nuclear genomes are capable of forming stable amphiploid nuclear hybrids. Organogenesis from hybrid callus will then result in the regeneration of somatic hybrid plants with both sets of parental chromosomes. Total chromosome counts are most frequently used in these assessments since it is usually not possible in the genera most studied so far, such as *Datura*, *Nicotiana* and *Petunia*, to distinguish between the chromosomes of the parents.

As discussed by Smith and Mastrangelo-Hough (1979), regeneration of true-breeding somatically stable hybrid plants, frequently a major aim in interspecific cell fusions, can sometimes be hindered by pertubations in chromosome number in the hybrid cells. Our experience is that the use of protoplasts isolated directly from the plant, coupled with rapid plant regeneration, minimises these pertubation tendencies, which may be caused by conditions *in vitro*, hybridity itself, or a combination of both.

In our studies within the *Petunia* genus (Cocking 1979) we

have produced a high percentage of amphiploid somatic hybrid plants by fusing wild-type leaf protoplasts of one species with albino protoplasts from cell suspension cultures of the other species. This has resulted in the production of flowering plants, with 28 chromosomes, of the somatic hybrid *Petunia parodii* (2n=14) ⊗ *Petunia hybrida* (2n=14) and of *Petunia parodii* (2n=14) ⊗ *Petunia inflata* (2n=14). Whilst *P. parodii* and *P. hybrida* can be crossed sexually, it is known that *P. parodii* and *P. inflata* cannot be crossed sexually by the standard procedure, since they posses pre-zygotic unidirectional sexual incompatibilities.

Recently we have investigated the consequences of fusion of *Petunia parodii* leaf protoplasts with albino protoplasts from cell suspensions of *Petunia parviflora*. These two species are sexually incompatible probably due to both pre-zygotic and post-zygotic isolation mechanisms, and all previous attempts at sexual bybridisation have failed. Our somatic protoplast fusions have enabled us to produce somatic hybrid plants with 32 chromosomes, *P. parodii* (2n=14) ⊗ *P. parviflora* (2n=18) which are amphidiploids (4n=32), and some with 31 chromosomes (Power *et al*. 1980). Differences in size and morphology of the chromosomes of these two species have proved sufficient to enable us to establish the presence of both parental chromosome sets in the somatic hybrid nuclei.

The behaviour of the chromosomes in this novel somatic hybrid, for which no sexual hybrid counterpart exists, will now be of interest, particularly meiotic pairing considerations. Currently we are trying to determine using various treatments, including p-fluorophenylalanine, to see if we can induce random chromosome loss - a method so successfully employed in fungal studies by Pontecorvo and his colleagues. Thereby it may be possible to find out whether a complete parasexual cycle can operate for flowering plants analogous to that observed in certain of the fungi. We are also attempting to cross this novel somatic hybrid sexually with the other *Petunias*, particularly with *P. hybrida*. This combination of somatic and sexual genetics may enable us to produce a horticulturally useful hybrid combining the 'hanging basket' branching habit of *P. parviflora* with the attractive flower characteristics of *P. hybrida*.

In our recent Fraction-1 protein biochemical analysis of the somatic hybrid plant developed between *P. parodii* and *P. parviflora* (Kumar, Wilson and Cocking 1980), we have found the expression of only *P. parodii* chloroplasts. The reason seems to be because in this somatic hybridisation procedure we have used *P. parodii* protoplasts from wild type mesophyll cells, and *P. parviflora* protoplasts from albino callus. This observed unidirectional chloroplast segregation, when using albino mutants for selection, may be useful in controlling the direction of plastid genotype segregation in somatic hybrids, particularly as in this instance sexual hybridisation is not possible.

ACKNOWLEDGEMENTS

Original work on somatic hybridisation described in this review was supported by a grant from the Agricultural Research Council

REFERENCES

Cocking, E.C. 1979.Parasexual reproduction in flowering plants. *New Zealand Journal of Botany* 17, 665-71.

Cocking, E.C. 1980.Concluding remarks and outlook. In *Plant Cell Cultures: Results and perspectives*,F. Sala, B. Parisi, R. Cella and O. Ciferri, eds., 419-25. Elsevier/North-Holland Biomedical Press.

Cocking, E. C. and Peberdy, J. F. 1974.*The use of protoplasts from fungi and higher plants - a practical handbook*. Department of Botany, University of Nottingham.

Dudits, D., Hadlaczky, G., Lazar, G. and Haydu, Z. 1980.Increase in genetic variability through somatic hybridization of distantly related plant species. In *Plant Cell Cultures: Results and Perspectives*, F. Sala, B. Parisi, R. Cella and O. Ciferri, eds., 207-14. Elsevier/North-Holland Biomedical Press.

Haldane, J. B. S. 1955.Some alternatives to sex. In *New Biology* 19, M. L. Johnson, M. Abercrombie and G. E. Fogg, eds, 7-26. Penguin Books Ltd.

Kao, K. N. 1977.Chromosomal behaviour in somatic hybrids of soybean - *Nicotiana glauca*. *Molecular and General Genetics* 150, 225-30

Kumar, A., Wilson, D. and Cocking, E. C. Polypeptide composition of Fraction 1 protein of the somatic hybrid between *Petunia parodii* and *Petunia parviflora*. *Biochemical Genetics* (in press).

Power, J. B., Berry, S. F., Chapman, J. V. and Cocking, E. C. 1980.Somatic hybridization of sexually incompatible *Petunias*: *Petunia parodii*, *Petunia parviflora*. *Theoretical and Applied Genetics* 57, 1-4.

Schwartz, A. G., Cook, P. R. and Harris, H. 1971.Correction of a genetic defect in a mammalian cell. *Nature (New Biology)* 230 5-8.

Smith, H. H. and Mastrangelo-Hough, Iris A. 1979.Genetic variability available through cell fusion. In Plant Cell and Tissue Culture Principles and Applications, W. R. Sharp, P. O. Larsen, E. F. Paddock and V. Raghaven, eds., 265-86. Ohio State University Press, Columbus.

Vasil, I. K., Ahuja, M. R. and Vasil, V. 1979.Plant tissue cultures in genetics and plant breeding. Advances in Genetics 20, 127-215.

CHROMOSOMES AND MALIGNANT CHANGE

Inherited chromosome instability in man – abstract

D. G. Harnden

Department of Cancer Studies, University of Birmingham, Birmingham B15 2TT

There is always a low background level of spontaneous chromosome breakage and rearrangement in preparations of normal human cells and this remains fairly constant. Occasionally, there are inexplicably high levels in individual cultures of lymphocytes from normal subjects, but subsequent cultures show the normal pattern. In addition to the normal background, however, fibroblast cultures from normal subjects sometimes contain clones, which may be quite large, of cytogenetically abnormal cells (Harnden et al, 1976). The reason for this is not known.

Sometimes aberrations may be seen regularly at a specific site on a particular chromosome in a normal subject. These are, however, more likely to be related in mechanism to the specific chromosome gap seen in some patients with X-linked mental retardation than to any inherited instability of the chromosomes in general.

Chromosome aberrations in normal subjects may be found in some premalignant condition such as carcinoma-in-situ and in conditions where there is a strong association with malignancy such as polycythaemia rubra vera, but in these cases the abnormalities are usually confined to the involved tissue (Sandberg, 1980). In only one case, scleroderma, is there good evidence that chromosome abnormalities may be found regularly in a disease in which association with malignant disease is weak and where there is no clear mode of inheritance (Emerit et al, 1976).

Induced chromosome aberrations in normal subjects may be found following exposure to a number of different environmental agents. Radiation induced damage shows a remarkably constant and dose related pattern. Clones may emerge in peripheral lymphocytes of irradiated subjects, but usually after a long delay (Buckton et al, 1978). Chromosome aberrations may be induced by chemical substances following in vivo exposure, but the aberration levels are not usually high and dose response relationships hard to demonstrate for a variety of reasons (Evans and O'Riordan, 1977). Likewise, virus infection in vivo may produce chromosome aberrations, but these seem to be both inconsistent and transient (Harnden, 1974a).

Spontaneous inherited aberrations

Before concluding that spontaneous chromosome breakage is an integral part of an inherited syndrome it is important to be sure that none of the situations described above apply. For this reason xeroderma pigmentosum, basal cell naevus syndrome and porokeratosis of Mibelli should probably not be considered as 'chromosome breakage syndromes' since aberrations have been described only in cultured fibroblasts. In Werner's syndrome where aberrations are found only in fibroblasts the frequency is such that it must be considered a feature of the disease (Salk, 1980). Reports of chromosome aberrations in the X-linked dominant condition, incontinentia pigmenti, are not well documented. This means that there are only 3 clear cases of spontaneous inherited chromosome aberrations, Bloom's syndrome, Ataxia telangiectasia (AT), and Fanconi's anaemia. Each has a characteristic aberration pattern of aberrations though there is often considerable variation from patient to patient. In Bloom's syndrome there is an increase of several different types of aberrations, but in particular there is a remarkably high frequency of chromatid interchanges between homologous chromosomes (German, 1974). Sister chromatid exchanges are also more frequent than in controls. Fanconi's anaemia patients also have an increase in chromosome and chromatid aberrations, but they do now show the specific aberrations in Bloom's syndrome. They do, however, have a high frequency of non-homologous chromatid exchanges (Schroeder and German, 1974). In ataxia telangiectasia there is an increase in cells with dicentrics and with chromatid and chromosome gaps and breaks. In many of these patients large clones of cytogenetically marked cells are found in cultured lymphocytes; the chromosome rearrangement in these clones frequently involves the band 14q12 (Harnden, 1974b).

Inherited predisposition to induced chromosome aberrations

Patients with a number of different clinical syndromes are clearly unusually sensitive to some specific environmental agent (Hecht and Kaiser McCaw, 1977). In some of these there is as yet no clear indication of the cellular nature of this sensitivity, e.g. patients with basal cell naevus syndrome are clearly susceptible to the induction of basal cell carcinomas by ionising radiation (Strong, 1977), but there is no clear evidence that cells from these patients are sensitive to ionising radiation. The classical example is xeroderma pigmentosum where clinical sensitivity to UV light is accompanied by an unusual sensitivity to the induction of chromosome aberrations in cultured cells by UV light (Gianelli, 1976). They are also sensitive to chromosome damage and SCE induction by a range of chemicals. There is some evidence of sensitivity to induction of chromosome damage by UV in Fanconi's anaemia, Bloom's syndrome and Cockayne's syndrome, again reflecting a clinical sensitivity. However, cells from Fanconi patients are extremely sensitive to some drugs and chemicals, e.g. mitomycin and diepoxybutane, so it is not too surprising to find clinical evidence of unusual sensitivity in Fanconi patients to drugs such as cyclophosphamide. AT patients are clinically sensitive to X-rays and cells in culture from these patients are unusually sensitive to the induction of chromosome damage by X-rays. Certain types of aberration are elevated more than others and this suggests a defect which involves failure to repair single strand lesions before the cells enter S-phase (Taylor, 1978). Patients with retinoblastoma may be sensitive to the radiation induction of osteosarcoma. There have been reports of radiosensitivity as measured by cell killing of retinoblastoma cells in culture (Weichselbaum et al, 1978). These results, however, are not consistent. There is a little evidence that retinoblastoma cells are sensitive to the induction of chromosome aberrations by ionising radiation.

The mechanisms underlying the induction of aberrations are not always clear. In the case of xeroderma pigmentosum it seems probable that the defect of excision repair of DNA is related directly to the induction of chromosome aberrations. In AT there is recent evidence which suggests that failure of the normal mechanism which inhibits S-phase DNA synthesis after exposure to ionising radiation may be responsible for the occurrence of chromosome aberrations of specific types (Edwards and Taylor, 1980). In Fanconi's anaemia failure to repair DNA cross-links could be directly associated with the high induced levels of chromosome aberrations following exposure to bifunctional alkylating agents.

Relationships to cancer

All the conditions which show either inherited spontaneous chromosome aberrations or an inherited susceptibility to induced aberrations show an unusually high incidence of cancer (Harnden and Taylor, 1978, 1979). In the case of xeroderma pigmentosum the occurrence of skin cancers (and few others) correlates very well with the observed sensitivity to UV light, but does suggest that chemicals with a UV like mode of action are not important in cancer induction in these patients. In AT more cancers occur than would be expected and these are of several different types though a majority are lymphomas. This is not the pattern that one would expect from a simple increase in radiosensitivity and the mechanisms must therefore be complex. Fanconi's anaemia patients get a myeloid or myelomonocytic leukaemia and a few other cancers, but again there is no clear relationship between the occurrence of cancer and the observed pattern of cellular and chromosomal abnormalities. Patients with Bloom's syndrome get many different kinds of cancer though there is a preponderance of leukaemias and lymphomas. Mechanisms are again unknown.

Further study of these diseases at the cellular and molecular, as well as at the clinical level may provide insight into the relationships between chromosome aberrations and cancer.

REFERENCES

Buckton, K.E., Hamilton, G.E., Paton, L. and Langlands, A.O. Chromosome aberrations in irradiated ankylosing spondylitis patients. In Mutagen-induced Chromosome Damage in Man, H.J. Evans and D.G. Lloyd, eds. p.142. Edinburgh University Press.

Edwards, M.J. and Taylor, A.M.R. 1980 Unusual levels of (ADP-ribose) and DNA synthesis in ataxia telangiectasia cells following γ-ray irradiation. Nature (In press).

Emerit, I. 1976 Chromosomal breakage in systemic sclerosis and related disorders. Dermatologica, 153, 145-156.

Evans, H.J. and O'Riordan 1977 Human peripheral blood lymphocytes for the analysis of chromosome aberrations in mutagen tests. In Handbook of Mutagenicity Test Procedures, B.J. Kilby, M. Legatar, W. Nichols and C. Ramel, eds. p.261-274. Amsterdam, New York, Oxford Elsevier.

German, J. 1974 Bloom's syndrome. II. The prototype of human genetic disorders predisposing to chromosome instability and cancer. In Chromosomes and Cancer, J. German, ed. p.601-618. John Wiley & Sons, New York.

Gianelli, F. 1976 Xeroderma Pigmentosum. In Scientific Foundations of Oncology, T. Symington and R.L. Carter, eds. p.476. Heinemann, London.

Harnden, D.G. 1974a Viruses, chromosomes and tumours: The interation between viruses and chromosomes. In Chromosomes and Cancer, J. German, ed. J. Wiley, New York.

Harnden, D.G. 1974b Ataxia telangiectasia syndrome: cytogenetic and cancer aspects. In Chromosomes and Cancer, J. German, ed. John Wiley & Sons, New York.

Harnden, D.G., Benn, P.A., Oxford, J.M., Taylor, A.M.R. and Webb, T.P. 1976 Cytogenetically marked clones in human fibroblasts cultured from normal individuals. Som. Cell Gen., 2, 55-62.

Harnden, D.G. and Taylor, A.M.R. 1978 The effects of radiation on the chromosomes of patients susceptible to cancer. In Mutagen Induced Chromosome Damage in Man, H.J. Evans and D.C. Lloyd, eds. p.52-61. Edinburgh University Press.

Harnden, D.G. and Taylor, A.M.R. 1979 Chromosomes and neoplasia. In Recent Advances in Human Genetics, vol. 8, K. Hirschhorn and H. Harris eds. p.1. Plenum, New York.

Hecht, F. and Kaiser McCaw, B. 1977 Chromosome Instability Syndromes. In Genetics of Human Cancer, J.J. Mulvihill, R.W. Miller and J.F. Fraumeni, p.105-123. Raven Press, New York.

Salk, D.J. 1980 Variegated translocation mosaicism in Werner syndrome. In Proceedings of the 7th International Chromosome Conference, Oxford, p.112.

Sandberg, A.A. 1980 The Chromosomes in Human Cancer and Leukaemia. Elsevier, New York and Amsterdam.

Schroeder, T.M. and German, J. 1974 Bloom's syndrome and Fanconi's anaemia: Demonstration of two distinctive patterns of chromosome disruption and rearrangement. Humangenetik, 25, 299-306.

Strong, L.C. 1977 Theories of pathogenesis: mutation and cancer. In The Genetics of Human Cancer, J.J. Mulvihill, R.W. Miller and J.F. Fraumeni, eds. p.401-416. Raven Press, New York.

Taylor, A.M.R. 1978 Unrepaired single and double strand breaks shown cytogenetically following X-irradiation of lymphocytes from patients with ataxia telangiectasia. Mut. Research, 53, 274.

Weichselbaum, R.R., Nove, J. and Little, J.B. 1978 X-ray sensitivity of diploid fibroblasts from patients with hereditary or sporadic retinoblastoma. Proc. Natl. Acad. Sci., USA, 75, 3962-3964.

The role of chromosomes in tumorigenicity

H. P. Klinger

Department of Genetics, Albert Einstein College of Medicine, 1300 Morris Park Avenue, Bronx, New York

Is the primary alteration which causes a normal cell to become malignant a genetic or nongenetic change? If genetic, does this involve loss of information or the gain of new types of information? The large amount of evidence favoring varied answers to these questions cannot be discussed in this short review. Instead, only a brief summary is presented of evidence which indirectly supports the view that malignant transformation involves the loss of genetic information which is essential for normal cellular responsiveness to growth-controlling mechanisms of the cell's environment. An example would be genes specifying for membrane-associated growth control receptors (Klein, 1975).

The early work of others related to that summarized here can be found in: Harris (1971); Wiener et al., (1971, 1974); Ephrussi (1972); Strauss et al. (1976); Jonasson et al. (1977); Klinger (1978); Marshall and Dave (1978) and Stanbridge and Wilkinson (1978), to list only a few.

The work of the author and associates has been published in part, but much of it is now in preparation (Klinger et al., 1978; Klinger and Shows, 1979; Klinger, 1980).

Supported by USPHS NIH Grant Nos. CA-16720 and GM-19100.

The results from this work of several groups, including ours, reveals that:

1. Hybrids of nontumorigenic diploid and tumorigenic heteroploid cells that retain all or many of the chromosomes of the diploid parent are nontumorigenic. (Primarily the work of Harris and associates cited above.) The most stable ones presently known are intraspecific hybrids made with human cells. These retain the suppressed phenotype permanently, yet have an infinite life-span (Stanbridge, 1976; Stanbridge and Wilkinson, 1978; Klinger, 1980).
2. These suppressed hybrids can be forced to segregate chromosomes. Some that lose chromosomes of the diploid parent re-express the tumorigenic phenotype which is defined here as the ability to grow progressively in nude mice (Klinger, 1980).
3. In some interspecific hybrid systems suppression is rarely observed. These are generally chromosomally unstable hybrids in which the nondiploid parental line is highly tumorigenic (Klinger et al., 1978; Kucherlapati and Shin, 1979).
4. In chromosomally more stable interspecific systems, particularly those utilizing a less tumorigenic parent, both tumorigenic and nontumorigenic hybrids are found. Our analyses of about 140 hybrids encompassing some 900 cells from such a human diploid x tumorigenic heteroploid Chinese hamster ovary cell system reveals that individually none of the human chromosomes can cause suppression. However, specific combinations of human chromosomes are consistently present in suppressed hybrids but are never found in tumors resulting from nonsuppressed hybrids. There also appear to be several alternate suppressor combinations, some of which share a chromosome in common.
5. Hybrids which contain the human No. 6, or the 6 and the 12, but no suppressor combinations, are sometimes more tumorigenic than the parental hamster cells.
6. A few clones which have greatly reduced, or completely lost their tumorigenic potential were isolated from the tumorigenic hamster line. (Klinger and Shows, 1979; Klinger et al., in preparation, for last three points).

These findings suggest that:

1. Chromosomes of normal cells contain genetic information which exerts positive (dominant) suppressor control of the tumorigenic phenotype, at least in those cell systems discussed here.
2. This suppressor information may represent normal gene products which impart to a cell the ability to respond to normal environmental stimuli that regulate growth.
3. Consequently, suppression of tumorigenicity in hybrids need not require complementation of defective genes of the tumorigenic parent cell but simply the presence of some of the postulated growth regulatory loci. This would explain why combinations of different chromosomes of a normal cell are able to effect suppression.
4. Some chromosomes of normal cells seem to carry still other types of information that enhances tumorigenicity in hybrids. These may be genes that normally promote cell growth and that would be expected to be under the control of regulatory elements not functional in the tumorigenic parent.
5. On the other hand, tumorigenic cells appear to contain information essential for the continued expression of tumorigenicity which they can sometimes lose. They then revert to the nontumorigenic state, but do not lose their ability to grow indefinitely *in vitro*.

These tentative conclusions are compatible with the view that at least two mutations are required for a cell to undergo malignant transformation. These might be at the postulated loci which allow a cell to respond to growth regulatory stimuli. Additional mutations could provide such cells with an added growth advantage if they affected loci that normally turn off growth promoters, such as those which must function in growing tissues and during differentiation and development. Tumorigenic cells which revert to the nontumorigenic state may have lost these growth promoters, or may be able to again suppress them. The chromosomes of normal cells, which enhance tumorigenicity of hybrids, may be carriers of genes which promote growth. Thus, malignant transformation is viewed as a disturbance in the balance of normal genetic regulatory mechanisms resulting primarily from the loss or inactivation of genes that cause a cell to stop growing at an appropriate point in response to environmental stimuli. Coupled with this may be a loss or malfunction of yet other genes that normally turn off or regulate growth promoters. It should be possible to test these concepts.

REFERENCES

Ephrussi, B. 1972. _Hybridization of Somatic Cells_. Princeton University Press, Princeton, N.J.

Harris, H. 1971. Cell fusion and the analysis of malignancy. The Croonian Lecture. _Proc. Roy. Soc. B_ 179, 1-20.

Jonasson, J., S. Povey and H. Harris, 1977. The analysis of malignancy by cell fusion. VII. Cytogenetic analysis of hybrids between malignant and diploid cells and of tumors derived from them. _J. Cell Sci_. 24, 217-254.

Klein,G. 1975. Mechanisms of carcinogenesis. _Internat. Congress of Radiation Research, Vth Seattle, 1974_. pp. 869-878, Academic Press, N.Y.

Klinger, H.P. 1978. Genetic analysis of cell malignancy - evidence from somatic cell genetics. Bull. _Swiss Acad. Med. Sci_. 34, 377-388.

Klinger, H.P. 1980. Suppression of tumorigenicity in somatic cell hybrids. I. Suppression and reexpression of tumorigenicity in diploid human x D98AH2 hybrids and independent segregation of tumorigenicity from other cell phenotypes. _Cytogenet. Cell Genet_. 27, 254-266.

Klinger, H.P., A.S. Baim, C.K. Eun, T.B. Shows and F.H. Ruddle 1978. Human chromosomes which affect tumorigenicity in diploid human x heteroploid human and rodent cell hybrids. In: Human Gene Mapping 4: Fourth International Workshop on Human Gene Mapping. Birth Defects: Original Article Series XIV, 4, 1978, The National Foundation, New York, also in Cytogenet. Cell Genet. 22, 245-249.

Klinger, H.P. and T.B. Shows 1979. Human chromosomes which in cell hybrids suppress tumorigenicity of heteroploid Chinese hamster (CHO) cells. In: Human Gene Mapping 5: Fifth International Workshop on Human Gene Mapping. Birth Defects: Original Article Series, XV, 11, 1979, The National Foundation, New York, also in Cytogent. Cell Genet. 25, 172-173.

Kucherlapati, R. and S. Shin 1979. Genetic control of tumorigenicity in interspecific mammalian cell hybrids. Cell 16, 639-648.

Marshall, C.J. and H. Dave 1978. Suppression of the transformed phenotype in somatic cell hybrids. J. Cell Sci. 33, 171-190.

Stanbridge, E.J. 1976. Suppression of malignancy in human cells. Nature, Lond. 260, 17-20.

Stanbridge, E.J. and J. Wilkinson 1978. Analysis of malignancy in human cells: Malignant and transformed phenotypes are under separate genetic control. Proc. natn. Acad. Sci. USA 75, 1466-1469.

Straus, D.S., J. Jonasson and H. Harris 1976. Growth in vitro of tumour cell x fibroblast hybrids in which malignancy is suppressed. J. Cell Sci. 25, 73-86.

Wiener, F., G. Klein and H. Harris 1971. The analysis of malignancy by cell fusion. III. Hybrids between diploid fibroblasts and other tumor cells. J. Cell Sci. 8, 681-692.

Wiener, F., G. Klein and H. Harris 1974. The analysis of malignancy by cell fusion. V. Further evidence of the ability of normal diploid cells to suppress malignancy. J. Cell Sci. 15, 177-183.

INDUCED CHROMOSOME VARIATION

Induced chromosome variation

Sheldon Wolff

*Laboratory of Radiobiology and Department of Anatomy,
University of California at San Francisco, San Francisco, CA 94143*

Shortly after it became known that X rays could "transmutate" the gene (Muller 1927), it also became known that gross chromosomal aberrations could be induced (Sax 1938). The variety and types of aberrations formed could be accommodated by the hypothesis that the radiation first broke chromosomes and that the broken ends in a cell then could either remain unrejoined to form terminal deletions, or could reunite in a variety of ways to form the multitude of possible aberrations such as inversions, interstitial deletions, translocations, dicentrics, and rings (Sax 1940). Most of the breaks, however, simply restituted or rejoined in the original configuration (Lea 1946). This rejoining was later shown to be under metabolic control (Wolff and Luippold 1955) and constituted the first documented case of genetic repair. By analogy, rejoining with other broken ends could be considered to be a case of "misrepair" (Evans 1968).

Some of the physical mutagens, such as X rays, interact with the cell nucleus to produce chromosome breaks at any stage of the cell cycle. Thus, if the cells are irradiated in G_1, the chromosomes react to radiation as though they are single-stranded and the unit of breakage is the whole unreplicated G_1 chromosome, even though this chromosome is most likely a DNA double helix. Thus, a chromosome break can be equated with a double-strand break in DNA (Wolff 1973, 1978a; Evans 1977). The broken ends produced in G_1 can undergo repair to form aberrant chromosomes that, after replication in S, lead to the formation of full chromosome aberrations affecting both chromatids alike. If, however, S cells or G_2 cells are irradiated, then the already-replicated chromatids are the unit of breakage and rejoining, which leads to chromatid aberrations.

With some physical mutagens, such as ultraviolet radiation (Griggs and Bender 1973), and most chemical mutagens (Evans and Scott 1969) the situation is considerably different (see Wolff 1978a for review), for these agents produce lesions in chromosomal DNA that lead to chromatid aberrations only when the cells pass through S. Those lesions that are unrepaired, and so remain in the chromosomes, retain their ability to lead to chromatid aberrations in any successive S phase.

The production of chromosome aberrations by physical mutagens such as sparsely ionizing radiations lent itself to kinetic analysis because those aberrations requiring only one break increase as the first power of the dose, whereas those that require two breaks, such as translocations, dicentrics, or rings, increase as the square of the dose. This type of analysis, which was made on objects that could be seen directly under the microscope, was invaluable in the development of the target theory of radiation effects (Lea 1946) because it differed from the usual target theory analysis, e.g., of cell survival, in which observations are made of those cells not hit in order to make inferences about the nature of the damage in unobserved dead cells.

The production of aberrations and rearranged chromosomes also led to a resurgence in the field of cytogenetics because translocations, deficiencies, duplications, and other aberrations could be produced for studies of chromosome mechanics and genetic mechanisms. In later years we were also able to use the induction of aberrations in long-lived human lymphocytes as a biological dosimeter to indicate the amount of ionizing radiation to which a person had been exposed.

More recently, we have seen an explosion of studies dealing with another cytogenetic endpoint, the sister chromatid exchange (SCE), which can be visualized in chromosomes that have sister chromatids that are physically (Taylor 1958) or chemically (Latt 1973; Ikushima and Wolff 1974; Perry and Wolff 1974) different from one another.

SCEs, like chromatid aberrations induced by S-dependent agents, are formed by unrepaired lesions that are present when the cell passes through S and the chromosome replicates (Wolff et al. 1974). Although both aberrations and SCEs can be induced by many of the same agents, there are several differences between the two genetic endpoints indicating that they are the result of different lesions in DNA and that different mechanisms are involved in their production (Wolff et al. 1977; Wolff 1978a). In particular, the formation of SCEs is much more sensitive to chemicals than is the formation of aberrations and can be found after exposures one-hundredth those required to cause significant increases in aberrations (Latt 1973; Solomon and Bobrow 1975; Perry and Evans 1975).

It is this difference in sensitivity, along with some other features of SCE formation, that has allowed us to use SCEs to determine several features of the mammalian cell's response to mutagenic carcinogens. Like chromatid aberrations, SCEs can be produced by mutagens that interact directly with DNA without chemical modification (Perry and Evans 1975), as well as by promutagens that need to be converted to their proximate or ultimate mutagenic form by metabolic processes (Stetka and Wolff 1976a,b; Natarajan et al. 1976). Furthermore, once lesions are produced in DNA they must remain in the cell until the S period or no SCEs will be induced. Thus, the DNA repair capacity of the cell will affect the yield of SCEs, as will the cell's ability to activate promutagens. Therefore, several studies have been carried out to determine 1) which of the metabolites of a weak carcinogen (benzene) are the most likely to be biologically active, 2) at what stage of development (embryogenesis) do cells genetically capable of producing aryl hydrocarbon hydroxylase become capable of activating promutagens or procarcinogens, 3) how long lesions induced by a short-lived highly electrophilic proximate carcinogen last in cells of differing repair capacity, and 4) whether or not mammalian cells exhibit the adaptive response previously found in *Escherichia coli* by which a nontoxic dose of a mutagenic carcinogen renders a cell less susceptible to a higher dose of such chemicals.

1. Determination of the active metabolites

Benzene, a weak carcinogen that has a direct association with human leukemia, did not induce SCEs in human lymphocytes, leading to the postulate that its metabolites, rather than benzene itself, might be the major mutagenic or carcinogenic substances (Gerner-Smidt and Friedrich 1978). Consequently, we have carried out experiments with benzene and its major metabolites, phenol, hydroquinone, and catechol, to determine which of these attack DNA, as indicated by the induction of SCEs, and which affect cell division kinetics in human lymphocytes (Morimoto and Wolff 1980).

In these experiments human lymphocytes in culture were grown in the presence of bromodeoxyuridine (BrdUrd), which not only allows detection of SCEs in cells that have divided twice in the presence of the thymidine analog, but also, by the chromosomes' staining pattern, allows one to distinguish whether the cells have divided once, twice, or three times in culture (Wolff and Perry 1974; Tice et al. 1976; Crossen and Morgan 1977). Thus, in the same cultures one can determine whether or not a substance induces SCEs and affects cell proliferation kinetics. In control cultures of lymphocytes grown in Roswell Park Memorial Institute tissue culture medium 1640 containing 15% fetal calf serum and 1% phytohemagglutinin, some cells have already divided twice by 48 hr in culture (Fig. 1). With longer times in culture the number of cells dividing twice increases up to a peak at about 56 hr in culture. As this occurs, the percentage of cells dividing for the first time decreases and the frequency of cells that have divided three times begins to increase and continues to do so with increasing time in culture. This increase is accompanied by a concomitant drop in the percentage of cells dividing once or twice. The yield of SCEs observed in harlequin cells, which have divided twice, is constant at all fixation times (Fig. 1).

To study the effects of a compound on cell proliferation kinetics, 72-hr cultures were observed. In control cultures 77% of the cells were dividing for the third time by 72 hr, 19% of the cells were dividing for the second time, and only 4.3% were dividing for the first time. If the addition of a compound at time zero slowed down cell proliferation, then at 72 hr one would

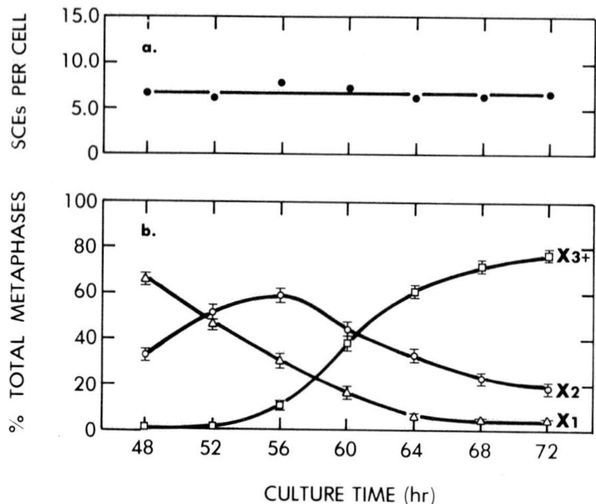

FIGURE 1. Top: the number of SCEs induced in second division human lymphocytes after various times in culture. Bottom: the relative proportion of human lymphocytes dividing for the 1st, 2nd, and 3rd time after various times in culture.

expect to see the relative numbers of cells dividing for the first, second, or third time that were observed at earlier fixation times in controls. In fact, one can measure the amount of delay from the proportions of these cells. Thus, if after 72 hr in culture with a compound, the pattern ordinarily obtained after 56 hr in controls is observed, e.g., 30% first-division cells, 59% second-division cells, and 11% third-division cells, it indicates that there had been a 16-hr delay in treated cells.

When this experiment was carried out with various concentrations of benzene, phenol, hydroquinone, or catechol (Fig. 2), it was found that benzene had very little effect on the proportion of first-, second-, and third-division cells found in 72-hr cultures, even at extremely high concentrations. Phenol had an effect only at concentrations as high as 10^{-3} M. Hydroquinone was more active, and catechol the most active in inhibiting cell proliferation. When SCEs were tested in second division cells observed in 72 hr cultures (Fig. 3), it was found that benzene was inactive over the full range of concentrations, as was phenol. In contrast, hydroquinone, and particularly catechol, were exceedingly effective inducers of SCEs. These data indicate that

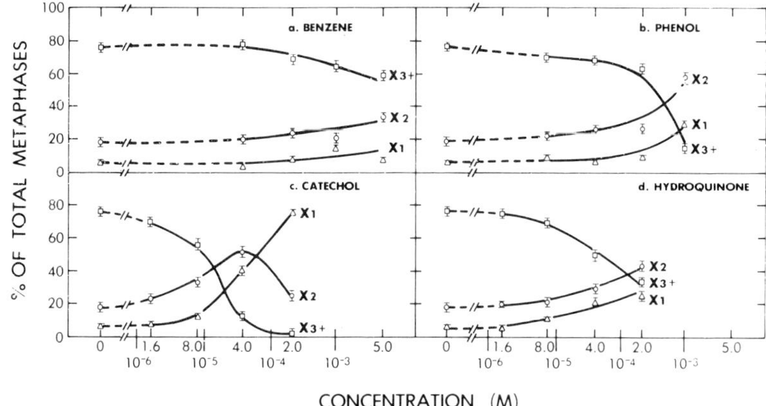

FIGURE 2. the relative proportion of human lymphocytes dividing for the 1st, 2nd, or 3rd time in 72 hr cultures with benzene, phenol, hydroquinone, or catechol.

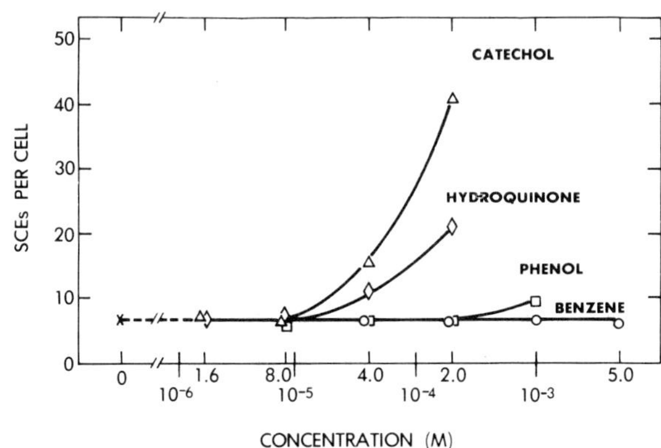

FIGURE 3. SCEs in human lymphocytes cultured 72 hrs with benzene, phenol, hydroquinone, or catechol.

benzene's mutagenic and cytotoxic effects are most likely to be caused by catechol, which is by far the most active metabolite in both the induction of SCEs and the inhibition of cell proliferation and turnover rates. The data indicate that hydroquinone, a relatively active compound, could also contribute to the effects. The sensitivity of the SCE test therefore allows us to make some inferences about which of the many compounds formed during the metabolism of a promutagen or procarcinogen are likely to be the mutagenic intermediates.

2. Determination of stage of development for proficiency in metabolic activation

The enzymes responsible for the conversion of promutagens and procarcinogens to their active forms are the mixed-function oxidases found mainly in the liver. These include the cytochrome P-450-mediated monooxygenases, whose activities are inducible by polycyclic and halogenated aromatic compounds. These same enzymes are also responsible for the detoxification of many compounds. In mice, the degree of inducibility differs among inbred strains and is under control of the Ah locus, whose gene product is a cytosolic receptor that mediates the induction of several structural gene products, including many of the cytochrome P-450 enzymes, such as aryl hydrocarbon hydroxylase. When pregnant mice are injected intraperitoneally with polycyclic hydrocarbons, the earliest that aryl hydrocarbon hydroxylase activity is detectable in fetal tissues is 12-14 days of gestation. Actually, a large dose of benzo(a)pyrene on day 7 or 10 of gestation induced more resorptions, stillbirths, and congenital anomalies in genetically responsive fetuses than in nonresponsive fetuses (Shum et al. 1979), but because the benzo(a)pyrene persists in the body for more than a week, it was not known if the enzymes were actually present as early as day 7 of gestation.

Experiments now have been carried out by Galloway et al. (1980) on the induction of SCEs in mouse embryos explanted at 7 days of gestation. These embryos were cultured in medium containing benzo(a)pyrene and BrdUrd. When benzo(a)pyrene was administered for 26-30 hr to embryos obtained from the genetically responsive inbred strains BALB/cDub, C3H/AnfCum, or C57BL/6N, a dramatic increase in SCEs per cell was found (Table 1), whereas the genetically nonresponsive inbred strains AKR/J and DBA/2J did not give such increases. Similar results were found when the embryos were obtained from an Ah responsive recombinant inbred mouse strain, B6NXAKN-12, but not from the nonresponsive recombinant inbred strain B6NXAKN-3. The results demonstrate that the inducible P-450 enzyme system is expressed in mouse embryos explanted from the uterus at 7½ days of gestation. They also imply that the regulatory gene product, which is the Ah receptor, and the struc-

TABLE 1. SCEs induced in cultured mouse embryos of 7½ days gestational age (From Galloway et al. 1980).

Benzo(a) pyrene (μM)	Ah-responsive inbred strains[1]		Ah-nonresponsive inbred strains[2]	
	#SCE/#chromosomes	SCE/cell[3]	#SCE/#chromosomes	SCE/cell[3]
0	782/4370	7.2 ± 0.3	586/3576	6.6 ± 0.3
0.1	3868/7322	21 ± 0.3	1072/3798	11 ± 0.3
0.32	1865/1871	40 ± 0.9		
1.0	3239/3483	37 ± 0.7	855/2689	13 ± 0.4
3.2	1167/867	54 ± 1.6	95/554	6.9 ± 0.7
10.0	215/134	64 ± 1.1	1045/2192	12 ± 0.6

[1]BALB/cDUB, C3H/AnfCum, C57BL/6N
[2]AKR/J, DBA/2J
[3]Because many cells were broken, the results are expressed as SCE per chromosome and then multiplied by 40 to give the average number of SCE per diploid cell.

tural gene product, cytochrome P-450, were both functional from an early embryonic age, even though they could not be detected by conventional fluorometric, radiometric, or spectrophotometric techniques. The results disprove the idea that basal and inducible cytochrome P-450 and associated monooxygenase activities appear only at or shortly before birth. In fact, preliminary experiments by Galloway et al. (1980) indicate that benzo(a)pyrene can cause SCEs in genetically responsive animals at 3½ days of gestation. The data, which show that the highly sensitive SCE test can be used to determine at which stage of development these enzyme systems are active, also indicate that embryos at a critical stage of early organogenesis could possibly be at risk from maternal exposures to polycyclic hydrocarbons, drugs, and other environmental pollutants that could be metabolized by cytochrome P-450.

3. Determination of lifetimes of lesions

The induction of SCEs in cells can be used not only to determine which metabolites might be responsible for the detrimental effects of a substance and whether or not cells are capable of carrying out this metabolism, but also to see how long lesions in the DNA can exist in cells with differing repair capacities. To determine the lifetime of lesions induced in cells, experiments were carried out in which it was possible to determine if an SCE was induced in the first, second, or third cycle after a chemical was administered. To determine if an SCE was induced in the first or second cycle, Colcemid is added to cells shortly after treatment, a method first developed by Taylor (1958). After two rounds of replication in the presence of Colcemid the cells containing harlequin chromosomes are tetraploid rather than diploid. In such cells any SCE induced in the first round of DNA replication after treatment with the chemical would affect both daughter chromosomes similarly, and thus be recorded as a twin SCE. Any SCE induced in the second round of replication, i.e., after the two daughter chromosomes are formed, would be independent and affect only one of the two chromosomes and thus be recorded as a single SCE. When such experiments were carried out with Chinese hamster ovary (CHO) cells, which are relatively repair-deficient, SCEs (Table 2) were induced in both the first cell cycle and the second cell cycle after treatment with a variety of chemicals (Wolff 1978b). One of these (Table 2) was N-acetoxyacetylaminofluorene (AAAF), an extremely short-lived electrophilic compound that has a half-life in water of only 7½ minutes (Miller 1970). The scoring in this case was restricted to the large acrocentric chromosome that is present only once in "diploid" CHO cells and thus present only twice in tetraploid cells, thus obviating the problem of false twins (Heddle 1969) that arises when there are four similar chromosomes in a tetraploid cell. However, in third-division cells (Table 3), in which only half of the chromatin is harlequinized, the lesions induced by AAAF did not persist and the SCE level was the same as in control cells, indicating that the lesions could persist for two cell cycles but not three. When the experiments were repeated

TABLE 2. Sister chromatid exchanges induced in Chinese hamster ovary cells: SCEs per large acrocentric chromosome in first and second cell cycles after treatment for 30 min in G_1 with various chemicals.

Treatment*	1st cycle (twins)		2nd cycle (singles)		Ratio of singles to twins in 4 n cells
	No. of SCEs / No. of chromosome pairs	SCEs per chromosome pair	No. of SCEs / No. of chromosomes	SCEs per chromosome	
Control	69/283	0.24	132/566	0.23	1.9
EMS, 10^{-4} M	109/281	0.39	192/562	0.34	1.8
MMS, 10^{-5} M	92/284	0.32	182/578	0.32	2.0
4NQO, 10^{-8} M	126/288	0.44	184/576	0.32	1.5
Control	29/98	0.30	52/196	0.27	1.8
AAAF, 10^{-8} M	26/97	0.27	69/194	0.36	2.7
AAAF, 5×10^{-8} M	41/95	0.43	74/190	0.39	1.8
AAAF, 10^{-7} M	55/96	0.57	108/192	0.56	2.0

*EMS, ethyl methanesulfonate; MMS, methyl methanesulfonate; 4NQO, 4-nitroquinoline-l-oxide; AAAF, N-acetoxy-acetylaminofluorene.

TABLE 3. Sister chromatid exchanges induced in Chinese hamster ovary cells: SCEs per chromosome in third cell cycle after treatment for 30 min in G_1 with AAAF. All chromosomes in cell scored.

Treatment	No. of SCEs/ No. of chromosomes	SCEs per chromosome*
Control	457/2048	0.45
AAAF, 10^{-8} M	431/2066	0.42
AAAF, 5 x 10^{-8} M	487/2075	0.47
AAAF, 10^{-7} M	512/2053	0.50

*Ratio obtained by multiplying quotient from preceding column by two, since only one-half of the genome contains differentially stained chromatids in third-cycle cells.

with Bl4FAF Chinese hamster cells, which are more repair-deficient than CHO cells, the lesions persisted not only for one and two cycles, but also for the third cycle (Table 4). In repair-proficient human lymphocytes (Table 4) and in a transformed human fibroblast line GM637 derived from cells with a normal excision-repair capacity (Table 4) AAAF was very inefficient at inducing SCEs. When transformed fibroblasts from the repair-deficient disease xeroderma pigmentosum were used, however, SCEs were induced readily (Table 4).

The data show the utility of the sensitive SCE test for determining how long lesions last in different cell types. They further indicate that the lifetimes of lesions induced in DNA are strongly dependent upon the DNA repair capacities of the cells and that repair-proficient human cells are far less susceptible to the effects of mutagenic carcinogens than are repair-defective cells.

4. Determination of novel repair systems

Experiments have now been carried out by Samson and Schwartz (1980) in which the sensitive SCE test was used to show that the adaptive DNA repair response previously noted in *E.coli* (Samson and Cairns 1977) also exists in CHO and human cells. They chronically exposed cells to low-nontoxic concentrations of N-methyl-N'-nitro-N-nitrosoguanidine (MNNG) to induce the adaptive response and then challenged the cells with exposure to high concentrations

TABLE 4. SCEs induced by AAAF.

Concentration (M)	Cells scored in 2nd cycle: SCEs from 1st and 2nd cycle		Cells scored in 3rd cycle: SCEs from 1st and 2nd cycle		Cells scored in 3rd cycle: SCEs from 3rd cycle	
	No. of SCEs / No. of chromosomes	SCEs per chromosome per cycle	No. of SCEs / No. of chromosomes	SCEs per chromosome per cycle	No. of SCEs / No. of chromosomes	SCEs per chromosome
B14FAF						
0	1152/2127	0.271	831/2184	0.190	210/2184	0.192
10^{-7}	4312/2163	0.997	3066/2169	0.707	883/2169	0.814
Human Lymphocytes						
0	1440/4598	0.157	1059/4597	0.115	355/4597	0.154
2×10^{-7}	1599/4600	0.174	1140/4596	0.124	435/4596	0.189
4×10^{-7}	1652/4600	0.179	1174/4599	0.128	422/4599	0.18
6×10^{-7}	2121/4599	0.231	1197/4002	0.149	475/4002	0.237
8×10^{-7}	1752/4600	0.190	693/2760	0.126	278/2760	0.201
10^{-6}	2139/4600	0.233	367/1194	0.154	145/1194	0.243
GM637						
0	335/1015	0.165	183/924	0.099	92/924	0.200
10^{-7}	908/1899	0.239	292/959	0.152	129/959	0.268
XP12RO						
0	2079/4776	0.218	1237/4883	0.127	877/4883	0.358
10^{-7}	4896/5186	0.474	2774/5139	0.270	2251/5137	0.876

of MNNG, methylnitrosourea, or ethylnitrosourea. Their results indicated that, if the challenge was given shortly after the adaptation was complete, the cells were resistant to alkylation damage, but not ultraviolet light damage. This resistance was manifested by a reduction in both the killing and the SCEs induced by the challenge doses. They were able to rule out effects of possible changes in cell cycle distribution, permeability to the mutagens, and degrees of alkylation, and thus to deduce that chronic exposures to MNNG enabled both CHO and GM637 cells to handle alkylation damage more efficiently and so become resistant to alkylating agents.

Consequently, their results with two mammalian cell lines paralleled the adaptation previously observed in *E.coli*, i.e., a chronic treatment that neither kills cells nor disturbs cell growth induces a resistance to alkylation damage, but not ultraviolet damage, that decays once the chronic treatment is stopped. It is presumed that, as in *E.coli*, this adaptive DNA repair pathway is error-free.

Conclusion

Over the years the induction of cytogenetic effects has proved to be one of the most sensitive methods for determining whether or not an agent could damage DNA and thus potentially be biologically hazardous. Ordinary chromosome aberrations still constitute the most sensitive endpoint for certain mutagens such as X rays or x-ray-like chemicals. For S-dependent agents like nonionizing radiations and most chemicals, however, the SCE is by far the more sensitive endpoint and can be used to answer a variety of questions about the lesions induced and the cell's ability to handle them. Thus, it has been possible to estimate what metabolites might be responsible for an agent's effect, at what stage of development the cells are proficient in making these metabolites, how long the DNA exists in a damaged condition before DNA repair mechanisms cause a return to normal, and whether novel DNA repair mechanisms exist in mammalian cells. But this is just the beginning, for the unparalleled sensitivity of the SCE test and the ease in collecting the data have led to a tremendous resurgence of cytogenetic studies.

REFERENCES

Crossen, P.E. and Morgan, W.F. 1977. Analysis of human lymphocyte cell cycle time in culture measured by sister chromatid differential staining. Exp. Cell Res. 104, 453-457.

Evans, H.J. 1968. Repair and recovery at chromosome and cellular levels: Similarities and differences. In Recovery and Repair Mechanisms in Radiobiology. Brookhaven Symposia in Biology, #20. Brookhaven National Laboratory, Upton, L.I., New York, 111-133.

Evans, H.J. 1977. Molecular mechanisms in the induction of chromosome aberrations. In Progress in Genetic Toxicology (eds. D. Scott, B.A. Bridges, and F.H. Sobels) Elsevier/North-Holland, 57-74.

Evans, H.J. and Scott, D. 1969. The induction of chromosome aberrations by nitrogen mustard and its dependence on DNA synthesis. Proc. Lond. Roy. Soc. B. 173, 491-512.

Galloway, S.M., Perry, P.E., Meneses, J., Nebert, D.W., and Pedersen, R.A. 1980. Cultured mouse embryos metabolize benzo(a)pyrene during early gestation: Genetic differences detectable by sister chromatid exchange. Proc. Nat. Acad. Sci. USA 77, 3524-3528.

Gerner-Smidt, P. and Friedrich, U. 1978. The mutagenic effect of benzene, toluene and xylene studied by the SCE technique. Mutat. Res. 58, 313-316.

Griggs, H.G. and Bender, M.A. 1973. Photoreactivation of ultraviolet-induced chromosomal aberrations. Science 179, 86-88.

Heddle, J.A. 1969. Influence of false twins on the ratios of twin and single sister chromatid exchanges. J. Theoret. Biol. 22, 151-162.

Ikushima, T. and Wolff, S. 1974. Sister chromatid exchanges induced by light flashes to 5-bromodeoxyuridine and 5-iododeoxyuridine substituted Chinese hamster chromosomes. Exp. Cell Res. 87, 15-19.

Latt, S.A. 1973. Microfluorometric detection of deoxyribonucleic acid replication in human metaphase chromosomes. Proc. Nat. Acad. Sci. USA 70, 3395-3399.

Lea, D.E. 1946. Actions of Radiations on Living Cells. Cambridge University Press, Cambridge, England.

Miller, J.A. 1970. Carcinogenesis by chemicals: An overview - G.H.A. Clowes Memorial Lecture. Cancer Res. 30, 559-576.

Morimoto, K. and Wolff, S. 1980. Increase of sister chromatid exchanges and perturbations of cell division kinetics in human lymphocytes by benzene metabolites. Cancer Res. 40, 1189-1193.

Muller, H.J. 1927. Artificial transmutation of the gene. Science 66, 84-87.

Natarajan, A.T., Tates, A.D., van Buul, P.P.W., Meijers, M., and deVogel, N. 1976. Cytogenetic effects of mutagens/carcinogens after activation in a microsomal system *in vitro*. I. Induction of chromosome aberrations and sister chromatid exchanges by diethylnitrosamine (DEN) and dimethylnitrosamine (DMN) in CHO cells in the presence of rat-liver microsomes. *Mutat. Res.* 37, 83-90.

Perry, P. and Evans, H.J. 1975. Cytological detection of mutagen-carcinogen exposure by sister chromatid exchange. *Nature*, London 258, 121-125.

Perry, P. and Wolff, S. 1974. New Giemsa method for the differential staining of sister chromatids. *Nature*, London 251, 156-158.

Samson, L. and Cairns, J. 1977. A new pathway for DNA repair in *Escherichia coli*. *Nature*, London 267, 281-283.

Samson, L. and Schwartz, J.L. 1980. Evidence for an adaptive DNA repair pathway in Chinese hamster ovary and human skin fibroblast cell lines. *Nature*, in press.

Sax, K. 1938. Chromosome aberrations induced by X-rays. *Genetics* 23, 494-516.

Sax, K. 1940. An analysis of X-ray induced chromosomal aberrations in Tradescantia. *Genetics* 25, 41-68.

Shum, S., Jensen, N.M. and Nebert, D.W. 1979. The murine Ah locus: In utero toxicity and teratogenesis associated with genetic differences in benzo(a)pyrene metabolism. *Teratology* 20, 365-376.

Solomon, E. and Bobrow, M. 1975. Sister chromatid exchanges - A sensitive assay of agents damaging human chromosomes. *Mutat. Res.* 30, 273-278.

Stetka, D.G. and Wolff, S. 1976a. Sister chromatid exchange as an assay for genetic damage induced by mutagenic carcinogens. I. In vivo test for compounds requiring metabolic activation. *Mutat. Res.* 41, 333-342.

Stetka, D.G. and Wolff, S. 1976b. Sister chromatid exchange as an assay for genetic damage induced by mutagen-carcinogens. II. In vitro test for compounds requiring metabolic activation. *Mutat. Res.* 41, 343-350.

Taylor, J.H. 1958. Sister chromatid exchanges in tritium labeled chromosomes. *Genetics* 43, 515-529.

Tice, R., Schneider, E.L., and Rary, J.M. 1976. The utilization of bromodeoxyuridine incorporation into DNA for the analysis of cellular kinetics. *Exp. Cell Res.* 102, 232-236.

Wolff, S. 1973. Chromosome aberrations: Mechanisms of cell death. In *Advances in Radiation Research*, vol. 1 (eds. J.F. Duplan and A. Chapiro) Gordon and Breach, New York, 457-465.

Wolff, S. 1978a. Relation between DNA repair, chromosome aberrations, and sister chromatid exchanges. In *DNA Repair Mechanisms* (eds. P.C. Hanawalt, E.C. Friedberg, and C.F. Fox) Academic Press, New York, 751-760.

Wolff, S. 1978b. Chromosome effects of mutagenic carcinogens and the nature of the lesions leading to sister chromatid exchange. In *Mutagen-Induced Chromosome Damage in Man* (eds. H.J. Evans and D.C. Lloyd) Edinburgh University Press, 208-215.

Wolff, S., Bodycote, J., and Painter, R.B. 1974. Sister chromatid exchanges induced in Chinese hamster cells by UV irradiation of different stages of the cell cycle: The necessity for cells to pass through S. Mutat. Res. 25, 73-81.
Wolff, S. and Luippold, H.E. 1955. Metabolism and chromosome-break rejoining. Science 122, 231-232.
Wolff, S. and Perry, P. 1974. Differential Giemsa staining of sister chromatids and the study of sister chromatid exchanges without autoradiography. Chromosoma 48, 341-353.
Wolff, S., Rodin, B., and Cleaver, J.E. 1977. Sister chromatid exchanges induced by mutagenic carcinogens in normal and xeroderma pigmentosum cells. Nature 265, 347-349.

ACKNOWLEDGEMENT

Work supported under the auspices of the U.S. Department of Energy.

DNA repair and its consequences in cultured mammalian cells

C. F. Arlett

MRC Cell Mutation Unit, University of Sussex, Brighton

The repair of DNA has been the subject of a large number of recent reviews. These may be general (Lehmann and Bridges, 1977; Hanawalt et al., 1979) or more specific relating to the repair of chemical damage (Roberts, 1978), radiation damage (Lehmann, 1978) DNA replication (Cleaver, 1978), the enzymology of DNA repair (Lindahl, 1979) and genetic disorders with defects in repair (Arlett and Lehmann, 1978; Setlow, 1978; Bootsma, 1978; Sasaki, 1978; Friedberg et al., 1979; Paterson and Smith, 1979; Pawsey et al., 1979; Kraemer, 1980). In order to avoid excessive referencing in this mini-review, the reader is directed to these more substantial reviews.

DNA is regarded as a vitally important cellular constituent. It would not be surprising, therefore, to anticipate that mechanisms might be found to protect it from damage or repair it if damaged. The molecule is uniquely susceptible to damage because of its large size, its complexity, and the need to conserve its base composition. It may thus be seen to be at risk during replication, as a consequence of covalent bond breakage and in response to external damaging agents.

The study of protection rather than repair has not been fashionable, evidence for the existence of protective mechanisms comes from a consideration of the effects of clastogenic factors isolated from cells from patients suffering from Blooms syndrome (BS). The original observations of Tice et al. (1978) showed that conditioned medium from fibroblast cultures of BS induced sister chromatid exchanges (SCE) in lymphocyte culture from normal donors and that co-cultivation of BS fibroblasts with normal fibroblasts increased SCE frequency in the latter. A number of groups have attempted to repeat these observations and have obtained conflicting results. Emerit and Cerruti (1980) have provided impressive evidence that concentrated ultra-filtrates of conditioned medium from six deficient BS cell strains possess clastogenic activity when tested on lymphocytes from healthy donors. The clastogenic activity of the ultra-filtrates was strongly suppressed when bovine superoxide dismutase was added. This allows us to propose that BS cells may be deficient in the detoxification of active oxygen species which in turn cause the formation of a clastogenic factor. Thus it may be an increase in the formation of DNA damage (lack of protection) rather than a decrease in repair capacity which causes the observed chromosome abnormalities in BS cells. This syndrome may, therefore prove to have a mutation in a protection rather than repair process. Clastogenic factors have been reported in two other chromosome breakage syndromes, Fanconi's anaemia (Keck and Emerit, 1979) and ataxia telangiectasia (AT) (Shaham *et al.*, 1980), and thus defects in radical scavenging activity might provide a unifying explanation.

The study of repair owes much to investigators of bacteria sensitive to DNA damaging agents such as UV, indeed sensitivity is now often regarded as indicative of a defect in repair. A basic scheme can be constructed whereby damage can be reversed, excised or tolerated, this last process often being described as post-replication or daughter strand repair.

Reversal of damage is seen in the monomerisation of UV light-induced pyrimidine dimers by photoreactivating enzyme. The demonstration of photoreactivating activity (PR) in human cells is dependent upon the composition of the medium. Despite claims that PR activity is reduced in xeroderma pigmentosum and has been claimed to reduce the frequency of UV-induced transformants to anchorage-independence in normal human fibroblasts (Sutherland *et al.*, 1980) no clear *in vivo* role for PR enzyme has been demonstrated.

Excision repair usually acts before DNA is replicated. Damaged regions are removed by a multistep enzymatic process and replaced by a new sequence of nucleotides using the undamaged strand as a template. The first, incision, step revealed in micro-organisms, the existence of damage-specific endonucleases. In T4 phage an endonuclease which is specific for UV-induced pyrimidine dimers makes incisions on the 5' side of the dimers resulting in 3'-OH and 5' phosphate ends. Dimer specific endonucleases from E.coli which act only on double-stranded DNA seem also capable of recognising damage inflicted by chemicals such as mitomycin C or 4-nitroquinoline oxide which produce bulky adducts on the DNA (a dimer produces a large distortion in the helix). An alternative mode of initiating excision repair is as a consequence of the loss of a base either as the result of the action of an N-glycosidase or non-enzymatic loss from undamaged or from alkylated DNA. Apurinic endonucleases have been isolated from animal cells and these nick in the region of the site of the missing base to provide a substrate for the subsequent steps of excision repair.

The second step of excision is carried out by exonucleases, they initiate hydrolysis from the 5' end of a DNA strand releasing oligonucleotides. DNA polymerase I from E.coli has both 5'-3' exonucleolytic activity and polymerase activity and may simultaneously remove damage and fill in the resulting gap.

The filling in of the gaps or repair replication requires polymerisation and is distinguished from semi-conservative DNA replication by labelling procedures. Detection of this "unscheduled" repair synthesis is a direct method for revealing DNA repair by excision using isopycnic labelled density gradients.

The final, ligation, step in excision repair is carried out by polynucleotide ligase, an essential enzyme responsible for joining fragments manufactured during normal DNA replication.

The evidence for excision repair in human cells rests largely with the study of the autosomal recessive sun-sensitive syndrome xeroderma pigmentosum (XP). Patients suffering from this disease exhibit an array of symptoms, both dermatological and neurological. Notable amongst the dermatological effects are:- the marked acute sun-sensitivity in infancy with pigmented macules and achromic spots and telangiectasia in exposed areas followed, ultimately, with basal cell carcinoma, squamous cell carcinoma and malignant melanoma. Similar skin changes may be seen in later life in normal Caucasian adults who have occupations or live in regions where extensive exposure to sunlight is experienced. XP may then be regarded as an extreme example of what might happen in normal individuals. In 1932 De Sancis and Cacchione gave a description of a sib-ship where in addition to the cutaneous and occular changes there were neurological abnormalities. These changes included microcephaly with progressive mental deterioration, low intelligence, areflexia, ataxia, dwarfism and immature sexual development. All of these symptoms are rarely present but many XP patients have one or more of the neurological features.

Cells from most but not all XP patients as shown originally by Cleaver (1968) are defective in the excision of cyclobutane pyrimidine dimers, the principal lesion observed in DNA following treatment with UV. The defect may be assayed as unscheduled DNA synthesis - synthesis in cells in the G_1, G_2 or mitotic phases of the cell cycle or as repair replication by caesium chloride or sodium iodide density gradient centrifugation.

Cell fusion studies using Sendai virus or poly ethylene glycol have made it possible to describe 7 (A-G) complementation groups amongst the excision-defective XPs. It is not clear whether these complementation groups represent a number of different genes operating in the control of excision or different mutations in a large gene complex. Each group is, in general, characterized by a specific residual level of excision repair and there is a rough correlation with the severity of the clinical symptoms. Clear exceptions exist, XP8LO which is a cell strain from complementation group A(0-5% excision repair) has 30-40% residual excision repair capacity and both representatives of group G (Arlett _et al._, 1980) with effectively zero excision repair have, as yet, no tumours (one is almost 20 years old).

A defect in repair replication implies a defect in the excision repair system prior to the action of the ligase step and XPs are usually considered to be defective at the level of the endonuclease. This is supported by the observations of Tanaka _et al._ (1975) that if a UV-specific endonuclease from T4 infected

E.coli is introduced into XP cells the rest of the excision repair processes can be completed by the cell. This endonuclease may also enhance the ability of XP cells to modify the lethal effects of UV damage. The defect may not simply be attributed to the absence of endonuclease activity since extracts of some XP cells are able to excise dimers from exogenously added DNA (Mortelmans *et al.*, 1976). The defect appears to be an inability to incise DNA while it is combined as chromatin, thus it may be more of a question of accessibility rather than deficiency in the enzyme.

Not all XP patients show the defect in excision repair, in the "variant"form cells show normal excision but are defective in their ability to synthesise DNA on a template with unexcised pyrimidine dimers when compared with normal cells. This process is referred to as post-replication or daughter strand repair (DSR) and in the variant cells it is specifically sensitive to inhibition by methylated xanthines. Excision-defective XP cells, with the exception of group E, show less marked defects in DSR. The mechanism of DSR remains subject to debate, however, despite the observations of Waters and Regan (1976) a recombination-type process such as can be inferred from *recA*$^-$ bacteria does not seem to operate in human cells.

In addition to the defects in excision or DSR, defects in apurinic endonuclease activity have also been reported for some excision defective XP cells from complementation groups A and D.

While it is not appropriate to describe XP as a chromosome breakage syndrome excision-defective cells are hypersensitive to the induction of chromosome damage and SCE after treatment with UV. They also show a reduced capacity to reactivate UV-irradiated viruses, which confirms that the defects are concerned with the repair of DNA damage. Excision-defective XP cells are also hypersensitive to the lethal effects of UV light and some chemicals which may be described as "UV-like" such as 4-nitro quinoline oxide. XP variant cells show normal or near normal sensitivity to the lethal effects of UV. This implies that the defects in excision repair have more serious consequences for the survival after UV than defects in DSR.

Andrews *et al.*, (1976) showed that XP cells from complementation groups A and D were generally more sensitive to the lethal effects of UV than other groups. They pointed out that the extreme hypersensitivity of these groups was correlated with the most severe neurological manifestations, our observations on group G individuals support this contention (Arlett et al., 1980).

In our studies (Arlett, 1980) of the induction of 6-thioguanine resistant variants by UV light it is clear that all XP cells, both excision-defective and proficient, are hypermutable when compared with normal cells. This result provides us with evidence that the repair of damage in daughter strands, which is defective in both classes of XP cells, is error prone. An equally plausible alternative, however, is that the hypermutability of XP cells reflects the action of an error-prone component of excision repair. Others (Maher et al., 1976; Glover et al., 1979) have suggested that for the excision-defective XPs the relative hypersensitivity of XP cells is similar for both cell killing and mutation. They have also produced compelling evidence for the error-free action of excision repair.

This summary of results with XP allows us to construct a simplified scheme of relationships placing a key role on DNA repair.

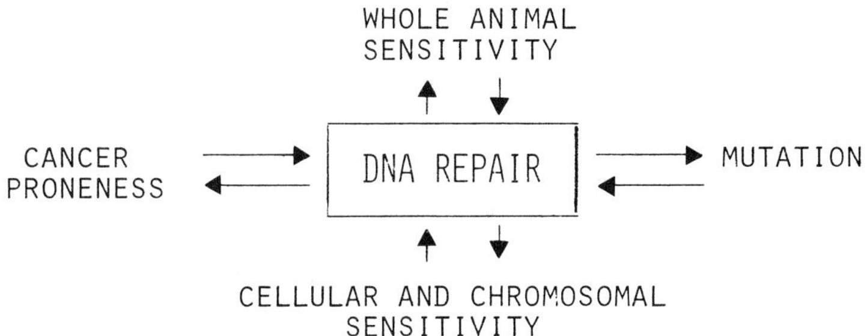

It is then necessary to determine how widely we can apply the model which associates the diverse features of XP.

There are other syndromes of interest in man with an undoubted actinic component and the results of our and other studies with Cockayne syndrome (CS) Blooms syndrome (BS), a sun sensitive child (11961), Rothmund-Thompson syndrome (RTS), Ferguson-Smith syndrome (FSS) and Dariers disease (Der Kaloustien and Kurban, 1979) are summarised in Table 1. Unequivocal sensitivity to the lethal

TABLE 1. The response of a variety of cell strains to 254 nm UV light (identified as at risk on the basis of whole animal sensitivity)

	Cell killing	Mutation	Chromosomal
Xeroderma pigmentosum	S	S	S
XP variant	S/R	S	R?
Blooms syndrome	S/R		?
11961	S	S	R
Fanconi's anaemia	R		?
Rothmund-Thompson syndrome	R		
Dariers disease	R		
Ferguson-Smith syndrome	R		

effects of UV are shown by CS and 11961, both also exhibit hypermutability although the enhancement factor is small for 11961. The sun-sensitive child (11961) is only a few years old and has not yet developed tumours, there is no evidence for increased tumour incidence in CS thus, hypermutability is not correlated with increased tumour incidence in these two conditions. No defects in excision or DSR for UV-induced damage have been detected in either condition. We are, therefore, obliged to invoke the existence of some as yet undescribed repair processes to accommodate these sensitivities. Such a possibility has been suggested by the demonstration that following treatment with UV both types are defective in the recovery of DNA synthesis when compared with normal cells. The possibility still remains that the techniques used to measure excision or DS repair may not be sensitive enough to discriminate CS and 11961 from normal.

The absence of any measurable defects or sensitivity in the other syndromes does not exclude the possibility of defects in DNA repair being associated with the "whole animal" sensitivity (vide the original observation on XP variants) but the case for them must be regarded as not proven.

Ionising radiation produces a considerable spectrum of damage in mammalian cells and the sensitivity of cells from ataxia telangiectasia (AT) patients suggests that they might be defective in the repair of some part of this damage. Whole animal sensitivity is revealed by the reports of morbidity following radiotherapy in three such patients. Although AT is undoubtedly a cancer-prone syndrome the tumours are of the lympho-reticular system and unlikely to be a direct consequence of the radiosensitivity. The frequent immune defects both humoral and cell-mediated seen in this syndrome suggests that the tumours may arise because of the failure of immune surveillance. Furthermore, and in direct contrast to the response of XP cells to UV, there is no hypermutability in AT following treatment with ionising radiation. Indeed the data indicate that such cells may even be hypomutable. Such a situation has analogies in E.coli where bacteria with the $LexA^-$ or $RecA^-$ phenotypes are hypersensitive to UV for cell killing but are also immutable. The absence of induced mutation which has also been observed in cells from Fanconi's anaemia patients after treatment with mytomycin C can be explained if the two syndromes are defective in error-prone repair processes which confer mutability on normal cells. An alternative explanation for the hypomutability of AT cells follows from the high proportion of deletion events which have been recorded amongst the hypoxanthine-guanine ribosyl transferase minus mutants picked up after treatment of normal cells with ionising radiation. AT cells are particularly susceptible to chromosome breakage by ionising radiation and the majority of induced mutants may carry lethal chromosome deletions (Cox, 1980).

A further contrast to XP (with the exception of bleomycin) is the lack of unequivocal evidence in AT for cross sensitivity to radiomimetic chemicals (Table 2). This implies that any repair defect in AT may be more damage specific than is the case for XP.

The evidence for defects in repair and molecular mechanisms in AT is confusing.The most substantial claims are those of Paterson and Smith (1979) who conclude that there are defects in repair synthesis in some AT cell strains when irradiated under anoxia. This defect correlated with a defect in the ability of these same cells to excise gamma-ray induced base damage from their DNA. Heterogeneity in the excision of endonuclease-sensitive sites revealed the possibility of at least two genetically distinct complementation groups. Those cells which do not show the defect are not analogous to the XP variant since they also show the characteristic

TABLE 2. Cellular sensitivity to DNA damaging agents in AT cell strains.

Agent	Response	Source	Comment
Ionizing radiation	S[a]	1,2	
UV	R	2	
AAF	R	2	
MMS	R/S	2	conflicting
EMS	R	2	
MC	R/S	2	"
AD	S	2	
MNNG	R/S	2 and Teo[b]	"
BL	S	Lehmann & Stevens (1979)	

R = resistant, normal response; S = sensitive;
UV = ultraviolet light; AAF = acetylaminofluorene;
MMS = methyl methanesulphonate; EMS = ethyl methanesulphonate;
MC = mitomycin C; AD = actinomycin D; MNNG = N-methyl-N'-nitro-N-nitrosoguanidine; BL = bleomycin.

1. Arlett & Lehmann (1978). 2. Friedberg et al. (1979).

[a]under oxic or anoxic conditions; [b]personal communication.

hypersensitivity to the lethal effect of gamma irradiation. To date no defects in the repair of ionising radiation-induced strand breaks have been demonstrated using either sucrose gradients or the more sensitive alkaline elution technique. Normal cells when gamma irradiated show an immediate reduction in DNA synthesis which recovers to its pre-irradiation level after five hours. Ataxia telangiectasia cells, however, do not show this radiation induced inhibition of DNA synthesis (M. James, personal communication).

AT qualifies as a chromosome breakage syndrome on the basis of the existence of stable chromosome rearrangements involving chromosome 14q12 which are commonly encountered in the circulating lymphocytes from these patients, other spontaneous chromosome aberrations are also increased. These cells also show an increased sensitivity to induced chromosome damage following treatment with ionizing radiation. In particular it was noted that when AT lymphocytes are irradiated at G_0 or G_1 chromatid type aberrations are observed in addition to the anticipated chromosome-type aberrations. Taylor et al. (1976) speculated that the existence of this class of aberrations is a consequence of defective repair in AT cells. It is of some interest to note the correlation between the existence of the chromatid aberrations in G_0 cells and the absence of inhibition of DNA synthesis in AT cells. The post-irradiation inhibition of DNA synthesis seen in normal cells might well be a period in which there is time to repair lesions which would otherwise appear as chromatid aberrations.

Claims for cellular radiosensitivity have been made for a number of syndromes. These include Fanconi's anaemia, Gardners syndrome (Little et al., (1980), Huntingtons disease (Arlett and Muriel, 1978; Moshell et al. 1980), Hutchinson-Gilford progeria, Familial retinoblastoma and some, but not all, AT heterozygotes. Cells from Fanconi's anaemia patients are specifically sensitive to cross-linking agents such as mitomycin C and evidence for a defect in the repair of DNA cross-links has been produced. Insofar as ionizing radiation induces a wide spectrum of lesions which will include cross-links a correlated sensitivity to ionizing radiation might be anticipated. Fanconi's anaemia qualifies as a "chromosome breakage syndrome" and is undoubtedly cancer prone, an extreme immune deficiency is also present, these features provide criteria which justify an examination of the cells for sensitivity to DNA damaging agents.

Retinoblastoma may also qualify both as a cancer-prone and chromosome breakage syndrome on the basis of the increase of tumours in sites outside the orbit and frequent involvement of deletions on chromosome 13.

Gardners syndrome, an autosomal dominant, qualifies as being cancer prone and the observations of Little et al. (1980) show that cells from a single individual are sensitive to UV, gamma irradiation and mitomycin C. We have been unable to confirm such sensitivity in a set of cell strains established from other polyposis coli patients.

In both AT and XP patients a common feature is the involvement of neurological defects. Both Freidreichs ataxia and Huntingtons disease were selected for examination on the basis of their neurological defects. Only limited data has been produced with respect to Freidreichs ataxia that these indicate sensitivity to ionizing radiation (Lewis et al. 1979).

Two groups have claimed radiation sensitivity in HD (Arlett and Muriel, 1979; Moshell et al., 1980). While some cell strains, notably those from the Camden culture collection, are sensitive to ionizing radiation, we have been able to demonstrate the existence of strains with normal sensitivity (Arlett, 1980). Our experience with HD emphasises a particular point, most of these conditions are extremely rare (HD is exceptional in being represented by 1 in 10^3 in Northern European populations) and it is, therefore, often difficult to survey large populations. A consequence of this limitation is that heterogeneity within a syndrome might well be missed - a random sample of XPs should be expected to include some variants which would show little if any hypersensitivity to the lethal effects of UV.

In none of these gamma sensitive syndromes, with the exception of Fanconi's anaemia, is there any direct evidence for defects in repair, thus the sensitivity is the only indication that repair defects might exist. It should be emphasised, therefore, that direct evidence for genetically impaired repair of radiation damage in human cells is particularly weak despite the existence of a considerable range of radiosensitive cell strains. It is of some interest to speculate that the existence of this range might indicate the presence of a considerable number of genes able to modulate radiation sensitivity in man.

ACKNOWLEDGEMENTS

I am indebted to Professor B. A. Bridges for critical comments and to S. A. Harcourt, B. C. Broughton and W. J. Muriel for their continued experimental support. This work is supported in part by Euratom Contract 166-76-1-BIO UK.

REFERENCES

Andrews, A. D., S. F. Barrett and J. H. Robbins 1976. Relation of DNA repair processes to pathological ageing of the nervous system in xeroderma pigmentosum. Lancet I. 1318-20.

Arlett, C. F. 1980(a). Presymptomatic diagnosis of Huntington's disease? Lancet 540.

Arlett, C. F. 1980(b) Mutagenesis in repair-deficient human cell strains. In Progress in Environmental Mutagenesis, M. Alacevic, ed., 161-174. Amsterdam:Elsevier.

Arlett, C. F., S. A. Harcourt, A. R. Lehmann, S. Stevens, M. A. Ferguson-Smith, and W. N. Morley 1980. Studies on a new case of xeroderma pigmentosum (XP3BR) from complementation group G with cellular sensitivity to ionizing radiation. Carcinogenesis (in press).

Arlett, C. F. and A. R. Lehmann 1978. Human disorders showing increased sensitivity to the induction of genetic damage. Ann. Rev. Genet. 12, 95-115.

Arlett, C. F. and W. J. Muriel 1979. Radiosensitivity in Huntington's chorea cell strains: a possible pre-clinical diagnosis. Heredity 42, 276.

Bootsma, D. 1978. Xeroderma pigmentosum. In DNA Repair Mechanisms P. C. Hanawalt, E. C. Friedberg and C. F. Fox, eds., 581-601. New York:Academic Press.

Cleaver, J. E. 1968. Defective repair replication of DNA in xeroderma pigmentosum. Nature 218, 652-56.

Cleaver, J. E. 1978. DNA repair and its coupling to DNA replication in eukaryotic cells. Biochim. Biophys. Acta. 516, 489-516.

Cox, R. 1980. Comparative mutagenesis in cultured mammalian cells. In Progress in Environmental Mutagenesis, M. Alacevic, ed., 33-46. Amsterdam:Elsevier.

Der Kaloustian, V. M. and A. K. Kurban 1979. Genetic Diseases of the Skin, Berlin, Springer-Verlag.

De Sanctis, C. and A. Cacchione, A. 1932. L'idiozia xerodermica. Riv. Sper. Freniatr. 56, 269-92.

Emerit, I. and P. Cerutti. Clastogenic activity from Bloom's syndrome fibroblast cultures. (In press)

Friedberg, E. C., U. K. Ehmann and J. I. Williams 1978. Human diseases associated with defective DNA repair. Adv. in Radiat. Biol. 8, 85-174.

Glover, T. W., C. C. Chang, J. E. Trosko and S. S. L. Li 1979. Ultraviolet light induction of diphtheria toxin-resistant mutants in normal and xeroderma pigmentosum fibroblasts. Proc. Natl. Acad. Sci. USA 76, 3982-86.

Hanawalt, P. C., P. K. Cooper, A. K. Ganesan and C. A. Smith 1979. DNA repair in bacteria and mammalian cells. Ann. Rev. Biochem. 48, 783-836.

Keck, M. and I. Emerit 1979. Human Genet. 50, 277-83.

Kraemer, K. H. 1980. Xeroderma pigmentosum. In Clinical Dermatology, D. J. Dennis, R. L. Dobson and J. McGuire, eds., New York:Harper and Row, (in press).

Lehmann, A. R. 1978. Repair processes for radiation-induced DNA damage. In Effects of Ionising Radiation on Nucleic Acids J. Huttermann et al. eds., 312-34, Berlin:Springer Press.

Lehmann, A. R. and B. A. Bridges 1977. DNA Repair. In Essays in Biochemistry. P. N. Campbell and W. N. Aldridge, eds., 71-119. London:Academic Press.

Lehmann, A. R. and S. Stevens 1979. The response of ataxia telangiectasia cells to bleomycin. Nucleic Acids Res. 6, 1953-60.

Lewis, P. D., J. B. Corr, C. F. Arlett and S. A. Harcourt 1979. Increased sensitivity to gamma irradiation of skin fibroblasts in Friedreich's ataxia. Lancet 474-75.

Lindahl, T. 1979. DNA glycosylases, endonucleases for apurinic/apyrimidinic sites and base excision repair. Prog. Nucleic Acids Res. and Mol. Biol. 22, 135-92.

Little, J. B., J. Nove and R. R. Weichselbaum 1980. Abnormal sensitivity of diploid skin fibroblasts from a family with Gardner's syndrome to the lethal effects of X-irradiation ultraviolet light and mitomycin C. Mutation Res. 70, 241-50.

Maher, V. M., D. J. Dorney, A. L. Mendrala, B. Konze-Thomas and J. J. McCormick 1979. DNA excision-repair processes in human cells can eliminate the cytotoxic and mutagenic consequences of ultraviolet irradiation. Mutation Res., 62, 311-23.

Mortelmanns, K., E. C. Friedberg, H. Slor, T. Thomas and J. E. Cleaver 1976. Defective thymine dimer excision by cell-free extracts of xeroderma pigmentosum cells. Proc. Natl. Acad. Sci., USA, 73, 2757-61.

Moshell, A. N., S. F. Barrett, R. E. Tarone and J. H. Robbins 1980. Radiosensitivity in Huntington's disease: Implications for pathogenesis and presymptomatic diagnosis. Lancet I, 9-11.

Paterson, M. C. and P. J. Smith 1979. Ataxia telangiectasia: An inherited human disorder involving hypersensitivity to ionizing radiation and related DNA-damaging chemicals. Ann. Rev. Genet. 13, 291-318.

Pawsey, S. A., I. A. Magnus, C. A. Ramsay, P. F. Benson and F. Gianelli 1979. Clinical, genetic and DNA repair studies on a consecutive series of patients with xeroderma pigmentosum, Quart. J. Med. (new series) 48, 179-210.

Roberts, J. J. 1978. The repair of DNA modified by cytotoxic, mutagenic and carcinogenic chemicals. In Advances in Radiation Biology, J. T. Lett and H. Adler, eds., 211-434, New York: Academic Press.

Sasaki, M. S. 1978. Fanconi's anaemia a condition possibly associated with a defective DNA repair. In DNA Repair Mechanisms, P. C. Hanawalt, E. C. Friedberg and C. F. Fox, eds., 675-84, New York:Academic Press.

Setlow, R. B. 1978. Repair deficient human disorders and cancer, Nature 271, 713-17.

Shaham, M., Y. Becker and M. Cohen 1980. A diffusable clastogenic factor in ataxia telangiectasia. Cytogenet.Cell Genet. 27, 155-161.

Sutherland, B. M., J. S. Cimino, N. Delihas, A. C. Shih and R. P. Oliver 1980. Ultraviolet light-induced transformation of human cells to anchorage-independent growth, Cancer Res., 40, 1934-39.

Tanaka, K., M. Sekiguchi and Y. Okada 1975. Restoration of ultraviolet induced unscheduled DNA synthesis of xeroderma pigmentosum cells by the concomitant treatment with bacteriophage

T4 endonuclease V and HVJ (Sendai virus). Proc. Natl. Acad. Sci. USA, 72, 4071-75.

Taylor, A. M. R., J. A. Metcalfe, J. M. Oxford and D. G. Harnden 1976. Is chromatid-type damage in ataxia telangiectasia after irradiation at G_0 a consequence of defective repair? Nature 260, 441-43.

Tice, R., G. Windler and J. Ray 1978. Effect of cocultivation on sister chromatid exchange frequencies in Blooms syndrome and normal fibroblast cells. Nature 273, 538-40.

Waters, R. and J. D. Regan 1976. Recombination of UV-induced pyrimidine dimers in human fibroblasts. Biochem. Biophys. Res. Comm., 72, 803-807.

HUMAN CYTOGENETICS

H-Y antigen and sex determination in mammals

Ulrich Wolf, Ulrich Müller

Institut für Humangenetik der Universität, 7800 Freiburg i.Br., Germany

and Susumu Ohno

City of Hope Research Institute, Duarte, CA 91010

This topic raises the question of the connection between the sex chromosomes, gonadal differentiation, and the role of H-Y antigen. What we ultimately want to understand is the mechanism of sex determination, and it may turn out that understanding the function and genetics of H-Y antigen is a key to the solution of this problem.

Therefore, some aspects of the function of H-Y antigen shall be discussed here, as well as some genetics, with preference to the cytogenetics of H-Y antigen, since this is a chromosome conference.

It must be said that we have only little knowledge on the mode of action of H-Y antigen at the early developmental stage when the gonadal blastema becomes differentiated into either testis or ovary. An impressive demonstration of the effect of H-Y antigen at the still indifferent stage is the conversion of the embryonal architecture by exogeneous H-Y antigen (Nagai et al., 1979). Similarly, in birds (Müller et al., 1979, 1980) and amphibians (Wachtel et al., 1980), with the ZW-mechanism of sex determination, H-Y antigen production, experimentally induced in the homogametic male sex by estrogen treatment, results in the conversion of the embryonal gonad into an ovotestis or ovary, respectively.

Apart from these experiments, there are no other studies on the action of H-Y antigen at this critical embryonal stage of gonadogenesis. We only know that H-Y antigen is already detectable in the 8-cell embryo of male mammals (Krco and Goldberg, 1976).

As a model to study the function of H-Y antigen, the capacity of a cell suspension derived from an organ, to reorganize in vitro into histotypic architecture, was used (Moscona, 1957). It was shown that dissociated gonadal cells of the newborn reaggregate to form tubular or follicular structures under appropriate culture conditions (Ohno et al., 1978; Zenzes et al., 1978a,b). With this experimental design, the morphogenetic effect of H-Y antigen was demonstrated: Addition of H-Y antigen to an ovarian cell suspension results in the formation of testicular tubules (Table 1).

Table 1. Histological structure of dissociated gonadal cells after reorganization in vitro (newborn rats)

dissociated cells	reorganized cells		
	control	H-Y ("induction")	H-Y and anti-H-Y
ovary	follicular	tubular	follicular
testis	tubular		

Interestingly enough, newborn ovarian cells release a factor into the culture medium which prevents reorganization of testicular cells into tubular structures. In the presence of this inhibitory factor, testicular cells form follicles (Zenzes et al., 1980).

This antagonism of H-Y antigen and an ovary-derived factor prompted us to study heterogonadal cocultures at various proportions of testicular and ovarian cells (Urban et al., subm.). A striking similarity to results obtained in hetero-sexual mouse chimaeras was found: A minority of 20 % of male cells still results in the formation of a uniform testicular aggregate in most of the cases. Exceptionally, a mixed ovarian and testicular histology is observed at that proportion. At 15 % of male cells, however, a uniform ovarian aggregate is formed. From these findings, we conclude that a threshold for effective H-Y antigen action exists, and that below this threshold, ovarian differentiation takes place as in the absence of H-Y antigen:

Tab. 2: Heterogonadal co-cultures in the dissociation-reorganization experiment (newborn rats)

	Percentage of testicular:ovarian cells	histological structure of the aggregate formed
	80 : 20	tubular
	50 : 50	tubular
threshold	20 : 80 (2 experiments)	tubular
range	20 : 80 (1 experiment)	mixed tub. and foll.
	15 : 85	follicular

Cocultures of male non-gonadal cells (spleen, liver) and ovarian cells do not result in tubular formation.

The mode of action of H-Y antigen in these co-cultures remains unclear: The antigen is a component of the cell membrane of male cells, but it is also secreted by testicular Sertoli cells (Zenzes et al., 1978c). We have shown before that H-Y antigen in soluble form binds to the gonad-specific receptor, presumably inducing the target cells to undergo morphogenetic changes (Müller et al., 1978). To clarify whether male cells are able to interact directly with ovarian cells, co-cultures of male non-gonadal cells derived from spleen and liver, and of ovarian cells were performed. Here, no tubular organization took place (Urban et al., subm.). Therefore, we assume that H-Y antigen acts via the humoural system only. The consequences for the origin of the bovine freemartin gonad are at hand: also in this case, humoural transport of H-Y antigen will be responsible for the gonad conversion.

For the embryonic stage of primary testicular differentiation, it would follow as a consequence that here again, H-Y antigen must be available in the extracellular fluids at a certain concentration, either secreted by special cells or shed into the milieu from the cell surface. Since cells of the early male embryo are H-Y positive even before the onset of gonad differentiation, active secretion of the antigen may mark the stage when the indifferent gonadal anlage starts to develop into the male direction.

Finally, we used this model system to demonstrate that male germ cells do not participate in the organization of testicular tubules. It is known from other studies that male mice devoid of germ cells nevertheless develop testicles (Mintz, 1957). In our experiments, male rats were treated with busulphane to suppress germ cell proliferation, and the testicles devoid of germ cells were dissociated and put under reorganization conditions in vitro. These cultures resulted in perfect tubular organization, though without germ cells in the lumen (Wolf and Zenzes, 1979).

In fact, we have shown earlier that male germ cells at the diploid stage are H-Y negative and not able to bind the antigen (Zenzes et al., 1978 c). With respect to tubular differentiation, therefore, they will not play an active role. Table 3 summarizes the general conclusions we draw from the series of experiments briefly reported here.

Tab. 3: Conclusions based on the dissociation-reorganization experiments

1. Independent of the sex chromosome constellation, H-Y antigen acts on the gonadal cells of both sexes.

2. H-Y antigen exerts its morphogenetic effect as a humoral factor by binding to the gonad-specific receptor, and most probably not as an integral part of the cellular membrane.

3. Testis differentiation is independent of the germ cells. Only the somatic elements of the gonad are targets for H-Y antigen.

4. Testicular morphogenesis depends on a certain threshold of H-Y antigen concentration. Below that threshold, an ovary is formed. Ovotestis formation is a rare event occurring within the threshold range of H-Y antigen concentration.

By the evidence reviewed here, in addition to other data not mentioned (Ohno, 1979), it seems rather well established that H-Y antigen, indeed, is an essential factor in testicular morphogenesis. Therefore, the assumption is at hand that the sex chromosomes are in some way involved in the genetic control of H-Y antigen. It is to be expected that aberrations of the sex chromosomes, structural as well as numerical, should provide some insight into this complex. Our own studies which shall be summarized here, are restricted to aberrations of the X chromosome.

Individuals with structural aberrations of the X chromosome were tested for H-Y antigen. It turned out that deletions of the short arm of one X chromosome as in 46,XXp- or 46Xi(Xq) cases result in the appearance of H-Y antigen, while deletions of the long arm (46,XXq-) do not. Since H-Y antigen was also detected in a fertile female with only the very end of the short arm of one X chromosome deleted (the band Xp 223), the gene involved in H-Y antigen expression was mapped on this segment (Wolf et al., 1980a). Interestingly enough, the duplication of this segment in female sibs with gonadal dysgenesis and the karyotype 46,Xp+Y resulted in absence of H-Y (Bernstein et al., 1980).

Thus, with the deletion of the distal short arm of the X, H-Y becomes expressed, while with the duplication of this segment, H-Y becomes suppressed. These phenomena can be interpreted by the assumption of a controlling gene on the X chromosome, interfering with the expression of the H-Y structural gene. There is another implication in these observations: if it makes a difference whether this controlling gene exists in uniplex dose as in the case of a deletion, or in duplex dose as in normal females, this gene must escape X-inactivation. Indeed, on the distal short arm of the X another gene has been mapped escaping inactivation which is involved in the expression of steroid sulfatase (X-linked ichthyosis gene; Tiepolo et al., 1980). The same may be true for the gene of the Xg blood group. Thus, this chromosome segment including several genes may not become inactivated, at least not completely (see below). Furthermore, these findings strongly favour the assumption that the H-Y structural gene is not localized on the Y chromosome, since H-Y antigen is expressed in various female karyotypes with X deletions, but lacking the Y or any trace of it. Therefore, the Y chromosome may be endowed with another gene controlling H-Y antigen expression instead.

Finally, numerical aberrations of the sex chromosomes are briefly to be discussed. In the 45,X Turner syndrome, H-Y antigen was also found to be present (Wolf et al., 1980b).

This should be the consequence of an uniplex dose of the X-linked controlling gene, as in the XXp- cases.

In the Klinefelter series including 2XY, 3XY, and 4XY, H-Y antigen is consistently found, but the titer apparently decreases with the number of X chromosomes (Fraccaro et al., in prep.) Under the assumption of an X-linked controlling gene suppressing H-Y antigen expression, this finding is only to be expected. However, in contrast to the duplication of the terminal Xp segment mentioned before (Bernstein et al., 1980), in X-polysomies H-Y antigen is still produced, though at a lower rate. The difference between these conditions is that on the one hand, the duplication is regional and present on a single active X, while in the polysomies the additional X chromosomes are inactivated. It seems that inactivation of the chromosome as such reduces the gene dosage of the assumed H-Y repressor gene on the "permanently active segment" on it. Thus, we are left with two apparently contradictory observations: 1) XO as well as XXp- women express appreciable amounts of H-Y antigen, yet they remain females. 2) XXY and XXXY men express progressively less H-Y antigen. Yet they show only minor failures of testicular organogenesis. It seems to us that there are only two alternative explanations: 1) This difference, again may point to the existence of a critical threshold in H-Y antigen levels: H-Y antigen titers below the threshold do not induce testicular organogenesis and do not necessarily interfere with ovarian organogenesis. In that event, H-Y antigen levels of XO and XXp- women should automatically be below the above threshold, whereas H-Y antigen levels of even 4XY men should be above the threshold. 2) The assumed X-linked locus for the H-Y repressor may control the expression of a H-Y antigen-like plasma membrane protein which cross-reacts with H-Y antibody but has no testis-organizing function.

In favour of the latter view is the finding that in experimentally sex-reversed birds and amphibians, H-Y antigen is induced in gonadal tissues only, but not in other organs (Müller et al., 1980; Wachtel et al., 1980).

While evidence has been presented on the existence of controlling genes on the X chromosomes, the localization of the H-Y structural gene still remains an open question. In view of various familial and pedigree data on autosomally inherited abnormalities of H-Y antigen expression, the H-Y structural gene may turn out to be of autosomal localization (Wolf, 1978; Fraccaro et al., 1979; Dagna Bricarelli et al., in press).
The conclusions we draw from the studies of X chromosome aberrations on H-Y antigen are presented in Table 4.

Table 4: Conclusions based on H-Y antigen studies in aberrations of the X chromosome

1. Structural aberrations

1.1. 46,XXp- (deletion of at least Xp223) and 46,Xi(Xq) individuals are H-Y positive (titer reduced). A gene controlling H-Y antigen is located on Xp223.

1.2. The X-linked controlling gene shows a gene-dosage effect: if present in uniplex, H-Y antigen is still produced, though at a reduced rate; if present in duplex (as in normal XX females), H-Y antigen production is completely repressed. Consequently, this controlling gene escapes X-inactivation.

1.3. The presence of H-Y antigen in individuals lacking the Y chromosome excludes the H-Y structural gene from this chromosome. On the Y, another controlling gene is postulated to exist.

2. Numerical aberrations

2.1. The 45,X Turner syndrome is H-Y positive (titer reduced) because of the presence of the X-linked controlling gene in uniplex only.

2.2. In X polysomies including the Y (Klinefelter series) the titer of H-Y antigen decreases with increasing number of X chromosomes. Inactivation may influence the permanently active segment on distal Xp.

Acknowledgements. This work was supported by NIH grant R01 ATT5620 and the Deutsche Forschungsgemeinschaft (SFB 46 and Si 46/4).

References

Bernstein, R., Koo, G.C., and Wachtel, S.S. (1980). Abnormality of the X chromosome in human 46,XY female siblings with dysgenetic ovaries. Science 207, 768

Dagna Bricarelli, F., Fraccaro, M., Lindsten, J., Müller, U. et al. (1980). Sex reversed XY females with campomelic dysplasia are H-Y negative. Hum. Genet., in press.

Fraccaro, M., Lindsten, J., Pawlowitzki, H., Mayerová, A., Wolf, U. Sex chromosome polysomies and H-Y antigen titer: Positive/negative correlations with the number of Y/X chromosomes. In preparation.

Fraccaro, M., Tiepolo, L., Zuffardi, O., Chiumello, G., Di Natale, B., Gargantini, L., Wolf, U. (1979). Familial XX true hermaphroditism and the H-Y antigen. Hum. Genet. 48, 45

Krco, C.J., Goldberg, E.H. (1976). H-Y (male) antigen: Detection on eight-cell mouse embryos. Science 193, 1134

Mintz, B. (1957). Embryological development of primordial germ cells in the mouse: Influence of a new mutation W^{jl}. J. Embryol. exp. Morphol. 5, 396

Moscona, A.A. (1957). The development in vitro of chimaeric aggregates of dissociated embryonic chick and mouse cells. Proc. Natl. Acad. Sci. USA 43, 184

Müller, U., Aschmoneit, I., Zenzes, M.T., Wolf, U. (1978). Binding studies of H-Y antigen in rat tissues. Indications for a gonad-specific receptor. Hum. Genet. 43, 151

Müller, U., Zenzes, M.T., Wolf, U., Engel, W., Weniger, J.P. (1979). Appearance of H-W (H-Y) antigen in the gonads of oestradiol sex reversed male chicken embryos. Nature 280, 142

Müller, U., Guichard, A., Reyss-Brion, M., Scheib, D. (1980). Induction of H-Y antigen in the gonads of male quail embryos by diethylstilbestrol. Differentiation 16, 129

Nagai, Y., Ciccarese, S., Ohno, S. (1979). The identification of human H-Y antigen and testicular transformation induced by its interaction with the receptor of bovine fetal ovarian cells. Differentiation 13, 155

Ohno, S. (1976). Major regulatory genes for mammalian sexual development. Cell 7, 315

Ohno, S. (1979). Major sex determining genes. Springer: Berlin Heidelberg, New York

Ohno, S., Nagai, Y. and Ciccarese, S. (1978). Testicular cells lysostripped of H-Y antigen organize ovarian follicle-like aggregates. Cytogenet. Cell Genet. 20, 351

Tiepolo, L., Zuffardi, O., Fraccaro, M., Natale, D. di., Gargantini, L., Müller, C.R., and Ropers, H.H. (1980). Assignment by deletion mapping of the steroid sulfatase X-linked ichthyosis locus to Xp 223. Hum. Genet. 54, 205

Urban , E., Zenzes, M.T., Müller, U., Wolf, U. Cell-reorganization in vitro of heterosexual gonadal cocultures. Submitted.

Wachtel, S.S., Bresler, P.A., Koide, S. (1980). Does H-Y antigen induce the heterogametic ovary? Cell 20, 859

Wolf, U. (1978). Zum Mechanismus der Gonadendifferenzierung. Bull. Schweiz. Akad. Med. Wiss. 34, 357

Wolf, U., Fraccaro, M., Mayerová, A., Hecht, T., Maraschio, P., and Hameister, H. (1980). A gene controlling H-Y antigen on the X chromosome. Tentative assignment by deletion mapping to Xp223. Hum. Genet. 54, 149

Wolf, U., Fraccaro, M., Mayerová, A., Hecht, T., Zuffardi, O., and Hameister, H. (1980). Turner syndrome patients are H-Y positive. Hum. Genet. 54, 315

Wolf, U., Zenzes, M.T. (1979). Gonadendifferenzierung und H-Y-Antigen. Verh. Anat. Ges. 73, 379

Zenzes, M.T., Müller U., Aschmoneit, I., Wolf, U. (1978c). Studies on H-Y antigen in different cell fractions of the testis during pubescence. Immature germ cells are H-Y antigen negative. Hum. Genet. 45, 297

Zenzes, M.T., Urban, E., Wolf, U. (1980). Inhibition of testicular organization in vitro by newborn rat ovarian cell supernatants. Differentiation 16, 193

Zenzes, M.T., Wolf, U., Engel, W. (1978a). Organization in vitro of ovarian cells into testicular structures. Hum. Genet. 44, 333

Zenzes, M.T., Wolf, U., Günther, E., Engel, W. (1978b). Studies on the function of H-Y antigen: Dissociation and reorganization experiments on rat gonadal tissue. Cytogenet. Cell Genet. 20, 365

The origin of chromosome abnormalities in man

P. A. Jacobs

Department of Anatomy, University of Hawaii, Honolulu, HI 96822

Variation in size, position or staining properties of heteromorphic chromosome regions, that is regions of chromosomes comprised largely or wholly of highly repetitive non-transcribed DNA, is ubiquitous in the human population and apparently without phenotypic effect. The majority of heteromorphisms of human chromosomes are at, or very near, the centromere and are minimally affected by crossing over. Furthermore this type of variation has a very low mutation rate and is a stable feature of a given chromosome or chromosome lineage (Jacobs 1977). Therefore, although the origin and biological significance of variations of heterochromatic chromosome regions are not understood, their properties make them ideal markers for determining the origin of many different types of cytogenetic abnormalities. These include the parental origin of structural rearrangements and trisomies involving heteromorphic chromosomes, the parental origin of triploids and the elucidation of developmental abnormalities such as tetraploidy, ovarian teratomas and hydatidiform moles.

Heteromorphisms are particularly valuable in determining the origin of events that involve a whole haploid complement because information from all heteromorphic chromosomes can be brought to bear on the problem. In this paper the origin of human triploidy and tetraploidy based on data from our Hawaiian survey of spontaneous abortions will be discussed and the origin of ovarian teratoma and hydatidiform mole based on published reports and our own data reviewed.

Triploidy

In our study of 1,000 karyotyped spontaneous abortions 70 were found to be triploid. Parental blood was obtained from 57 in order to determine the parental origin of the additional haploid set by comparison of the centromeric heteromorphisms of the chromosomes of the parents and the triploids. In all but four, information from the heteromorphic chromosomes allowed us to determine the mechanism of origin of the triploidy. As can be seen from Table 1 the majority were paternal in origin, 29 being due to dispermy and 13 due either to dispermy or to fertilization of a haploid egg by a diploid spermatozoan resulting from failure of the first meiotic division. Only 11 triploids were maternal in origin; in six the diploid ovum resulted from failure of the first meiotic division and in five from failure of the second meiotic division. Our data are in agreement with those of other surveys in finding the additional haploid set in the majority of human triploids to be paternal. Failures of the first or the second meiotic division in the male cannot formally be distinguished from dispermy but maximum likelihood estimates based on analysis of chromosome heteromorphisms suggest that 20-25% of triploids may be the result of failure the first paternal meiotic division and 4% the result of failure of the second paternal meiotic division (Jacobs et al. 1978).

TABLE 1. Hawaii triploids - parental origin.

Origin	Number	%	
Dispermy	29	55	79
Dispermy/Pat I	13	25	
Dispermy/Pat II	-	-	
Maternal I	6	11	21
Maternal II	5	9	

In the Hawaiian series of triploid parents two fathers were found to have a balanced translocation and in each case the triploid also carried the translocation (Table 2). In neither instance could the exact mechanism of origin be determined but in both diplospermy due to failure of the first meiotic division was by far the most likely. As we have examined the chromosomes of only some 70 parents of triploids in which the triploidy could have arisen as a result of a meiotic error rather than dispermy, and as the frequency of translocations in the population is about one in 500, our observations suggest that there may be an excess of translocation carriers among triploid parents. The presence of such a translocation may interfere with the orderly segregation of bivalents at the first meiotic anaphase, resulting in the failure of the first meiotic division and the formation of a diploid gamete.

TABLE 2. Structural chromosome abnormalities in triploids

		Conditional probability of heteromorphism observations x10^3				
No.	Karyotype	2♂	♂I	♂II	♀I	♀II
K321	69,XXY t(4;12)(ql;pll)pat.	15.6	1,000	0	15.6	15.6
K1363	68,XXY Rob t(14;15)pat.	125	1,000	0	0	0

A surprising finding in our triploid series was a highly significant correlation between the mechanism of origin of the triploid and the gestational age at the time of its abortion (Table 3). The mean gestational age for the triploids arising by dispermy was 128 days, almost twice as long as those arising by failure of the second meiotic division which was only 69 days. The gestational age of triploids arising by failure of the first maternal meiotic division and those that possibly arose by failure of the first paternal meiotic division lay between these extremes. The reason for the correlation between the mechanism of origin and gestational age is not obvious but it may be the result of an "inbreeding" effect. Failure of the second meiotic division will result in a diploid gamete homozygous for all loci between the centromere and the most proximal chiasmata, failure of the first meiotic division will result in a diploid gamete homozygous for some loci distal to the most proximal chiasmata, while dispermy will be associated with less homozygosity than failure of either meiotic division. Homozygosity for deleterious recessive genes at even two of the three loci in triploids may well have a very disadvantageous effect on development and result in early death of the fetus and its subsequent abortion.

TABLE 3. Hawaii triploids - gestational age by parental origin

Origin	Number	Gestational age (days ±S.E.)
Dispermy	29	128.1 ± 4.8
Dispermy/Pat I	13	114.3 ± 14.3
Dispermy/Pat II	-	-
Maternal I	6	94.2 ± 16.1
Maternal II	5	69.0 ± 5.5

Tetraploidy

In our study of 1,000 karyotyped spontaneous abortions we found 28 to be tetraploid with no evidence of a diploid cell line, and five to be diploid/tetraploid mosaics. Chromosome heteromorphisms were examined in 14 of the tetraploids and in all 14 the observations were consistent with an origin by duplication of a diploid cell. Thus the great majority of human tetraploids appear to arise as a result of an error of cell division of a chromosomally normal zygote. This is borne out by the finding of approximately equal numbers of XXYY and XXXX tetraploids and by the absence of other more exotic sex chromosome complements.

Ovarian teratoma

In a series of papers published in the 1960's Linder and his colleagues showed that human ovarian teratomas, i.e. benign tumors of germ cell origin, had a 46,XX constitution and that they originated from maternal germ cells that had already undergone their first meiotic division (Linder 1969; Linder et al. 1970). This conclusion was reached on the basis of enzymatic differences between the teratoma and the host mother. The teratomas were homozygous for all loci for which the mother was homozygous, but were either homozygous or heterozygous for loci for which the mother was heterozygous. Linder postulated that this might be the result of failure of the second meiotic division or alternatively to fusion of the products of second meiosis. This suggestion was confirmed in 1975 by Linder et al. using chromosome heteromorphisms. Eight centromeric heteromorphisms and three enzymes were studied in each of five teratomas. The mothers were homozygous for 23 and heterozygous for 17 of the centromere markers, while the tumors were homozygous for all 40. In contrast the mothers were homozygous for nine enzyme loci and heterozygous for six while the tumors were homozygous for twelve and heterozygous for three loci. These are exactly the observations that would be expected if the tumor indeed arose by failure of the second meiotic division. Ovarian teratomas are very common and abnormal development of the resulting oocyte must be a frequent occurrence in our species. Whether the second meiotic failure and subsequent abnormal development is merely the consequence of the egg failing to be released from the ovary at the appropriate time or whether it is the result of a basic abnormality in the meiotic process itself is not known. However preliminary attempts at gene mapping using ovarian teratomas as the data source suggest that there may be less crossing over in teratomas than in normal gametes (Patil et al. 1978). If this suggestion is substantiated it implies that oocytes that give rise to ovarian teratomas are abnormal from at least the pachytene stage of development and therefore that human ovarian teratomas are the result of an abnormality of the meiotic process itself.

Hydatidiform moles

One of the most exciting uses of chromosome heteromorphisms has been in the elucidation of the etiology of hydatidiform moles. Gestational trophoblast disease, which in its benign form is known as hydatidiform mole and in its malignant form as choriocarcinoma, is a disease that is unique to man. It is a condition of a conceptus in which the placenta is abnormally large with grossly swollen chorionic villi and pronounced hyperplasia of the trophoblast and in which there is no visible embryo. The great majority of such moles have a 46,XX chromosome constitution. In 1977 Kajii and his colleagues published their observations on the chromosome heteromorphisms of such moles and their parents. They showed that the conceptuses contained no maternal chromosomes but appeared entirely homozygous for a single set of paternal centromere markers. These observations could be explained by the fertilization of an effectively empty egg by a normal haploid sperm that subsequently divided without the egg cleaving, to restore the diploid number of 46. Such conceptuses would be completely homozygous. Alternatively, the observations could be explained by fertilization of an effectively empty egg by a diploid sperm arising as a result of failure of the second paternal meiotic division. Such conceptuses would be the male counterparts of ovarian teratomas; they would be homozygous for all centromere markers and heterozygous for those loci heterozygous in the father and which had undergone crossing over.

In order to determine the precise mechanism of origin of hydatidiform moles we studied the centromeric heteromorphisms and the enzyme phosphoglucomutase-1 (PGM_1) in a series of moles and their parents (Jacobs et al. 1980). PGM_1 has two common alleles with gene frequencies of approximately .76 and .24. Its locus is on the short arm of chromosome 1 and maximum likelihood estimates suggest that in males it is 50 centimorgans from the centromeric heteromorphic band at q12. We restricted our analysis of non-centromeric markers to PGM_1 because it was the only locus available to us 1) whose genotype could be determined reliably both in parental blood and fetal tissue 2) that had a high frequency of parental heterozygosity and 3) that was situated sufficiently far from the centromere to ensure frequent recombination with it.

We studied the cytogenetic status of 20 moles and both parents and a further four moles in which we obtained chromosome preparations from the mother alone. In 22 of the 24 moles the centromeric heteromorphisms in all informative chromosomes appeared homozygous and clearly of paternal origin. The PGM_1 genotype of the mole and both parents were determined for 14 of these 22 moles and in a further three cases from the mole alone. In all 17 cases, including six in which the father was found to be heterozygous, the mole was homozygous. Based on gene frequencies alone it can be estimated that if the moles originated from a diploid sperm resulting from failure of the second meiotic division 6.2 of the 17 tested moles would be heterozygous at the PGM_1 locus as would 4.0 of the six in which the father is known to be heterozygous. The absence of heterozygosity at the PGM_1 locus is significant both for the total moles tested ($p < 0.001$) and for the offspring of known heterozygous fathers ($p < 0.01$) and is therefore strongly supportive of a haploid sperm origin for the great majority of 46,XX moles. Our observations therefore supported the preliminary data of both Lawler et al. (1979) and Yamashita and his colleagues (1979).

Thus, gestational trophoblast disease appears to be a condition resulting from the production and subsequent normal fertilization of an egg with no effective genome. Such an "empty" or anucleate egg could result from an abnormality of the first or second meiotic division with the exclusion of the chromosomes from the ovum itself or it could result from a disintegration of the maternal haploid complement subsequent to completion of the second meiotic division. Numerous etiologic factors have been reported to be associated with gestational trophoblast disease and thus with the production of anucleate eggs (Bagshawe 1969). First, the frequency of constitutional structural rearrangements is 20-30 times higher in women who have had a molar pregnancy than in the general population (Kajii et al. 1977; Lawler et al. 1979). The presence of such a rearrangement may well interfere with the orderly segregation of chromosomes at meiosis I. If all chromosomes are included in the polar body an anucleate egg will be produced which, if fertilized, will give rise to a hydatidiform mole. The second etiologic factor associated with hydatidiform moles and therefore anucleate eggs is extreme reproductive age. Thus moles are much more frequent in pregnancies occurring in teenagers and women over 40 than in women in their 20's and 30's. Thirdly, moles appear much more prevalent in certain areas of the world than in others. For example, hydatidiform moles occur in about one pregnancy in 200 in Japan, the Philippines and Taiwan, but in only one pregnancy in 2,000 in the continental U.S.A. and in western Europe. Fourthly, it has been suggested that socio-economic factors and diet may be important causes of gestational trophoblast disease as it appears to be more prevalent among the lower socio-economic groups and among those whose diets are low in protein. If the above factors do indeed play a part in the etiology of hydatidiform mole they must affect, either directly or indirectly, the meiotic process in the human female.

SUMMARY AND CONCLUSIONS

Studies of chromosome heteromorphisms have demonstrated three common conditions in our species to be associated with failure of one or other meiotic division; namely some 40% of triploids and virtually all ovarian teratomas and hydatidiform moles.

Direct evidence is provided by chromosome heteromorphisms that failure of both the first or second meiotic division in the ovum leads to triploidy, and there is strong statistical evidence that the failure of the first meiotic division in the spermatocyte also leads to triploidy. However evidence implicating the second paternal meiotic division in the genesis of human triploidy is as yet rather sparse.

Ovarian teratomas result from the abnormal development of ova that have undergone the first meiotic division but not completed the second. However it is not known whether the abnormal development of the egg is a consequence of a meiotic aberration or merely the result of the egg being retained in the ovary instead of being shed. Hydatidiform moles are associated with the fertilization and subsequent abnormal development of an egg devoid of an effective maternal genome. It is not yet known whether the anucleate egg is the result of an abnormality of the first or second meiotic division or whether it results from the degeneration of the maternal genome subsequent to normal meiosis. However circumstantial evidence, in the form of an excess of structural chromosome rearrangements in the mothers of moles and perhaps also the strong maternal age effect, tend to favor abnormality of the first meiotic division as the method of production of the majority of anucleate eggs.

Whatever the true nature of the basic lesions underlying triploidy, ovarian teratomas and gestational trophoblast disease it is clear that rigorous comparative studies of the etiology of these conditions would shed light not only on the conditions themselves but also on factors affected the meiotic process in our species.

REFERENCES

Bagshawe, K. D. 1969. Choriocarcinoma. Baltimore: Williams and Wilkins.

Jacobs, P. A. 1977. Human chromosome heteromorphisms. In Progress in Medical Genetics, New Series Vol. 2, A. G. Steinberg, A. G. Bearn, A. G. Motulsky, B. Childs, eds., 251-274. Philadelphia: W. B. Saunders.

Jacobs, P. A., R. R. Angell, I. M. Buchanan, T. J. Hassold, A. M. Matsuyama and B. Manuel 1978. The origin of human triploids. Ann Hum Genet Lond 42, 49-57.

Jacobs, P. A., C. M. Wilson, J. A. Sprenkle, N. B. Rosenshein and B. R. Migeon 1980. Mechanism of origin of complete hydatidiform moles. Nature 286, 714-716.

Kajii, T. and K. Ohama 1977. Androgenetic origin of hydatidiform mole. Nature 268, 633-634.

Lawler, S. D., V. J. Pickthall, R. Fisher, S. Povey, M. W. Evans and A. E. Szulman 1979. Genetic studies of complete and partial hydatidiform moles. Lancet 2, 580.

Linder, D. 1969. Gene loss in human teratomas. P.N.A.S. 63, 699-704.

Linder, D. and J. Power 1970. Further evidence for post-meiotic origin of teratomas in the human female. Ann Hum Genet 34, 21-30.

Linder, D., B. K. McCaw and F. Hecht 1975. Parthenogenic origin of benign ovarian teratomas. New Eng J Med 292, 63-66.

Patil, S. R., B. Kaiser-McCaw, F. Hecht, D. Linder and E. W. Lovrien 1978. Human benign ovarian teratomas: chromosomal and electrophoretic enzyme studies. In *Birth Defects Original Article Series*, Vol. 14, 297-301, National Foundation.

Yamashita, K., N. Wake, T. Araki, K. Ichinoe and K. Makoto 1979. Human lymphocyte antigen expression in hydatidiform mole: androgenesis following fertilization by a haploid sperm. *Am J Obst Gynecol* 135, 597-600.

Chromosome structural rearrangements and reproductive failure

A. Boué and J. Boué

Groupe de Recherches des Biologie Prénatale, INSERM, Chateau de Longchamp, 75016 Paris, France

The estimates of the incidence of human chromosome structural rearrangements have been made using various population studies. Data on balanced chromosome rearrangements have been obtained from : 1 . published surveys of 59,452 liveborn children done before the availability of banding techniques ; the incidence of balanced rearrangements was 0.19 per cent.
2 . chromosome analysis of 5,726 spontaneous abortions from 7 different studies collected by P.Jacobs (1980); banding techniques were used in some studies ; the incidence of balanced rearrangements was 0.28 per cent.
3 . chromosome analysis of amniotic fluid cells from 2,330 consecutive prenatal diagnosis performed for other indications than structural rearrangement in a parent ; G banding techniques were routinely used (J. Boué unpublished data) ; among the 9 balanced structural rearrangements found, 5 were de novo ; the total incidence is 0.38 per cent.

The overall incidence of balanced rearrangements is similar in the three groups. There is a non significant increase of anomalies among the spontaneous abortion group compared to new-born surveys and among the prenatal diagnosis group compared to the two other groups : The use of banding techniques may explain this increase, especially of reciprocal translocations and inversions. From these surveys it can be estimated that in the general population balanced chromosome structural rearrangements of all types occur with a frequency of 1 per 250 to 500 subjects (1 per 125 to 250 couples). These surveys did not include minor structural anomalies and inversion of chromosome 9.

What are the consequences of these structural rearrangements on the reproductive fitness of these couples ?

Different aspects of reproductive failure may be considered : sterility, prenatal wastage including early subclinical losses and clinically detected spontaneous abortions, perinatal deaths and malformed infants. From studies performed in recent years, estimates of the relative frequency of these different aspects have been made ; their overall frequency represents at least fifty per cent of all conceptions.

Early losses represent more than one third of the conceptions (Miller 1980) but the study of these specimens is practically impossible and most of the cytogenetic studies of prenatal wastage have been done in spontaneous abortion specimens (Boué 1975 ; Kajii 1980; Hassold 1980).

The frequency of chromosome rearrangements involved in prenatal wastage, the different types of rearrangements which are observed, their inheritance, or their de novo apparance have been evaluated :

1. by cytogenetic studies of spontaneous abortions. 50 to 60 per cent of clinically recognizable abortions have abnormal karyotypes. Numerical anomalies represent most of these abnormalities and structural rearrangements have been detected in only 3 to 6 per cent of chromosomally abnormal specimens.

The data of 7 surveys collected by P.Jacobs (1980) show an increase of unbalanced rearrangements in abortuses compared to the incidence in population studies

(Table 1). In these abortuses different types of structural rearrangements are observed. About one half of these unbalanced structural anomalies were inherited and the other half appeared de novo.

Table 1 :

CHROMOSOME STRUCTURAL REARRANGEMENTS

	Total examined	Balanced rearrangements		Unbalanced rearrangements	
		No	%	No	%
in newborns (7 surveys)	59.452	113	0.19	31	0.05
in abortuses (7 surveys)	5.726	16	0.28 N.S.	88	1.54 x 30

(From P. JACOBS 1980).

2. by cytogenetic studies of couples with recurrent abortion. Table 2 shows the results of different European surveys of couples with 2 or more spontaneous abortions. A balanced structural rearrangement has been found in one member in 7.2 per cent of these couples.

Table 2 :

INCIDENCE OF CHROMOSOME STRUCTURAL REARRANGEMENTS in couples with recurrent abortions ($\geqslant$ 2 abortions).

		N° of couples studied	couples with balanced structural rearrangements. No	%
BARCELONA	(Antich 1980)	32	6	17.8
GENT	(Matton 1980)	96	8	8.3
LEIDEN	(Geraedts 1980)	67	9	13.4
PADOVA	(Bortotto 1980)	145	14	9.6
PARIS	(Turleau 1979)	315	16	5.1
ROTTERDAM	(Sachs 1980)	148	14	9.6
STRASBOURG	(Stoll 1980)	217	6	2.8
ZURICH	(Schmid 1980)	96	7	7.3
	Total	1,116	80	7.2

The analysis of the frequency of the different types of structural anomalies in these couples compared to the frequency in newborn surveys shows a twenty fold increase of these anomalies, the different types of rearrangement are involved in this increase (table 3).

Table 3 :

FREQUENCY OF CHROMOSOME STRUCTURAL REARRANGEMENTS.

Types of rearrangements	In newborn surveys (59452 individuals)		In couples with recurrent abortions (2232 individuals)		Increase
	N°	%	N°	%	
Robertsonian	52	0.087	20	0.89	x10
Reciprocal	52	0.087	39	1.75	x20
Inversion	9	0.015	13	0.58	x40
Others			8		
Total :	113	0.19	80	3.58	x20

3. by the analysis of the ascertainments of the anomaly in parents carrying a balanced structural rearrangements which are referred for a prenatal diagnosis. Table 4 shows the ascertainments in 158 couples studied in our laboratory ; 45 per cent were ascertained by a history of recurrent abortions.

Table 4 :

ASCERTAINMENT OF THE STRUCTURAL REARRANGEMENT IN 158 COUPLES REFERRED FOR PRENATAL DIAGNOSIS.

Rearrangements	Ascertainment				
	Infants with unbalanced anomaly	Abortions or sterility		Others	Total
		N°	%		
DqDq	5	22	71	4	31
DqGq	21	4	14	3	28
Reciprocal	30	31	40	16	77
Inversions	2	14	64	6	22
TOTAL	58	71	45	29	158

Comparison of the relative frequencies of the different types of rearrangements shows no significant difference between newborn surveys and the recurrent abortion groups, but there is a significant difference of the Robertsonian translocations frequencies in the unbalanced infants group (table 5).

From these different approaches it appears that the different types of structural rearrangements are responsible of reproductive failure. It should be noted that only some aspects of reproductive failure can be studied in humans.

Table 5 :

RELATIVE FREQUENCY OF DIFFERENT TYPES OF STRUCTURAL REARRANGEMENTS

Rearrangements	In newborn surveys (113)	In couples referred for prenatal diagnosis ascertained through: Abortions (71)	Unbalanced anomaly in infant (58)
DqDq	0.37	0.30	0.09
DqGq	0.10	0.06	0.36
Reciprocal	0.43	0.43	0.52
Inversions	0.10	0.20	0.03

( ) number of observations.

In structural rearrangements there is an apparent discrepancy between the frequency of unbalanced zygotes which are expected from the theoretical segregation of gametes of a balanced carrier and the relatively small number of unbalanced fetuses and newborn which are observed.

The experimental studies which have been performed on tobacco-mouse particularly those of A.Gropp clearly demonstrated that many unbalanced zygotes have a developmental arrest early in gestation and often before implantation, particularly those zygotes with a monosomic karyotype. Obviously such types of zygotes cannot be collected in human studies.

Some particular aspects of reproductive failure can be studied in relation to some types of structural rearrangements.

1. ROBERTSONIAN TRANSLOCATION.

Studies on the segregation of the rearranged chromosomes in families with Robertsonian translocations (Hamerton 1970) have shown that the risk of a heterozygous mother having an affected child is greater than the risk from a heterozygous father. Similar results were observed in data collected from prenatal diagnosis (European Collaborative Study, Boué 1979).

From the data collected in spontaneous abortion material it was observed that when the unbalanced Robertsonian translocation was inherited in spontaneously aborted fetuses the carrier was the mother in most of the cases (table 6). These observations seem to exclude the hypothesis of differences in the frequency of early losses of unbalanced fetuses in relation to the sex of the carrier of the balanced translocation.

Table 6 :

INHERITED UNBALANCED ROBERTSONIAN TRANSLOCATIONS.

		Parent carrying the balanced translocation	
		Mother	Father
Liveborn progeny (J.L.Hamerton)	DqDq	1	1
	DqGq	16	4
	GqGq	2	
Prenatal diagnosis (European survey)	DqDq	1	
	DqGq	9	
	GqGq	3	
Spontaneous abortions (J.Boué)	DqDq	6	1
	DqGq	5	
	GqGq		

These findings in humans can be compared with the results obtained by Gropp (1980) on tobacco mouse.

Studying the proportion of trisomies and of resorptions at days 12-15 they observed that the risk of unbalanced fetuses in almost all the different types of Robertsonian translocations is significantly higher in a heterozygous female carrier compared with male carriers of the same chromosome anomaly.

These observations can be correlated to the segregation data between balanced heterozygotes and normal subjects which have been obtained in the study of liveborn progeny (Hamerton) and in prenatal diagnosis (European Collaborative Study). In both studies an excess of heterozygotes was observed in DqDq families (table 7).

In the experimental model of Gropp the transmission of translocated chromosomes is equal in almost all heterozygous males, but the transmission is highly distorted in many of the heterozygous females with the same anomalies, where a prevalence of the homozygous type is observed in the progeny.

From the results obtained in man and in mouse for the segregation of Robertsonian translocations Gropp believes "there is a distortion of segregation of the rearranged chromosome. Comparing man and mouse the direction of distortion may be different. This may only be due to reversions or inversions of the respective mechanism which does not devaluate the basic principe".

Table 7 :

PROGENY OF BALANCED HETEROZYGOTES.

Liveborn progeny (J.L. HAMERTON)		Total	Normal	Balanced	Unbalanced
DqDq	Mat	149	67	81	1
	Pat	120	46	74	
Prenatal diagnosis (European survey)					
DqDq	Mat	61	20	40	1
	Pat	33	9	24	

2. RECIPROCAL TRANSLOCATIONS.

Some aspects of the consequences of reciprocal translocations have been studied in couples referred for prenatal diagnosis (European Collaborative Study Boué 1979 and couples referred to our laboratory, J.Boué unpublished data). Reciprocal translocations ascertained through a history of recurrent abortions were compared to those ascertained through a unbalanced malformed infant.

a) distribution of break points on the chromosomes is not significantly different from the expected random distribution when the translocation has been ascertained through prenatal wastage European survey (table 8).

These results are in contrast with the non random distribution when the anomaly was ascertained in unbalanced infants. Similar results were observed previously by Aurias (1978) and by Daniel (1979).

Table 8 :

RECIPROCAL TRANSLOCATIONS

Percentage distribution of break points in chromosome groups in relation to the methods of ascertainment.

Chromosome group	Malformed infant	Spontaneous abortions	Expected
	(188)	(86)	
A	9.6	22.1	21.7
B	16.5	12.8	11.7
C	36.7	33.7	37.2
D	14.4	10.5	10.5
E	10.6	9.3	9.3
F	3.2	5.8	5.1
G	9.0	5.8	4.4

( ) number of breaks.

b) the potential chromosome imbalance in these translocations was measured in units, considering that the haploid human karyotype consists of 300 bands (Aurias, 1978), for example the short arm of chromosome 6 measures 6 units.

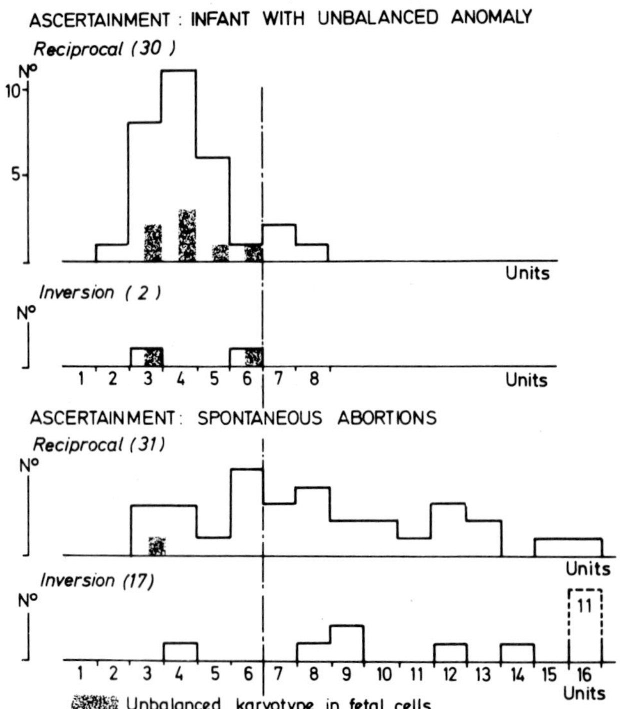

When the anomaly was ascertained through an unbalanced infant (30 families) the total length of chromosome segments which can be involved in the imbalance is usually small (less than 7 units in 27 out of 30). The mean imbalance is 4,26 units. (figure 1).

When the anomaly was ascertained through a history of recurrent abortions (31 families), the total length of chromosome segments is longer (less than 7 units in 12 out of 31). The mean imbalance is 7.84 units. These findings may be compared to those of Daniel (1979) and of Aurias (1978).

In the prenatal diagnosis performed in these families a fetus with an unbalanced karyotype was found only in the anomalies in which the total potential imbalance was 6 units or less.

INVERSIONS.

Few data have been collected on chromosome inversions and their consequences.

In 22 couples referred for prenatal diagnosis a parent was a carrier of a pericentric inversion.(figure 1).

Most of these inversions were ascertained through a history of recurrent abortion and in this group the total potential imbalance is usually larger than 6 units

One interesting observation is that some of the inverted chromosomes were analogous to some chromosomes of primates, in at least one third of the observations.

CONCLUSIONS.

The study of reproductive failures resulting from unbalanced structural rearrangements offers important results :

1. on fundamental aspects : the segregation of Robertsonian translocations and the distortions of segregation.

2. on the practical application of these findings for the genetic counselling of parents carrying these anomalies. The collection of more data will permit evaluation of the recurrence risks of the different types of rearrangements.

REFERENCES.

Antich J., Clusellas N., Twose A., Godo R.M. 1980. Chromosomal abnormalities in parents in cases of reproductive failure. Clin.Genet. 17, 52.

Aurias A., Prieur M., Dutrillaux B., Lejeune J.1978. Systematic analysis of 95 reciprocal translocations of autosomes. Hum.Genet. 45, 259 - 282.

Bortotto L., Baccichetti C., Lenzini E., Tenconi R., Delendi N., Caufin D. 1980. Cytogenetic survey of couples with habitual abortion and other reproductive wastage. Clin.Genet. 17, 56.

Boué A., 1979. European Collaborative Study on structural chromosome anomalies in prenatal diagnosis, Group report, in Prenatal Diagnosis, J.D. Murken, S.Stengel-Rutkowski, E.Schwinger eds. 34-46. Stuttgart, Enke.

Boué J., Boué A., Lazar P. 1975. Retrospective and prospective epidemiological studies of 1500 karyotyped spontaneous human abortions. Teratology. 12, 11-26.

Daniel A. 1979. Structural differences in reciprocal translocations Hum.Genet. 51, 171-182.

Geraedts J.P.M., Klasen E.C. 1980. Chromosomal studies and alpha-antitrysin phenotypes in recurrent abortions. Clin.Genet.17, 68.

Gropp A., Putz B, Zimmerman U., 1976. Autosomal monosomy and trisomy causing developmental failure. In Curr.Top.Pathol, vol 62 A.Gropp and K.Benirschke, eds, 177-182.Berlin,Springer.

Gropp A. 1980. Personal communication.

Hamerton J.L. 1970.Robertsonian translocation : evidence on segregation from family studies in Human population cytogenetics, P.A. Jacobs, W.H. Price and P.Law, eds, 64-80, Edinburgh, University Press.

Hassold T., Chen N., Funkhouser J., Jooss T., Manuel B, Matsuura J. Matsuyama A., Wilson C., Yamane J.A., Jacobs P.A. 1980. A cytogenetic study of 1000 spontaneous abortions.Am.Hum.Genet(in press)

Jacobs P.A. 1980. Mutation rates of structural chromosome rearrangements in man. Amer.J.Hum.Genet. (in press).

Kajii T., Ferrier A., Niikawa N., Takahara H., Ohama K., Avirachan S. 1980. Anatomic and chromosomal anomalies in 639 spontaneous abortuses.Hum.Genet. 55, 87-98.

Matton M., Verschraegen-spae M.R., De Bie S., Van den Wijngaert J. 1980. Incidence of T.Carriers amongst couples with repetitive abortion, after exclusion of any other etiology.Clin-Genet.17,78.

Miller J.F., Williamson E.,Glue J.,GordonY.B,Grudzinskas J.G., Sykes A. 1980. Fetal loss after implantation,Lancet.1., 554-556.

Sachs E.S.1980.Fertility of translocation carriers.Clin.Genet17,83.

Schmid W.1980.Cytogenetic results in 96 couples with repeated abortions.Clin.Genet.17,85.

Stoll C.,Flori E., Rumpler Y.,WarterS.1980.Cytogenetic findings in 217 couples with recurrent fetal wastage.Clin.Genet.17, 88.

Turleau C., Chavin-colin F., de Grouchy J. 1979. Cytogenetic investigation in 413 couples with spontaneous abortions.Europ.J.Obstet Gynec.Reprod.Biol. 9, 65-74.

Karyotype/phenotype correlations

J. de Grouchy

U.173 INSERM and ER.149 CNRS, Hôpital Necker-Enfants-Malades, Clinique Maurice Lamy, 149 rue de Sèvres, 75730 Paris, Cedex 15, France

Karyotype/phenotype correlations in man can be apprehended from different standpoints. Historically, the discovery that trisomy 21 is responsible for the phenotype of mongolism (Lejeune et al., 1959) was the first evidence of such a correlation and was observed at the level of the individual. With the fantastic development of cytogenetics, karyotype/phenotype correlations can now be studied at other levels of organisation : biochemical, cellular, evolutionary. Recent observations all tend to show the high degree of complexity of each of these different levels of organization.

BIOCHEMICAL LEVEL

The first demonstration of a gene dosage effect was in the case of the enzyme superoxide dismutase 1 (SOD1) and trisomy 21 (Sinet et al., 1976). Individuals monosomic or trisomic for segment 21q221 show a SOD1 activity respectively halved or sesquialter as compared to normal. Since this first observation many others have been reported, demonstrating a direct gene dosage effect in patients trisomic or monosomic for given chromosomes or chromosome segments. Some 20 localized human genes are now known to show such an effect (see Junien et al., 1980(b) for review). The most recent assignment by gene dosage effect is that of the gene for catalase (CAT) to band 11p13 in close association with the aniridia-Wilms' tumor or gonadoblastoma complex (Junien et al. 1980(c)).

Yet gene dosage effect may not be straightforward. The gene for peptidase A (PEPA) is assigned to 18q23, but there is a wide

Chromosomes today, volume 7 George Allen & Unwin 1981

range of PEPA activity in red blood cells due to quantitative polymorphism at this locus. A gene dosage effect is observed in patients trisomic or monosomic for 18q23 only if PEPA activity in the patient is compared to the mean of his parents' activities (Denesino *et al.*, 1978; Junien *et al.*, 1980(a)).

Genetic regulatory systems are well documented in micro-organisms since the pioneer work of Jacob and Monod (1961). Their demonstration in Mammalia and particularly in man is still very fragmentary. One example of a karyotype/phenotype correlation could be that of coagulation factor VII. A 50% deficiency of this factor was reported in trisomy 8 by Grouchy *et al.* (1974) and further confirmed by Fineman *et al.* (1975) and Stenbjerg *et al.* (1975). This deficiency is perhaps best explained, as suggested initially by Grouchy *et al.* (1974), by the presence of a regulatory gene on chromosome 8 responsible for the metabolism of factor VII.

If regulatory genes do exist in man it is reasonable to believe that they are not located on the same chromosomes as the corresponding structural genes. If this were not the case trisomies or monosomies would not show a gene dosage effect and individuals with, for instance, trisomy 21 would be normal. On the other hand if regulatory and structural genes are on different chromosomes, triploid organisms should be normal. And indeed triploid cells have been shown to have normal enzymatic activities (Junien *et al.*, 1976). Yet triploidy is a highly lethal condition in man.

Other fundamental aspects of genetic regulation are the biochemical mechanisms responsible for embryonic differentiation. Here again we know hardly anything of such mechanisms. One possible insight in these systems could be the persistence of the embryonic Gower-2 hemoglobin ($Hb\alpha^{A}_{2}\ \varepsilon 2$) in trisomy 13 (Hoehns *et al.*, 1964). An explanation could be the existence on chromosome 13 of a locus responsible for the switching from embryonic to fetal hemoglobin, since we now know that the structural genes for hemoglobin are located elsewhere in the karyotype, the α and α-like genes on chromosome 16 and the non-α genes on chromosomes 11 (Deisseroth *et al.*, 1977, 1978).

CELLULAR LEVEL

Trisomy 13 affords another example of a karyotype/phenotype correlation observable, this time, at the cellular level, namely the existence of abnormal projections, sessile or pediculate, of the polynuclear neutrophile nuclei (Huehns *et al.*, 1964). Still other examples are found in trisomy 21, such as impaired chromosomal repair mechanisms of X-ray induced damage (Countryman *et al.*, 1977) or abnormal cell ageing (Paton *et al.*, 1974).

The most remarkable instance of karyotype/phenotype correlation, strictly at the cellular level, is probably carcinogenesis. Cancer develops from a single cell and we now know that in many cases, if not in all, one of the very first steps of malignant evolution is a chromosomal rearrangement. This is discussed elsewhere in these meetings.

If cancer is most often a somatic event, there are however two situations where a congenital chromosomal rearrangement is specifically associated with neoplasia of a particular cell type. One is the association of the deletion of band q14 of chromosome 13 and retinoblastoma (Lele *et al.*, 1963; Yunis and Ramsay, 1978). The other is the association of the deletion of band p13 of chromosome 11, aniridia, and Wilms' tumor or gonadoblastoma. This association has been called the WAGR complex (Francke *et al.*, 1979; Human Gene Mapping 5).

Retinoblastoma is a rare tumor that occurs in infancy with a prevalence of the order of 1 p. 20,000. Some 90 to 98% of the cases are due to genic mutations which may be germinal and transmitted in a dominant fashion, or somatic and occurring in retinal cells. In 2 to 10% of the cases retionoblastoma is associated with a deletion of 13q which may vary in size but always includes band 13q14 (Vogel, 1979; Grouchy *et al.*, 1980). Recent observations have shown that fibroblasts from such patients have an increased sensitivity to cell killing *in vitro* by X-rays (Nove *et al.*, 1979) as well as an increased rate of sister chromatid exchanges (Turleau *et al.*, 1980). Patients with del(13q14) offer therefore an intriguing situation : on one hand they exhibit an abnormal sensitivity of their genetic material detectable in cells as common as fibroblasts and, on the other hand, they are at a high risk of developing malignancy, but only in a specific type of cells, the retinal cells.

Aniridia is usually a dominant disorder due to the mutation of a gene linked to ACP1 on 2p (Ferrell *et al.*, 1980). There are however instances when aniridia is associated with deletion of band 11p13 (close to the locus of ACP2), in patients with mental retardation and ambiguous genitalia, and who have a high risk of developing Wilms' tumor (nephroblastoma) or gonadoblastoma. No particular sensitivity of their genetic material has as yet been demonstrated in such patients.

Del(13)-retinoblastoma patients and del(11p)-Wilms' tumor or gonadoblastoma patients are remarkable examples of a specific karyotype/phenotype correlation at the cellular level. In both instances the tumors occur early in infancy and may be considered as embryonic tumors. It is conceivable that bands 13q14 and 11p13 are involved in the embryonic differentiation of retinal cells and of renal and gonadal cells, respectively.

THE ORGANISM'S LEVEL

When considering the organism, karyotype/phenotype correlations represent no less than the entire field of clinical cytogenetics and their description would not be possible here. We shall therefore discuss only recent observations which suggest a highly complex inner organization of the chromosomes with regard to their "phenotype mapping".

Trisomy 18 is one of the first reported trisomies in man (Edwards *et al.*, 1960). Main features are dolichocephaly with a protruding occiput, a slender even protruberant nose bridge, considerable micrognathia, low-set, "faunlike" ears, a short neck, a narrow pelvis, "rocker-bottom" feet, severe inner organ malformations, abnormal genitalia. Mean survival is 2-3 months for males and 10 months for females. Rare patients have survived childhood and lived to the age of 15 or 19 years. Patients with mosaicism have a prolonged survival rate.

Several partial trisomy 18 syndromes have recently been delineated. Trisomy 18qter (Turleau and Grouchy, 1977) is responsible for a syndrome which seems distinct and has in no case enticed the diagnosis of full trisomy 18. Patients are dolichocephalic with a high-bossed forehead and a receding hair-line. The face is elongated with poorly indicated angles of the mandible. The most conspicuous feature is the prominent nasal bridge with no naso-frontal angle. Visceral malformations are very rare. Life span does not seem to be impaired. Mental retardation is variable.

Trisomy 18p is responsible for a syndrome with mild dysmorphisms quite different from trisomy 18, with a chubby face, epicantic folds, a triangular mouth, a pinched nose, low-set ears, hypertonicity and spasticity (Turleau and Grouchy, 1977; Rocchi et al., 1979).

Trisomy 18q- (i.e. trisomy for 18p and the proximal third of half of 18q) is responsible for a syndrome which has many features of full trisomy 18 but some distinct features (Turleau et al., 1980). Cranio-facial dysmorphisms are a prominent occiput, small palpebral fissures slanting downwards, a pointed nose with a prominent bridge, severe micrognathia, low-set somewhat faunesque ears. The main difference with full trisomy 18 is the birdlike appearance and the severe micrognathia. Inner organ malformations are not constant and survival is more frequent.

Put together these observations and others suggest that the proximal segment of 18q, band 18q11, is crucial for the expression of the most characteristic symptoms of trisomy 18. It also appears that there is an intermediate segment which extends from 18q11 to 18q22 and that trisomy for this segment is not associated with the trisomy 18 phenotype, although severe mental retardation is present.

These examples as well as others from chromosome 13 (Schinzel et al., 1976), or chromosome 8 (Rethoré et al., 1977) point to a highly organized structure of the chromosome with possibly redundancy and a great degree of interaction between different segments.

Many other features of cytogenetic diseases, some of which have been described for some time now, point to the very complex karyotype/phenotype correlations at the individual's level. For instance the gravity of the phenotypic effect is often disproportional to the size of the aneusomic chromosome segment. The deletion of the very end of 4p (band p16) is responsible for the extremely severe 4p- syndrome (Grouchy, 1977) while trisomy for chromosome 8 can be responsible for relatively little impairment of the phenotype (Grouchy et al., 1971).

Another example is the great variability from patient to patient of the physical and intellectual impairment resulting from exactly the same aneusomy. Also, is the fact that any aneusomy, even of a small segment, has a very general effect affecting many organs and embryonic determinants.

These examples, and there are many others, suggest an organization of the chromosome which a cartesian mind has still difficulty to grasp. Yet, on the other hand, the now well-documented type and countertype correlations (Lejeune, 1966) point to a great logic of the system.

EVOLUTIONARY LEVEL

With the advent of the banding techniques, it has become possible to reconstruct the chromosomal phylogeny of practically all of the primates, from man to the New World monkeys (Turleau and Grouchy, 1972; Grouchy et al., 1979; Dutrillaux, 1979; see also Dutrillaux in these meetings). These studies show a considerable homology between the chromosomes, or rather chromosome segments, of most of the primate species. In other words, all primates possess the same visible chromosome material. Simply, evolution has rearranged differently this material in the various species, using such mechanisms as telomeric or centric fusions, para- or pericentric inversions, fissions, other inter- or intra-chromosomal rearrangements, and reorganization of the heterochromatic material.

This homology of chromosome material has also been confirmed by an identical homology of gene mapping. Homologous chromosome segments carry the same genes, or rather the same structural genes (Finaz et al., 1973; Human Gene Mapping 5, 1979).

In summary, the karyotypes of man and the primates are largely homologous. The chromosomes carry the same structural genes and manufacture the same proteins as shown by King and Wilson (1975). Yet the phenotypes of these species are different. The reasons for these different karyotype/phenotype correlations must probably be searched for in the different features of the genetic material we still know least of in higher organisms and which have been discussed in these meetings : DNA redundancy, the structure and role of heterochromatic material, genetic regulatory systems, embryonic differentiation. Only when these mysteries of biology will have been solved, shall we understand better how Homo sapiens has evolved by handling more efficiently the same basic genetic material than Pan troglodytes or any other of his fellow primate species.

REFERENCES

Countryman, P. I., J. A. Heddle and E. Crawford. 1977. The repair of X-ray-induced chromosomal damage in trisomy 21 and normal diploid lymphocytes. Cancer Res. 37, 52-58.

Danesino, C., A. D'Azzo, P. Maraschio and M. Fraccaro. 1978. The gene for human peptidase A is on band 18q23 and shows triplex and uniplex dosage effect. Hum. Genet. 43, 299-305.

Deisseroth, A., A. Nienhuis, P. Turner, R. Velez, W. F. Anderson, F. Ruddle, J. Lawrence, R. Creagan and R. Kucherla Pati. 1977. Localization of the human α-globin structural gene to chromosome 16 in somatic cell hybrids by molecular hybridisation assay. Cell 12, 205-218.

Deisseroth, A., A. Nienhuis, J. Lawrence, R. Giles, P. Turner and F. H. Ruddle. 1978. Chromosomal localization of human β-globin gene on human chromosome 11 in somatic cell hybrids. Proc. Natl. Acad. Sci. 75, 1456-2460.

Dutrillaux, B., E. Viegas-Pequignot, J. Couturier, and G. Chauvier. 1978. Identity of euchromatic bands from man to certopithecidae. Hum. Genet. 45, 283-296.

Edwards, J. H., D. G. Harnden, A. H. Cameron, V. M. Crosse and O. H. Wolff. 1960. A new trisomic syndrome. Lancet i, 787-790.

Ferrel, R. E., A. Chakravarti, N. Mintz Hittner and V. M. Riccardi. 1980. Autosomal dominant aniridia : probable linkage to acid phosphatase-1 locus on chromosome 2. Proc. Natl. Acad. Sci. 77, 1580-1582.

Finaz, C., C. Turleau, J. de Grouchy, Nguyen van Cong, R. Rebourcet and J. Frezal. 1973. Comparison of man and chimpanzee zyntenic groups by cellular hybridization. Preliminary report. Biomedicine 19, 526-531.

Fineman, R. M., R. C. Ablow, R. O. Howard, J. Albright and W. R. Breg. 1975. Trisomy 8 mosaicism syndrome. Pediatrics 56, 762-767.

Francke, U., L. B. Holmes and V. M. Riccardi. 1979. Aniridia-Wilms' tumor association: evidence for specific deletion of 11p13. Cytogenet. Cell Genet. 24, 185-192.

Grouchy, J. de, C. Turleau and C. Leonard. 1971. Etude en fluorescence d'une trisomie C mosaique probablement 8 : 46,XY/47,XY,+8+. Ann. Génét. 14, 69-72.

Grouchy, J. de, F. Josso, S. Beguin, C. Turleau, P. Jalbert and C. Laurent. 1974. Déficit en facteur VII de la coagulation chez trois sujets trisomiques 8. Ann. Génét. 17, 105-108.

Gròuchy, J. de, 1976. New Cytogenetic Syndromes and Chromosomes Organization. In: Human Genetics, Proceedings of the Fifth International Congress of Human Genetics, Mexico City, 10-15 October 1976. Excerpta Medica, Amsterdam, Oxford, p. 106-113.

Grouchy, J. de, C. Turleau and C. Finaz. 1978. Chromosomal phylogeny of the Primates. Ann. Rev. Genet. 12, 289-328.

Grouchy, J. de, C. Turleau, M. O. Cabanis and J. M. Richardet. 1980. Rétinoblastome et délétion intercalaire du chromosome 13. Arch. Fr. Pediat.

Huehns, E. R., M. Lutzner and F. Hecht. 1964. Nuclear abnormalities of the neutrophils in D1 (13)15)-trisomy syndrome. Lancet i, 589-590.

Huehns, E. R., F. Hecht, J. V. Keil and A. G. Motulsky. 1964. Developmental hemoglobin anomalies in a chromosomal triplication : D1 trisomy syndrome. Proc. Natl. Acad. Sci. 51, 89-97.

Human Gene Mapping 5. Edinburgh Conference. 1979. Cytogenetics Cell Genet. 25, 1-236.

Jacob, F. and J. Monod. 1961. Genetic regulatory mechanisms in the synthesis of proteins. J. Mol. Biol. 3, 318-356.

Junien, C., H. Rubinson, J. C. Dreyfus, M. C. Meienhofer, N. Ravise, J. Boue and A. Boue. 1976. Gene dosage effect in human triploid fibroblasts. Hum. Genet. 33, 61-66.

Junien, C., J. de Grouchy, C. Turleau and F. Serville. 1980(a). Confirmation of the regional assignment of peptidase A (PEPA) to 18q23 by gene dosage studies. Ann. Génét. 23, 89-90.

Junien, C., H. Rubinson-Skala, J. C. Dreyfus, N. Ravise, J. Boue, A. Boue and J. C. Kaplan. 1980(b). PK3 : a new chromosome enzyme marker for gene dosage studies in chromosome 15 imbalance. Hum. Genet. 54, 191-196.

Junien, C., C. Turleau, J. de Grouchy, R. Said, M. O. Rethore, C. Baccichetti and J. L. Dufier. 1980(c). Regional assignment of catalase (CAT) gene to band 11p13. Association with the aniridia-Wilms' tumor-gonadoblastoma (WAGR) complex. Ann. Génét.

King, M. G. and A. C. Wilson. 1975. Evolution at two levels in humans and chimpanzees. Science 188, 107-116.

Lejeune, J., M. Gautier and R. Turpin. 1959. Etude des chromosomes somatiques de neuf enfants mongoliens. C. R. Acad. Sci. 248, 1721-1722.

Lejeune, J. 1966. Type et contretypes. In: Journées Parisiennes de Pédiatrie. Paris, Flammarion et Cie, pp. 73-83.

Lele, K. P., L. S. Penrose and H. B. Stallard. 1963. Chromosome deletion in a case of retinoblastoma. Amer. J. Hum. Genet. 27, 171-174.

Nove, J., J. B. Little, R. R. Weichselbaum, W. W. Nichols and E. Hoffman. 1979. Retinoblastoma, chromosome 13, and in vitro cellular radiosensitivity. Cytogenet. Cell Genet. 24, 176-184.

Paton, G. R., M. F. Silver and A. C. Allison. 1974. Comparison of cell cycle time in normal and trisomic cells. Humangenetik, 23, 173-182.

Rethore, M. O., A. Aurias, J. Couturier, B. Dutrillaux, M. Prieur and J. Lejeune. 1977. Chromosome 8 : trisomie complète et trisomies segmentaires. Ann. Génét. 20, 5-11.

Rocchi, M., M. Stormi, N. Archidiacono and G. Filippi. 1979. Extra small metacentric chromosome identified as i(18p). J. Med. Genet. 16, 69-72.

Schinzel, A., K. Hayashi and W. Schmid. 1976. Further delineation of the clinical picture of trisomy for the distal segment of chromosome 13. Hum. Genet. 32, 1-12.

Sinet, P. M., J. Couturier, B. Dutrillaux, M. Poissonnier, O. Raoul, M. O. Rethore, D. Allard, J. Lejeune and H. Jerome. 1976. Trisomie 21 et superoxyde dismutase-1 (IPO-A). Tentative de localisation sur la sous-bande 21q22.1. Expt. Cell Res. 97, 47-55.

Stenbjerg, S., S. Husted, A. Bernsen, P. Jacobsen, J. Nielsen and K. Rasmussen. 1975. Coagulation studies in patients with trisomy 8 syndrome. Ann. Génét. 18, 241-242.

Turleau, C., and J. de Grouchy. 1972. Caryotypes de l'homme et du chimpanzé. Comparaison de la topographie des bandes. Mécanismes évolutifs possibles. C. R. Acad. Sci. 274, 2355-2357, série D.

Turleau, C. and J. de Grouchy. 1977. Trisomy 18qter and trisomy mapping of chromosome 18. Clin. Genet. 12, 361-371.

Turleau, C., M. O. Cabanis and J. de Grouchy. 1980(a). Augmentation des échanges de chromatides dans les fibroblastes d'un enfant atteint de del(13)-rétinoblastome. Ann. Génét. 23,

Turleau, C., F. Chavin-Colin, R. Narbouton, D. Asensi and J. de Grouchy. 1980(b). Trisomy 18q-. Trisomy mapping of chromosome 18 revisited. Clin. Genet. 17,

Vogel, F. 1979. Genetics of retinoblastoma. Hum. Genet. 52, 1-54.

Yunis, J. J. and N. Ramsay. 1978. Retinoblastoma and subband deletion of chromosome 13. Am. J. Dis. Child. 132, 161-163.

Index